AMERICAN CULTURAL STUDIES

American Cultural Studies

EDITED BY

CATHERINE A. WARREN AND

MARY DOUGLAS VAVRUS

UNIVERSITY OF ILLINOIS PRESS

URBANA AND CHICAGO

Manufactured in the United States of America
1 2 3 4 5 C P 5 4 3 2 1

This book is printed on acid-free paper.

Library of Congress Cataloging-in-Publication Data
American cultural studies / edited by Catherine A.
Warren and Mary Douglas Vavrus.
p. cm.
Includes bibliographical references and index.
ISBN 0-252-02699-3 (cloth : alk. paper)
ISBN 0-252-07008-9 (pbk. : alk. paper)
1. United States—Civilization—20th century—
Congresses. 2. United States—Intellectual life—20th
century—Congresses. 3. United States—Civilization—
20th century—Study and teaching (Higher)—Congresses.
4. Culture—Study and teaching (Higher)—United States—
Congresses. 5. National characteristics, American—
Congresses. I. Warren, Catherine A. II. Vavrus, Mary
Douglas. III. Title.
E169.1.W284 2001
973.9—dc21 2001002242

Contents

Acknowledgments

This collection is a truly collaborative project. We want to thank a number of people who were essential in making this book possible. First, Kim Rotzell, dean of the College of Communications at University of Illinois, Urbana-Champaign, and Clifford Christians, director of the Institute of Communications Research, were unstinting in their support of the conference and the book that came of it. The conference in November 1995, "Across Disciplines and Beyond Boundaries: Tracking American Cultural Studies," was possible only because of the generous financial, intellectual, and emotional contributions that both Kim and Cliff made. From thousands of dollars to clerical assistance and valuable advice, we felt supported from the very beginning.

Equally important, we thank Eve Stryker Munson, now at Penn State University, who cochaired the conference. This project was her brainchild, and she helped manage every single detail, from the intellectual ones of creating a vision of the conference and choosing presenters to making sure that the hundreds of tasks associated with running a conference went smoothly. We are deeply appreciative.

Then there is James Carey. He was the inspiration for this collection and continues to be an inspiration for all of us who were his graduate students. If ever the term *public intellectual* had credibility and meaning, he embodies it. He is simply a wonderful, thoughtful, provocative thinker and doer. Often, especially after this rancorous, intellectually bereft, and hypocritically religious presidential campaign, we could not help thinking, "What would J.C. do?" The answer is a guide to the next four years and beyond.

We also thank Dianne Tipps and Anita Specht (now retired) of the Institute of Communications Research and Nickie Dalton of the College of Communications, who provided hours of support, both clerical and emotional.

A number of colleagues provided services too numerous to mention. Thanks to Bruce Williams, Andrea Press, Larry Grossberg, Allan O'Connor, Joel Super, Nate Kohn, and Paula Treichler, among many others. Thanks also go the contributors, who provided support and encouragement far beyond the call of duty.

Last, we want to thank acquiring editors Karen Hewitt and Richard Martin of the University of Illinois Press, who supported this project and nursed it along, and especially Jane Frampton and Jane Mohraz, copy editors par excellence, who beat this manuscript into submission.

AMERICAN CULTURAL STUDIES

CATHERINE A. WARREN AND
MARY DOUGLAS VAVRUS

Introduction

Two major themes run through the essays in this volume. One is a meditation on what cultural studies is or what it should be in the United States. The second concerns what has been called, by James W. Carey and others, the "exceptionalism" of the United States. That is, does it mean something unique to live in this nation, with this particular political structure, in this particular time? If so, do we have any moral and social responsibility as its citizens and intellectuals?

The answers found in these essays are clear: despite globalization and diasporas, despite the Internet and cyborgs, despite the communications revolution that has overseen the seeming breakdown of any boundary one might imagine, those of us who live in the United States are subject to its history, its crime and violence, its racism, its media structures, its education, its economy, its communities. As scholars and intellectuals, we are also deeply implicated in its shape, present and future.

This does not mean that the intent of this collection is to study the United States in isolation or to impose any sort of unitary identity on it. It is simply to reaffirm that the nation-state still has meaning, despite postmodernism, and that generation after generation, the nation-state endures as a geographic, political, and symbolic entity. It is within the nation-state that media events find their greatest meaning and within the nation-state that significant change can take place. Columbine High School and the Amadou Diallo case are U.S. media events; their significance is not unitary, but it is bounded by our geopolitical and symbolic borders.

This collection is also partly an effort to return to some old disciplinary paradigms that have been neglected and, as argued herein, need to be embraced, while also acknowledging some of the new. The term *American cultural studies* in this context means simply that the United States is the home of these particular essays on cultural studies and that part of what is being examined is this peculiar and unique nation-state, with its policies, its media structures, and its disintegrating democracy.

From Joli Jensen's study of American intellectuals in the first half of this century to Lana Rakow's examination of the role of rural community in the United States, these essays struggle with finding an understanding of cultural studies that is grounded in history, in the specificity of experience, and in the perhaps vain hope of transformation.

Without eschewing theory, these essays call for a new understanding of political engagement—one that at least makes an effort to set aside the interminable debates over the boundaries of cultural studies. One of the central purposes of understanding culture is to fully engage in it. Instead of endlessly debating the extent of hegemony, the futility or creativity of resistance, or the shape of new technologies, these essays address the question, "What is to be done?" The answers are not simple or necessarily straightforward. Sometimes, they are only partial. Sometimes, the response is grim or oblique. Some call for an activism in which some of the essayists already engage.

One might argue that a progressive or radical politics is an overweening ambition on the part of scholars well ensconced in the academy. Nonetheless, several contributors to this volume can be considered public intellectuals, writ small and large. Their work is fully part of the public debate. James Carey has for decades used his vast intellectual grasp to move beyond the academy and engage in a very public conversation about how to sustain democracy in this country. Daniel Czitrom has brought his acuity and radical vision as a historian to public television and radio, putting the poor, the working class, and ethnic minorities back into the frame of American culture. The media historian and political theorist Robert McChesney has continually entered the national debate on the thorny issue of corporate media ownership and its implications for democracy. Lana Rakow practices what she preaches in her hometown in North Dakota. "We need to return to our communities as cultural studies scholars," encourages Rakow. "I am not suggesting we should become community activists who start domestic violence shelters. I am suggesting we need to figure out how to integrate our intellectual work with the other kinds of work performed by other members of our community."

These approaches to integrating academic and public life are not easy or obvious. The issues of theory versus practice and of private scholarship versus public life can be contentious. Some of the essays in this collection are pointed critiques of cultural studies, accusing certain strains of being smug and insular or indulging in vain postmodern theorizing. Earlier critiques of cultural studies have also stressed its general lack of sustained engagement with history, its overdependence on theoretical discussion, its rarefied vocabulary, and its tendency to become a kind of performance art. The people who contributed to this volume are actively struggling with the question of formulating a practice in cultural studies that is, in Robert McChesney's words, an "explicitly radical politics."

How does one inject progressive practice into cultural studies, especially since some might argue that it was always central to its definition? However, those were the days when Richard Hoggart and Raymond Williams used the study of culture as part and parcel of a progressive program, of a conversation with a wider public. But in the United States, as James Carey has argued in numerous essays, the academic Left, many of whom call cultural studies their home, has become increasingly irrelevant and isolated from the larger communities, allowing the Right to capture the hearts and minds of Americans. How, then, does one transform a discipline that has become increasingly textualized, self-obsessed, ironic, institutionalized, and superfluous into something that is politically engaged, committed, and responsive to understanding the state of the United States?

Daniel Czitrom, a media historian who has increasingly moved into the public arena, most recently being featured in PBS's history of New York, begins the collection with a plea to consider the importance of historical analysis—one of those older paradigms that, when well done, still provides enormous explanatory power. Cultural studies and historical analysis should be necessarily intertwined, as each approach to culture enriches the other. All too often, he notes, cultural studies is ahistorical. History, however, is sometimes blind to the inequalities to which cultural studies is sensitive. For Czitrom, historical narratives are not only more revealing but also more authentic when they take into account the ways in which power is exercised—often in a manner that exploits race, class, and gender. This analysis of power relations is fundamental to a cultural studies critique.

Czitrom notes, however, that cultural critique tends toward irrelevance when it is not sufficiently historical: "I worry that American cultural studies suffers from a kind of intellectual ventriloquism. Too often, history appears simply as an illustration for the real text—showing a command of Continental theory." Czitrom cautions against such an approach and against a view of citizens as political and cultural dupes. "We need an American cultural studies that brings a deeper, more historically informed engagement with the state and with how power relations get worked out in the realm of public policy," he argues. Such an engagement with, for instance, the history of race relations and public policy would enrich the public debate on welfare reform. The stakes are high: "We cannot afford to cede the public sphere, and historical analysis offers some effective tools for scholars and citizens in pressing this point."

Joli Jensen's essay is a concrete response to Czitrom's request for a historically informed cultural studies. Her explication of the intellectual-historical roots of American cultural studies shows that critical reflexivity, while much touted, has been accomplished only sporadically in the history of cultural studies. Yet, she argues, this reflexivity is "what American cultural studies does best." Jensen notes that historically the work of intellectuals on the issue of the arts' place in a democratic society has been enriched—and American cultural theory strengthened—when such reflexivity is practiced and assumes a prominent place in cultural analysis. To achieve this goal, she recommends that American cultural studies reexamine its foundation in pragmatism. She envisions a Deweyan pragmatism—dialogic in nature—that decenters the importance of the critic in research and teaching. Jensen notes, "One thing I especially like about the American cultural studies alternative is its potential for humility. Pragmatism offers us an alternative to the theoretical mandates that so haunt British cultural studies and have so captivated American departments of literature. With American cultural studies, we can turn away from the elitism and solipsism of elaborate theorizing and turn toward a more egalitarian and participatory discourse."

John Dewey's name has been invoked for decades as an ancestor of American cultural studies. This is no surprise. Carey (1989) invoked Dewey's name at the beginning of his first collection on cultural studies: "When I decided some years ago to read seriously the literature of communications, a wise man suggested I begin with John Dewey. It was advice I have never regretted accepting" (13). Dewey's insight, that communication was the way to create and sustain democracy in the United States, helped create the bedrock for Carey's engaged study of mass communications as ritual. Carey has repeatedly returned to Dewey's (1916) enigmatic comment: "Society exists not only by transmission, by communication, but it may fairly be said to exist in transmission, in communication" (5).

In his essay, Rick Tilman, a historian who is completing a trilogy on American theorists—Dewey, Thorstein Veblen, and C. Wright Mills—goes back to examine in depth Dewey's political thought and behavior. A resonant theme in these essays is the importance of being historical.

As Tilman points out, although Dewey threatens to become a cottage industry, little work has been done on his social and political activism.

Tilman turns to Dewey's social and political writings to reveal his significant contribution to American cultural studies. Tilman locates Dewey in what Currin V. Shields (1952) has called the "American tradition of empirical collectivism," a heuristic device that determines the appropriateness of collective action or individual action to social issues and problems. Tilman suggests that the effectiveness of Dewey's work—foundational to American cultural studies—was at least partially due to his ability to analyze American politics with keen prescience. Tilman illustrates this in some of Dewey's predictions about the American political-economic landscape: he identified, for example, a developing corporate-commercial hegemony and foresaw the consolidating potential of electricity. Both of these themes are taken up in contemporary American cultural studies work, perhaps because of the visionary Dewey.

Tilman constructs an intellectual chronology for Dewey's philosophy and politics and in so doing demonstrates why his thinking constitutes a crucial part of the historical root system underlying American cultural studies. Tilman's genealogy helps explain the development of Dewey's relation to empirical collectivism and thus to activism more generally in developing democracy in the United States.

Following Tilman's contribution, Robert W. McChesney's essay concerns the democratic promise of cultural studies work as well as its failure to fulfill that promise. Several years ago, as he points out in his essay, McChesney criticized cultural studies for "its ignorance of social theory and history, its insular nature, its lack of a critique of the academy, and its categorical disregard for journalism." There has, to his mind, been little recent progress: "I write this essay to share my honest concerns regarding what I see as basic flaws in U.S. cultural studies as it has developed over the past decade." Two factors have contributed to this condition, according to McChesney. First, the institutionalization of cultural studies has depoliticized it, turning it into a "lifeless caricature." Second, cultural studies has embraced theoretical principles of postmodernism, thereby "accepting the complete victory of capitalism and the repudiation of the possibility of socialism. In short, the politics of postmodernism are the rejection of radical politics."

To McChesney, postmodern theory is a dead end that distracts researchers from factoring class into their work. Cultural studies is moving away from radical politics, not toward it, and if it continues its present course, it will "finally and forever repudiate its charter." Cultural studies must be reconfigured, he argues, so that the issue of equitable distribution of income and resources is at front and center.

If cultural studies has ignored history, it has also tended to slight feminist methodologies that hold great promise for really understanding the research subject. Linda M. Blum, Andrea L. Press, and Linda Steiner offer nuanced and grounded methodologies that encourage cultural studies to expand by investigating the terrain between text and experience, what these authors show to be a richly revealing arena.

Linda Blum and Andrea Press talk about doing feminist fieldwork in "the age of cultural studies"—that is, of textuality and high theory—rather than experience-based research and methodology. As a sociologist, one author observes, she is often viewed by those in cultural studies as a "rank empiricist," unwilling and unable to make the necessary textual turn to theoretical sophistication. The authors are thus split, they note, between feminist research and cultural studies, between text-based and experience-based research.

Blum and Press suggest that feminist ethnographic research offers a way out of a bind produced by sociology's rejection of textual analysis and cultural studies' suspicion of social science. Feminist fieldwork, inflected with the "provocations of postmodernism," encourages examination of aspects integral to any cultural studies project: difference, experience, and the research text that results. Further, fieldwork—particularly feminist fieldwork—is resistant to acontextuality, influenced as it has been by decades of reflection on and reconsideration of the generative function of context in lived experience. Ethnographic work requires researchers to understand the places and spaces where informants live and work. This "thick description," advocated first by Clifford Geertz, demands more than merely recording details; researchers must take account of all the elements that could possibly affect their informants' lives through a dialogic process by which ethnographers come to know their informants and through which ethnographers examine their own place in the process. This further presupposes that a voice other than the researcher's will dominate the ethnographic text.

While Press and Blum believe the cultural studies critique of fieldwork is valid, they also believe that the textual turn is a blind alley where new insights are impossible, for texts are not dialogical. It is in the give-and-take of the relationship between researchers and the people with whom they are speaking that the taken-for-granted and the unspoken can emerge, and that ultimately leads to a more nuanced understanding.

Linda Steiner's essay shares Blum and Press's concern with voice; she is particularly interested in the explanatory power of biography. Steiner uses women's narratives to examine, in the words of Clifford Geertz (1973), what stories we tell ourselves about ourselves (448). Those stories are our culture, and their inclusion could enrich cultural studies, according to Steiner.

In this particular case, Steiner uses the stories of women journalists working in the early years of the twentieth century. Steiner stresses the importance of personal voice in cultural studies research and how voice can aid in explaining the powerful and complex interactions between personal and professional life, between writer and reader. "For all its attention to audiences," she declares, "recent cultural studies work often reads off cultural practices without reference to the people involved in cultural work. Imbedded in such research agendas is a dubiousness about people's self-assertions." To prevent such misanthropy from further creeping into cultural studies work, Steiner advocates the sensitive, yet critical, use of autobiography. "I suggest that life stories can enrich our understanding of cultural problems, including those inhering in media practices."

The next three contributors—Norman K. Denzin, Lana Rakow, and Clifford G. Christians—take on the question of how intellectuals contribute to the formation, cohesion, and, sometimes, deterioration of a variety of communities. Denzin, an early advocate for the interpretive, postmodern turn in sociology, opens the section by examining potentially productive overlaps between "new journalism" and cultural studies. He suggests that cultural studies might learn a great deal from the new journalists. "The purpose of cultural studies is clear," he notes; it is "to tell and perform critical stories about this society and the ways people make meaning in it." Yet many cultural theorists have failed in this, Denzin observes. As intellectuals, they position themselves far from their subjects, not as participants but as critics. Denzin suggests that the new journalists be considered an ideal model to "open a conversation that would bring this country back to its senses." He advocates a move away from a spectator model of narrative production to a participative, mutually interactive, and conversation-based model. By making themselves participants in events rather than bystanders, cultural critics will more likely tell stories that resonate with readers, thus increasing the chances that critique will "make a difference in the lives of those we study."

Lana Rakow's contribution asks for something seemingly straightforward but difficult to achieve. She asks that American cultural studies scholars return to their communities both to inform their work and to help transform those communities. Making this move from critique to action, she notes, is fraught. As scholars, we are all too aware of the contradictions between hegemony and human capacity for resistance. Nonetheless, she observes that "the world is being made and remade—to all of our detriment—while we are arguing on the sidelines."

What she proposes is not a new grand narrative or ultimate solution but communication solutions that place communities at their center. Rakow herself has been at the head of a project to provide her hometown of Grand Forks, devastated by floods and fires in 1997, with a new communicative infrastructure using computer technologies. A new concept of community, she argues, would move us beyond Robert Bellah et al.'s framing of middle-class white America toward communities at the margins, such as rural communities struggling against declining populations and prosperity. A study of these communities would bring a new richness to an already resurgent collection of community studies. While arguing against a "received history of nostalgia," Rakow suggests a new history of community, which would include "a history of communities destroyed, created, and sacrificed for."

Rakow asserts that the history of Native American communities provides a significant challenge to the typically told story of community in the United States, the story of the eclipse of small towns by large cities. She also notes that cultural studies work could be enhanced by examining community among African Americans, women, rural and working-class populations, gay and lesbian groups, and the developmentally disabled—to theorize how and where their voices have appeared in those communities.

Clifford Christians also places community squarely in the center of his discussion of the moral claims of cultural studies. He, like several other contributors, sees pragmatism and symbolic interactionism as cultural studies' theoretical predecessors. Within these groups, he notes, thinkers "worked from the inside out, from the backyard to the grass roots." Communities can develop and maintain these values through narratives, he argues, noting that American cultural studies embraces a narrative ethic that "has generally reflected a humanistic worldview."

But Christians also wants to argue for another tradition of American cultural studies: a theistic one. Here, Cornel West, Reinhold Niebuhr, and Paul Tillich are also part of an equation that creates a notion of public life with a center to it, one that values universal human dignity.

Community cohesion is Carolyn Marvin's concern as well, but in her view cultural studies can contribute to such cohesion in a different way: by understanding the media as performing a set of blood rituals crucial to social bonding and the preservation of the nation-state. Marvin argues that the struggle for dominance between bodies and texts—exemplified in media rituals—is one of the major dramas in advanced nations. Societal rituals help to preserve societies in space and time and to create and sustain nations; they are thus dependent on the material facts of human bodies. Into this material, bloody relationship come the media to superimpose a structure for interpreting the deaths, both actual and threatened, associated with such events as O. J. Simpson's trial, hurricanes, wars, and moon landings. The manner in which violence is framed in such events creates a parallel between the material body and the media body.

Media rituals are successful to the degree that they remodel primitive bloodletting and ensure the unity of the group, in this case, the nation-state. "By re-presenting the bodies at critical moments of group transformation," she asserts, "they play a critical role in keeping nation-states cohesive."

The final essay in the collection, and its wide-ranging and lengthy anchor, is James W. Carey's "The Sense of an Ending: On Nations, Communications, and Culture." He extends some of the work on which he has built his reputation for many years to consider the formation and survival of nations, especially the United States, under the influences of communications technology, transportation technology, immigration patterns, religion, economic imperatives, and cities, among others. Carey still deeply believes in the formative effect of nationhood, as well as the central role that the media play in forming the nation.

Here, he considers the history and trajectory of nationhood worldwide and the upheavals wrought by a communications and technological revolution that erases national boundaries. At the same time, he weaves through his essay the unique issues the United States faced as a still young nation.

Carey's essay is a significant contribution to a conversation about borders in an era when some academics are arguing that borders no longer exist. It is not a repudiation of the concepts of the postmodern but an argument about what survives in the midst of sweeping change. It is also a provocative and ambitious piece of work that shows once again Carey's great gift—to use an array of viewpoints, tools, and disciplines to synthesize something entirely new and yet hauntingly familiar, something that always goes well beyond the material used to create it.

This interdisciplinarity and breadth are, of course, nothing new. Carey was one of the first scholars to define the field of cultural studies in the United States, and he helped create an intellectual position defined in opposition to the conservative, empirical paradigm that reigned in communication studies through most of the twentieth century; he gave the new terrain the name of "cultural studies" after Richard Hoggart sent him a letter admiring one of his pieces, along with the first mimeographed working papers from the Centre for Contemporary Cultural Studies at Birmingham University in England. Carey's was an early and articulate voice for cultural studies here in the United States.

Like the intellectuals associated with the Birmingham Centre, Carey began with a firm belief in the importance of the specificity of nation-state for cultural experience. To substantiate his position, he relied on intellectual work by U.S. and Canadian theorists, such as John Dewey and Harold Innis, because he believed that there was a unique "American" cultural experience that could be analyzed best by those who had been shaped by that experience themselves.

Here, Carey depends on Innis's key insight, that Western history began in time and is ending in space. He extends this to ask other central questions about how nations themselves exist. The questions he asks and answers are both profound and fascinating:

> Nations, like all political and social organizations, have definite physical limits; that is, they live within geography or space. Similarly, they have definite temporal limits; that is, they live within history or time. This is so obvious that it usually goes without saying, but its implications are hardly explored. Duration and extent define the borders of social organization. But where are the origins and limits of these borders? What purposes do they serve? How do spatial and temporal borders act as technological containers shaping the lives of peoples consigned to different locations along them? How does technology, among other things, figure into the establishment and maintenance of these frontiers? How are spatial and temporal boundaries reciprocally related?

Carey sketches out his already familiar argument: beginning with the railroad and the telegraph and ending with television's conquest of national space with the large broadcasting organizations, the United States had—up until the mid-1970s—a well-defined sense of both geographic space and time and media space and time. "Television," he observes, "cemented and rendered visible what was less apprehensible in the age of the printing press: a particular structural relation between the state, technology, and the economy in which the authority of the state, the economy, and the national culture was nailed metaphorically to every tree via a television signal, dominating all the partial and particular cultures and authorities contained within national borders."

But this is no longer the case in the age of cable, satellite, and the web. The huge changes that new communication technologies bring with them are enigmatically contradictory. It is not, Carey notes, that we have moved completely, easily, and seamlessly from the modern to the post-modern. The print tradition, for instance, has not completely ceded to the electronic tradition. Nonetheless, we are in a "verge": "In the mid-1970s, we entered a new phase in the history of the compression of space and time. As telecommunications has burst the constraining boundaries of the nation-state, social structures that have defined the modern world and established its direction have been thrown into disarray, and national cultures have been forced into cognitive and affective melt-down." Amazingly, in the midst of this meltdown, nations survive. As Carey points out, nationalism, like it or not, is still "the principle power among men and women."

Carey's essay does not provide a rosy vision of the future. Complacency has never been one of his hallmarks. But it does help provide a new understanding of some of the tensions and forces at work at the turn of the century.

This collection is a group of essays that neither praise cultural studies nor bury it. The essays offer a different perspective, a fresh perspective on cultural studies from within and outside the field. They offer a fresh approach to thinking about what it means to practice cultural studies in the United States, using claims about communications, community, morality, and activism. They consider the meaning of cultural studies in terms of geography, theory, and methodology, and then they move on to do the kind of grounded work necessary if democracy is going to survive in this increasingly complex nation.

References

Carey, J. C. 1989. *Communication as Culture.* Boston: Unwin Hyman.
Dewey, J. 1916. *Democracy and Education.* New York: Macmillan.
Geertz, C. 1973. *The Interpretation of Cultures.* New York: Basic Books.
Shields, C. V. 1952. "The American Tradition of Empirical Collectivism." *American Political Science Review* 46:104–20.

DANIEL CZITROM

1 Does Cultural Studies Have a Past?

When I was asked to be a part of this project, I envisioned myself throwing down the gauntlet: what is it about the practice of American cultural studies that leads to the neglect of history? After immersing myself in some of the recent overviews of cultural studies and revisiting two comprehensive anthologies, I quickly realized that any formulation that posed "history versus cultural studies" was just too simplistic and would obscure more than it illuminated. I had to remind myself that my own relationship to cultural studies has been that of a fellow traveler. Twenty-five years ago I was a coeditor of the journal *Cultural Correspondence,* a thoroughly low-tech, unfunded, homemade effort at sympathetically treating popular culture from a Left perspective. Nor have I forgotten my difficulties convincing the University of Wisconsin's history department that the intellectual and cultural history of the American mass media was a legitimate topic for a dissertation.[1] Cultural studies obviously has a past, and on the evidence of the proliferating number of review essays, anthology introductions, and critical meditations, the self-consciousness about that past is more pronounced than ever. It is also a sure sign of its coming of age as an established force in American academia. One can fairly say, for example, that the peculiar institution known as American studies has for all intents and purposes become a branch of cultural studies. If you think I exaggerate, just check any issue of *American Quarterly* or, better yet, read aloud randomly from the session titles and paper topics listed in the annual American Studies Association programs.

This essay explores what I see as the uneasy connections between cultural studies and contemporary American historical scholarship by addressing three questions. First, what do the various overviews of cultural studies' own evolution tell us about its relationship with the discipline of history? Second, how has recent historical practice itself been transformed by the intellectual achievements of cultural studies? Finally, if, as I believe, much of the current practice of American cultural studies too often neglects American history, what advantages might accrue to cultural studies from a more explicitly historical approach? Let me begin with some insights gleaned from recent overviews. Joel Pfister, Michael Bérubé, Catharine Hall, and Fredric Jameson, among others, have pointed to what Pfister (1991) calls "an absence of sustained engagement with the matter of history" (206) and the "failure to see that history is inseparable from contemporary cultural studies" (207).[2] Insofar as what Simon During (1993) has called the "culturalist" strand of cultural studies—emphasizing forms of life, practices, and feelings—has been superseded by the "structuralist/semiotic" strand—analyzing codings and decodings—the ahistoricity of the cultural studies enterprise becomes more glaring.

A historical critique of cultural studies cannot be separated from the broader, sophisticated questioning of the postmodernist and poststructuralist turns in recent American intellectual life. It would be impossible for me to summarize quickly this important line of criticism, which includes a growing number of historians. But the key sticking point remains: what is lost when analyzing discourse and language becomes a substitute for analyzing changes in material conditions, consciousness, and power relations over time. Bryan D. Palmer (1990) put it well in his thoughtful study *Descent into Discourse,* a critical look at how that "body of critical writing which posits the centrality of discourse or language is constructing being, power, and consciousness" (xii) and how it has affected the writing of social history. "Historical materialism," Palmer argues, "has no difficulty accommodating an appreciation of the materiality of texts and the importance of discourse":

> It can accept that discourse plays a role in constructing social being, just as it can appreciate the importance language plays in the politics of labor and the process of revolutionary transformation. The opposition between discourse and materialism hardens into a this versus that countering of interpretive choice at the very point where discourse demands recognition of the totalizing and discursive determinations of language,

> writing, and texts, elevating itself to an all-encompassing authority that is both everywhere and nowhere. (215)[3]

Yet I think even Palmer would acknowledge that the hardening into "this versus that interpretive choice" is only part of the story. Recent historical scholarship, especially in the realm of cultural history, owes an enormous debt to cultural studies and shares very real common ground. By insisting on a greater sophistication about language and a more careful interrogation of how historical sources and categories have been constructed, cultural studies has surely influenced some of the pathbreaking cultural history of recent years. Among the works that I would include on my personal short list are George Chauncey's *Gay New York* (1994), David Roediger's *Wages of Whiteness* (1991), Lizabeth Cohen's *Making a New Deal* (1990), George Lipsitz's *Time Passages* (1990), Linda Gordon's *Pitied but Not Entitled* (1994), and Glenda Gilmore's *Gender and Jim Crow* (1996).

Let me use an example that is even closer to home for me. Having recently coauthored a new American history survey text, I know firsthand how cultural studies has pushed historians to rethink America's past. Both the organization and thematic approach in *Out of Many: A History of the American People* (2000) are harmonious with several of the perspectives associated with cultural studies. *Out of Many* reworks the traditional survey narrative in three key ways.

First, it deploys a dynamic understanding of community as one way of synthesizing social and political history, of integrating the history of the nation with that of its people. The term *community* is frequently used to convey a sense of harmony and social peace, but the historical process through which communities are defined, governed, and directed often includes a great deal of conflict. The underlying dialectic of American history locates unity in difference. Rather than assume a Whig perspective that posits the inevitable and steady progress of a glorious nation, we leave the question open. It is still unclear whether the E pluribus ends in a genuine Unum. Each chapter opens with a narrative vignette about a representative community in which local, everyday life struggles over, for example, politics, racial difference, citizenship rights, labor systems, or the control of new technologies refract conflicts played out on the regional, national, and global levels. The very notion of community itself, once defined spatially, becomes more complex the closer one gets to the present, as such new historical constructions as the nation-state, ethnic and racial groups, the corporation, professions, and the mass media emerge as bases for new kinds of communities.

Second, the book insists on a continental approach to American history and thus offers a radical decentering of traditional narratives driven by the westward march of white colonists from New England and Virginia. The community introduction for the founding of the first European settlements in the New World, for example, depicts the tensions between the Pueblo Indians and the Spanish colonists of seventeenth-century Santa Fe. We present early-nineteenth-century territorial expansion into the American West from the perspective of the Mandan villagers who encountered Lewis and Clark on the upper Missouri River. We introduce Reconstruction through the political, economic, and cultural strategies pursued by newly freed African Americans in Alabama's Hale County. The Progressive Era opens with a consideration of Lillian Wald and the extraordinary reform community of educated young women she gathered in New York City's Henry Street settlement. We lead the 1920s with a consideration of Hollywood the place and the national movie audience it created as models for new kinds of communities based on the culture of consumption.

Finally, *Out of Many* argues for the centrality of racial and ethnic difference and the gendered nature of historical experience in making sense of the American past. We try to get this across in several ways. In volume 1, for example, we devote a whole chapter to the origins of slavery and its relation to empire. Volume 2 has an entire chapter dedicated to the civil rights movement, arguably the most important domestic political event of the twentieth century and the culmination of a century-long tradition of black protest. We try to integrate the voices of women and their experiences as historical subjects throughout the entire narrative, instead of boxing them off in the textbook equivalent of "the woman's page" in a newspaper. We pay special attention to the historical migrations, voluntary and forced, that have peopled the continent and contributed to our fundamentally creole culture. We give serious attention to groups that are still underrepresented in survey texts, such as Mexican Americans, Native Americans, and Asian Americans. Beyond that, we show how at any of the critical turning points of the nation-state—the Revolution and constitutional period; the Civil War and Reconstruction; the New Deal and World War II; and the postwar era—inequality based on racial, ethnic, class, and gender difference was repeatedly inscribed in law and public policy.

Textbook writing is, however, only one form of historical practice, and it can make no claim for the sort of intellectual breakthroughs associated with cutting-edge scholarship. But it seems to me that the approach we take in *Out of Many* bears directly on those critiques of cultural studies that address the related issues of audience, language, and political intervention. Michael Denning (1992) reminds us that the original British project of cultural studies was "always an intervention in several publics—beginning in adult education, and moving into universities, polytechnics, the Open University, the magazines and journals of the Labor left, and the British Film Institute" (35). Denning carefully avoids a nostalgic plea for a return to the glory days of the Birmingham Centre for Contemporary Cultural Studies, and he rightly insists, "For better or worse, cultural studies in the United States will be what we make of it" (36).

What have we made of it? "Because cultural studies explicitly makes claims on public life," Michael Bérubé (1994) explains, "it is especially susceptible to challenges from academics and nonacademics alike whenever it seems to be getting too highfalutin and exclusionary, whatever that means" (138). In one of the most searing of these challenges Steven Watts (1991) argues that the "modern American Studies agenda, with its growing poststructuralist leanings, is in danger of lapsing into 'idiocy,' with its advocates speaking—or, perhaps, being spoken by—the discourse of idiots." Watts uses the term *idiot* in its original Greek meaning, "a peculiar and self-possessed individual, the opposite of a public minded citizen of the republic" (632). Frances Mulhern (1995) believes it "romantic to go on thinking of cultural studies as an 'intervention.' It is now an instituted academic activity, and academic activity, whatever its intrinsic merits, is inevitably not the same thing as a political project" (33). She questions what she calls a "culturalist reductionism" that "honors all manifestations of cultural difference as political, so encouraging particularism and a narcissistic dissolution of politics in the necessary stricter sense" (38).

I have not tried to present here or anywhere else the sort of extended, closely argued critiques made by Watts, Bérubé, and others. Nor am I entirely comfortable with this level of generalization about what is now quite clearly a sprawling body of intellectual work, of varied quality and spoken with a rich assortment of disciplinary accents. But the substance of these criticisms resonates for me. These days, when I read dissertation prospectuses, refereed articles, and book manuscripts, listen to conference papers, and read the journals, I worry that American cultural studies suffers from a kind of intellectual ventriloquism. Too often, history appears simply as an illustration for the real text—showing a command of Continental theory. Too many scholars seem to be putting their quarters into the academic jukebox and playing the same tunes. American cultural studies, having challenged so many of the "master narratives," is now in danger of substituting a "master methodology" that too frequently betrays a scandalously weak grounding in American history.

Regardless of where one stands on the questions of audience and political intervention, we are all invested in empowering our students to make more informed and critical choices about the world in which they live. In this respect I am very sympathetic to Donald Lazere's (1995) analysis of how poststructuralism has contributed to "depoliticizing politics." He writes tellingly of his experience teaching American literature at California Polytech:

> The majority of American students suffer not from an excess of logocentrism and humanistic culture but from a deficiency in the elements of them that are necessary for self-defense against manipulations by political, economic, and cultural elites. I have taken to giving vocabulary and factual quizzes in my junior level class in American literature from 1865 to 1918 since I discovered that few students could define words in the readings such as plutocracy, demagogue, the spoils system, populism, progressive and socialism, or identify any president during that period or date the Russian Revolution or World War I within twenty years. It is dreamily romantic to expect that the masses of young Americans today are eager or able to set their indigenous language and culture in opposition to the dominant language and culture when they have so little knowledge of the latter to begin with. (352)

American cultural studies needs to reclaim the idea of education for citizenship, in the broadest sense of that term. One way to do that is to get the state and public policy back onto its agenda. We need an American cultural studies that brings a deeper, more historically informed engagement with the state and with how power relations get worked out in the realm of public policy. This is one way, as well, to try to answer what Steven Watts (1991) identifies as "the massive unsolved problem at the heart of Foucauldian poststructuralism: what exactly connects the primacy of certain discourses to the domination of certain social groups?" (637).

Let me briefly try to flesh out the approach I am suggesting, first with an anecdote from teaching and then with some specific examples from American history. The anecdote comes from the Clarence Thomas–Anita Hill hearings in the fall of 1991. Recall the highly charged moment when Thomas played his version of the race card by accusing his critics of attempting a "high tech lynching." As I watched Strom Thurmond, one of Thomas's chief sponsors, nodding approvingly, the ghoulish irony of that scene was stunning. In 1948, of course, Thurmond had run for president on the States Rights Party ticket, winning thirty-nine electoral votes and polling a higher popular vote than Henry Wallace did that same year with the Progressive Party. And why had Thurmond, the Democratic governor of South Carolina, and his supporters bolted the Democratic National Convention? Because they vehemently opposed the civil rights plank the Democrats had adopted, including a provision to make lynching a federal crime.

I may have missed something, but in the blizzard of commentary on the hearings I do not recall anyone pursuing this point. The Thomas-Hill confrontation produced a great deal of theorizing about race and gender and their intersections, and I have no objections to that. But I thought it important to go to the microfilm reader, look up contemporary newspaper accounts of the 1948 presidential campaign, and read aloud to my class on post–World War II America some of what I found. This led to an extended, semester-long discussion on the centrality of the race issue in postwar politics, and I think it helped my students understand how the Thomas-Hill hearings could be linked to racialized political strategies of the last several decades.

For those of us still inspired by the original spirit of the Birmingham project, American cultural studies needs a fuller engagement with how power relations operate in the realm of public policy. We need to pay more attention to the state as a site for dynamic interplay between culture, politics, and economics. The contemporary forces of reaction, racism, and corporate power have been engaged in a wholesale and very successful attack on public life over the last generation. Part of their strategy for defunding and dismantling public institutions lies in persistently assaulting (and denying) the central role of government throughout American history. We cannot afford to cede the public sphere, and historical analysis offers some effective tools for scholars and citizens in pressing this point.

Just for example—think of the tight relationship between public policy and two historical realms that are hotly contested in current political and cultural discourse: race relations and economic inequality. So much of the public debate about America's racial divisions, affirmative action, or "welfare reform" betrays ignorance of the historical record. Above all, we avoid analysis of institutional racism, of the ways in which racial prejudice has been inscribed in public policy. As George Lipsitz (1995) argues in an article on what he calls "the possessive investment in whiteness," "Contemporary racism is not just a residual consequence of slavery and de jure segregation but rather something that has been created anew in our own time by many factors including the putatively race-neutral liberal social democratic reforms of the past five decades" (371–72).[4]

These public policies include the Social Security Act of 1935, which excluded domestics and farm workers, thus denying a disproportionately minority (and female) sector of the work force benefits routinely given to whites. After World War II, an expanded Federal Housing Administration (FHA) extended the government's role in subsidizing the housing industry. By insuring long-term mortgage loans made by private lenders, the FHA put the full faith and credit of the federal government behind residential mortgages and thus revolutionized the building industry. But the FHA required an "unbiased professional estimate" rating the property, the prospective borrower, and the neighborhood. In practice, these estimates resulted in blatant discrimination against communities that were racially mixed. The FHA's underwriting manual bluntly warned, "If a neighborhood is to retain stability, it is necessary that properties shall continue to be occupied by the same social and racial classes" (quoted in Jackson 1985, 208). The net effect was to help ensure racial segregation in the postwar suburban boom.

The current historical amnesia over the origins of the postwar economic boom is ominous, and it is also a clear measure of how the reactionary Right is winning the war for American memory. Our political culture evinces a deep denial about the crucial role played by publicly funded programs in the three decades following World War II. Yet that postwar boom, which helped millions of Americans achieve middle-class status, simply cannot be understood without acknowledging the historical reality of direct federal subsidy. Have we totally forgotten the tangible results of such entitlement programs? The 1944 Veterans Act, or the GI Bill of Rights, provided educational grants, low-interest mortgages, and business loans for ten million veterans. By 1961, one of every six owner-occupied houses in the United States (over 5 million) had been financed through Veterans Administration loans. By 1972, the FHA had helped 33 million families buy their own homes or improve their property. The 1956 Interstate Highway Act created the single largest public works program in our history. The National Defense Education Act (NDEA) of 1958 and the Higher Education Act of 1965 embodied a new consensus that defined publicly funded quality education as part of the national interest. The point here is not to celebrate these programs as unalloyed success stories—they were not. We must note the downside of the FHA policies in contributing to all-white suburbs; the GI Bill's negative impact on female college enrollment; the cold war context for the NDEA; and how the interstate system accelerated the decline of mass transit and devastated many urban neighborhoods. But the larger issue is to insist that this history be part of contemporary debates and policy decisions about education, housing, inequality, and race relations. That it generally is not impoverishes us all.

After nearly twenty years of teaching undergraduates, I am more convinced than ever that the study of history offers a unique kind of intellectual empowerment, one that is not sufficient but surely necessary. I mean here imparting not merely historical knowledge but historical method and critical habits of thinking as well. Some of the best students I see these days amaze me with their ability to deploy complex theory, sophisticated vocabularies, and conceptual models. But too often these same students discount the specifics of time and place, change over time, and the evolution of institutions. Can one truly unlock the power of high theory without basic knowledge of the historical referents contained therein? Is an engagement with critical theory somehow antithetical to critical engagement with primary sources? I do not think so. I used the term *intellectual ventriloquism* earlier, and I return to it now in closing, for if as teachers and writers of cultural studies we cannot find ways to make historical thinking a more central part of our enterprise, then we risk treating our students as if they were mere dummies.

Notes

1. For a collection of *Cultural Correspondence*'s "greatest hits," see Buhle (1987); see also Czitrom (1982).

2. See also Bérubé (1994, 137–60); Jameson (1993, 17–52); and Hall (1992, 270–76).

3. See also "In Defense of History," the special issue of *Monthly Review* 47 (July–August 1995), especially the articles by Wood; McNally; and Eagleton.

4. For similar arguments, see Sugrue (1996); and Hirsch (1995).

References

Bérubé, M. 1994. *Public Access: Literary Theory and American Cultural Politics.* New York: Verso.

Buhle, P., ed. 1987. *Popular Culture in America.* Minneapolis: University of Minnesota Press.

Chauncey, G. 1994. *Gay New York: Gender, Urban Culture, and the Making of the Gay Male World, 1890–1940.* New York: Basic Books.

Cohen, L. 1990. *Making a New Deal: Industrial Workers in Chicago, 1919–1939.* New York: Cambridge University Press.

Czitrom, D. J. 1982. *Media and the American Mind: From Morse to McLuhan.* Chapel Hill: University of North Carolina Press.

Denning, M. 1992. "The Academic Left and the Rise of Cultural Studies." *Radical History Review* 54:21–47.

During, S. 1993. Introduction to *The Cultural Studies Reader,* edited by S. During, 5–11. New York: Routledge.

Eagleton, T. 1995. "Where Do Postmodernists Come From?" *Monthly Review,* July–August, 59–70.

Faragher, J. M., M. J. Buhle, D. Czitrom, and S. Armitage. 2000. *Out of Many: A History of the American People,* 3d ed. Upper Saddle River, N.J.: Prentice Hall.

Gilmore, G. E. 1996. *Gender and Jim Crow: Women and the Politics of White Supremacy in North Carolina, 1896–1920.* Chapel Hill: University of North Carolina Press.

Gordon, L. 1994. *Pitied but Not Entitled: Single Mothers and the History of Welfare, 1890–1935.* New York: Maxwell Macmillan International.

Hall, C. 1992. "Discussion." In *Cultural Studies,* edited by L. Grossberg, C. Nelson, and P. Treichler, 270–76. New York: Routledge.

Hirsch, A. R. 1995. "Massive Resistance in the Urban North: Trumbull Park, Chicago, 1953–1966." *Journal of American History* 82:522–50.

Jackson, K. T. 1985. *Crabgrass Frontier.* New York: Oxford University Press.

Jameson, F. 1993. "On 'Cultural Studies.'" *Social Text* 34:17–52.

Lazere, D. 1995. "Cultural Studies: Countering a Depoliticized Culture." In *After Political Correctness: The Humanities and Society in the 1990s,* edited by C. Newfield and R. Strickland, 340–60. Boulder: Westview.

Lipsitz, G. 1990. *Time Passages: Collective Memory and Popular Culture.* Minneapolis: University of Minnesota Press.

———. 1995. "The Possessive Investment in Whiteness: Racialized Social Democracy and the 'White' Problem in American Studies." *American Quarterly* 47:369–87.

McNally, D. 1995. "Language, History, and Class Struggle." *Monthly Review,* July–August, 13–30.

Mulhern, F. 1995. "The Politics of Cultural Studies." *Monthly Review,* July–August, 32–40.

Palmer, B. D. 1990. *Descent into Discourse: The Reification of Language and the Writing of Social History.* Philadelphia: Temple University Press.

Pfister, J. 1991. "The Americanization of Cultural Studies." *Yale Journal of Criticism* 4 (2): 199–229.

Roediger, D. R. 1991. *The Wages of Whiteness: Race and the Making of the American Working Class.* New York: Verso.

Sugrue, T. 1996. *The Origins of the Urban Crisis: Race and Inequality in Postwar Detroit.* Princeton, N.J.: Princeton University Press.

Watts, S. 1991. "The Idiocy of American Studies: Poststructuralism, Language, and Politics in the Age of Self-Fulfillment." *American Quarterly* 43:625–60.

Wood, E. M. 1995. "What is the 'Postmodern' Agenda?" *Monthly Review,* July–August, 1–12.

JOLI JENSEN

2 Arts, Intellectuals, and the Public: The Legacies and Limits of American Cultural Criticism, 1910–50

This essay traces a conversation about the social power of art that American intellectuals conducted in the first half of the twentieth century as it relates to assumptions about democratic life. In this conversation, the arts are imagined as having the power to uplift, improve, salvage, redeem "the people"; it is through this power that they are presumed to benefit society. My interest is in tracing the consequences of these beliefs.[1] The cultural material I analyze are essays, articles, and debates; the social consequences I consider are what we as intellectuals do; the conversation I study is the conversation I believe is at the heart of American cultural studies—the nature and consequences of American democracy.

I use the work of four groups of American intellectuals to ground my analysis of the possibilities and limits of this heritage of American cultural and social criticism. I find in their discussions a complex concern with the public—what worries these critics is whether "the people" are what they need to be for democracy to work. I find that "the arts" are continually imagined as a magic factor in a critical equation that assumes that, if the arts are made right, the public will be made right, and thus democracy will flourish. This equation anoints the arts-savvy intellectual as seer and sage and, I argue, leads to intolerant and therefore impotent social criticism.

My analysis offers a cautionary tale for us as practitioners of cultural studies. I believe that we in cultural studies are always social critics, because our cultural analyses are inescapably social analyses, in relation to hopes and fears about contemporary life. We must avoid drawing on assumptions that appear generous and democratic but are in their consequences self-serving and elitist. We must be critical of the assumptions we use when we think about democracy, culture, media, society, and our roles in them. That critical reflexivity is, I have always believed, something American cultural studies does particularly well.

Passions and Convictions

In the early twentieth century, American intellectuals argued, prophesied, exhorted, and despaired about the prospects of modern American life. Virtually all of what are now believed to be postmodern themes appeared in the discourse of early-twentieth-century critics; the nature and consequences of fragmentation, mobility, capitalism, the cult of the new, mass communication, and technology were aspects of their developed critique of modern life. This critique of modernity animated a complex tapestry of debates about the role of art in social life.

This tapestry was, ultimately, about connections between culture, society, and politics. This means early-twentieth-century criticism offers a "usable past" for American cultural studies and contemporary cultural politics. To simplify drastically, debates centered on the connections between art and criticism in the 1910s, art and social renewal in the 1920s, and art and political action in the 1930s. Discussions about the necessary role of art in the modern age were simultaneously discussions of the role of the artist; the abstract thus became concrete and, by the 1930s, intensely personal.

This was a time of palpable social changes—nothing stood, and nothing stood still in this period of intellectual fervor, played out against World War I, the Russian Revolution, the Great Depression, and World War II. In this period, woven through with Freudian and Marxist thought against a backdrop of major economic and political change, a newly self-conscious American intelligentsia developed a series of positions about art and modern society.

While the concerns about politics and culture can seem contemporary, the faith and fervor of the essays can make them seem quaint, especially when set against current discursive styles. In the early twentieth century, passion and hope animated discussion—passion for new experiences, new living arrangements, new literatures, hopes for new people, new societies, new futures. Essays were filled with exhortations, and books ended with calls for action, exclamation points, and claims about the possibilities of a glorious future. There was an adolescent quality to this fervent rhetoric, both in the passion of the exhortations and in the totalizing nature of the explanations.

Many of the critics later dismissed their convictions and their fellow writers in just those terms—as "adolescent." The notion of "maturity" haunted the memoirs of intellectuals of the period, as they wrote accounts of their changing beliefs across time. The 1930s became "adulthood" for the bohemians of the 1910s and 1920s; the 1940s and 1950s became "adulthood" for the radicals of the 1930s. The level of intensity diminished, and debates took on a bookish air—arguments among gentlemen in cozy chairs rather than polemics in front of crowds on street corners. This indicates a shift in the imagined social location of intellectuals[2]—from the neighborhood and streets to the study—during the period.

The relationship between art and society was the touchstone for intellectual debate from the 1910s to the 1940s. In reading articles and books of the period and later memoirs and analyses, I found four distinct positions on the art-society relationship. These are necessarily simplifications, but they offer accounts that can be compared against each other and against the pragmatic position I suggest as an alternative. The differences among these positions fueled criticism throughout the period; what they have in common, still, is the presumption that something called art has great social power.

The first position can be called a *renewal* position. Associated with little magazines, experimental living, and Greenwich Village, a group of (mostly) men wrote, argued, and disagreed about the appropriate ways for art to energize, renew, and restore the promise of American life. The position is best characterized by the "Young American" critics who argued that a new art was necessary for a social renaissance. Their view can be contrasted with a more radical view of art as a revolutionary weapon.

This *revolutionary* view, with roots in the prewar years, became the major intellectual force in the 1930s, the so-called Red Decade. During this period of American economic and social upheaval, a number of intellectuals understood their role in response to versions of Marxism. What defined the radical position was a belief that art could and should be used as a direct weapon for social change. During a revolutionary period, artists must align themselves with the proletariat and find ways to further revolutionary aims to bring about a new society, where all people and true art can finally flourish. While individuals made different connections with the Left throughout the period (and endlessly justified, repudiated, and redefined them), the radical position, at its most fundamental, maintained that art had revolutionary power in conjunction with the forces of history.

Neither the renewal nor the revolutionary approach to art went unchallenged. The most clear-cut alternative to both claims about the social role of art and artists was offered by the New Humanists. This group argued that art was a repository of higher values to be sustained and protected and judged by standards other than immediate personal or social effect. For the New Humanists, uses of art for personal or social liberation were misuses. Art, especially in a modern, industrializing age, must function as a *conservator* of humane values, values that help men discipline and civilize themselves. To deploy art for liberation was to misunderstand its true value and power—to embody and sustain civilization. Art functions to maintain what makes individuals moral, our common life worthy, and civilization's advance possible.

The final take (in my account) on the role of art in early-twentieth-century American social thought was that of the avant-garde of the 1910s and 1920s, which became, in a transformed version, the *subversive* position of *Partisan Review* critics in the 1940s. It is a view that art and criticism are inherently challenging to the dominant culture. This means that whatever true artists and critics do is salutary, since it undercuts the dominant culture, known to be hollow, regressive, meretricious.

This last version of art's social power is extremely useful. It logically meshes with any other available version of art's supposed powers and puts the artist/critic in an enviable position of always working toward the social good, simply by doing art or criticism. The artist/critic is always, everywhere, making things better by restoring the world (the renewal position), changing the world (the revolutionary position), or maintaining truth in the world (the conservator position) through art's implicit or explicit power to challenge "what is" (the subversion position).

By the 1940s, the definition of art/criticism as inherently subversive allowed intellectuals to make their peace with the passions of their youth and the assumptions of their elders, while justifying their doing the work they wanted to do. It also served as an animating framework for the mass culture debates of the 1950s, when the mass media, rather than the arts, were at the center of intellectual debate.[3]

The Seven Arts *and the Promise of Renewal*

The Young American critics, including Randolph Bourne, Waldo Frank, Van Wyck Brooks, and Lewis Mumford, offered a vision of the arts as social renewal, a medium in and through which a new America could be created. Their project was most closely identified with the journal *Seven Arts* (1916–17) and various books that were written during the same period, including Van Wyck Brooks's *America's Coming of Age* and Waldo Frank's *Our America.*

These critics defined themselves against the central dichotomy they found in the American cultural heritage: a sterile choice between genteel culture and technocratic growth. They felt trapped between an elite, Puritan high culture and a commercial, philistine machine culture—both meretricious, and both soul-killing. For America to live up to its promise, a new form of culture had to be developed, one that was neither genteel nor commercial.[4]

This new form of culture was imagined to be democratic, American, liberating, enlivening, soul-building. Through it, new, freer, and more robust personalities could develop, and more authentic, organic, and restorative communities could be built. The imagined renaissance was a transformation of personality and thus of society—new selves grew from the new culture, to make possible a new society. Understandably, Walt Whitman was revered as an early figure in this quest.[5]

The new society was related to the best aspects of the past and of the people. These aspects, the Young Americans argued, were being choked and deflected by both genteel and commercial culture. The elite culture of the universities and museums was desiccated, unable to offer the energy needed for personal and social change. The tawdry culture of the emerging media was an extension of the machine age, offering only false pleasures.

The goal of the *Seven Arts* critics was a new, more grounded, more organic, and more experienced culture, one that allowed "mature" personalities to develop and flower. This culture was imagined as synthesizing dualities that had divided experience since the Enlightenment. The critics sought to overcome an American heritage laden with unnecessary divisions—reason from emotion, the arts from everyday life, the present from the past, the moral from the practical. These divisions were soul-destroying; if American society and the American people were to recover, the society and its people had to create and sustain a new, unifying culture (see, for example, Brooks 1917a and 1917b).

The nature and dimensions of such a culture remained vague and varied over time and among critics. Bourne is often cited for his argument, in "Trans-national America" ([1916] 1977), for a vivid cosmopolitan culture, making use of the forces of immigrant culture already at work (but deflected) in modern American life. Such a cosmopolitan culture would be not a melting pot but a way to release a synergistic pluralism that could offer integrity and purpose to American life.

Brooks, in his essay "Young America" (1916), sought a culture that could become a common ground between intellectuals and their generation, where they could develop matured sensibilities and strengthen their resistance to the developing commercial culture. Frank, in *Our America* (1919), offered a more radical version, where creative culture could fire the imagination of the people, whose modern existence was transforming them into a complacent herd.

In all these cases, the call was for a new form of American culture, one that could serve as a medium of social renovation. The arts had the power of social renewal because they had the power to create and sustain new personalities. These personalities, in community and in communion with one another, had the insight and imagination to withstand the grip of a genteel past and the lure of a mechanized future. The new culture offered the medium through which these new personalities were formed and sustained.

The defining aspect of the Young American critics was their engagement in self-transformation through cultural criticism. They saw themselves enacting the personal and social change they called for. They saw themselves as part of a new generation that had the potential to bring into existence America's true promise. They were engaged in an act of simultaneous creation and reclamation. Together, they could create a new culture, drawing from a "usable past" and enacting its best characteristics in a new, unique present. This was the way toward a social renaissance.

This cultural approach to social change is what gives these critics contemporary resonance. To change how we live and think, we must change how we think and live. Culture is the medium through which we do both, and since culture is humanly created, new forms of culture can be brought into existence and serve as an energizing and transforming force.

The Young American critics were thus (in a simplistic comparison) idealists, not materialists, in their beliefs about social change. Their critique of the consequences of capitalism was in relation to its spiritual and social costs, and their calls for reform were only vaguely economic or political. For them, since the quality of our common life is determined by institutions and practices that depend on beliefs and values, we can change the quality of our civic life by changing what we believe, value, and thus do.

It is important to see how this perspective of personal transformation leading to social change was different from the more radical approach of Marxists and other leftist intellectuals of the period. Waldo Frank concluded *Our America* with the recognition that "[t]he men who listen to Stieglitz have not yet quite joined him in their mind with the example of Bill Haywood. In other words, the impulse of New America is still unfused" (231). In 1919, for Frank, the necessary fusion was a creative act, one that is nonintellectual and "proceeds from love of life and love of being. It animated the Russian Revolution. It is the spiritual substance which moves mountains." He ended his book by exhorting the reader toward necessary social change: "Whitman foresaw it and sang of it and warned us. We must go through a period of static suffering, of inner cultivation. We must break our impotent habit of constant issuance into petty deed. We must begin to generate within ourselves the energy which is love of life. For that energy, to whatever form the mind consign it, is religious. Its act is creation. And in a dying world, creation is revolution" (232).

From Renaissance to Revolution

The social renewal the Young American critics imagined was an extension of the more general progressive spirit of the era, one that found the possibility of new syntheses between science and art, individual and machine, old and new. The progressive perspective placed great faith in human abilities to find new connections, new fusions, new harmonies among disparate forces. Those connections were usually contingent, designed to function well for now, always available for rethinking and revision. The Progressive Era, with its pragmatist heritage, valued the flexible over the rigid, the relative over the absolute.

To more radical critics, it looked like an ameliorative perspective, one that was always willing to become corrupt through compromise. To understand how Marxism charmed a generation of intellectuals, most of whom later repudiated their faith, it is important to recognize the ways in which the "renaissance" lost favor and a more rigorous revolutionary perspective gained appeal.

One way to understand this shift is to consider *Intellectual Vagabondage,* Floyd Dell's (1926) critique of his own generation, which he characterized as childlike, self-indulgent bohemians. In his analysis, the nineteenth-century heritage of "art for art's sake" became the excuse for Dell's generation to "play at life" as mere onlookers. The literature of the period, Dell argued, supported "the essentially homeless and childless and migratory life to which capitalism had largely condemned us" (176). Artists adopted and protected their role as idlers and onlookers, with the world a mere spectacle. They were intellectual vagabonds, "cut off from the world of reality by a magic circle," so that they "looked outside into the chaos of meaningless accident with a kind of divine scorn" (214).

This detached, distanced, immature attitude was first challenged, Dell claimed, by the work of H. G. Wells and the sense that an old world was dying and that a new world was waiting to be built; "nothing in the world was so calculated to throw the glamour of righteousness over our impulsive follies as the notion that we were the servitors of the Future" (227).

But, Dell implied, his generation could not serve the future, since it could not free itself from the vagabond attitude. Instead, it responded to the World War and the Russian Revolution by continuing to bemoan the chaos and spiritual emptiness of the times, to "foist off our own muddlement upon the universe itself" (247). What was needed? A new generation, one not "shell-shocked" by world events, which could scientifically explore the "real" reasons behind them.

Here we come to a key intellectual trope of the period—the "muddlement" and "chaos" of the 1910s and 1920s was giving way to the "science" and "laws" of Marx and Freud. The next generation, Dell believed, would have good working theories of the unconscious and of society. They would find "a definite kind of order . . . to correlate and explain all sorts of bewildering and painful discrepancies in outward conduct, previously inexplicable; they [will] have created an intelligible and practically demonstrable theoretic unity out of just those aspects of human life which have for fictional and other artistic purposes seemed in the past a hopeless jangle of contradictions" (248).

This new theoretic insight had not yet met with wide response from the intelligentsia because, in Dell's words, "it would be a reproach to us for our own failure" (249). The lessons that the Russian Revolution could and should have taught intellectuals—the value of such dull matters as honesty, sobriety, responsibility, and duty—were ignored. There was no actual social relation between artists and the masses, since artists had repudiated it through their isolated onlooker role. They had left the masses to be "fed" by the movies, the comic strips, and a literature that undertook only to "solace its audiences with simple wish-fulfillment of a quasi-infantile nature" (258). But the new generation would be different.

Those in the new generation, Dell believed, would "take themselves and their responsibilities more seriously and at the same time more joyously" (259). They would find "the political terms upon which they can accept and serve and use a machine civilization." And, he argued, "it may be quite natural for them to think of the arts as a means of communication rather than merely opportunities for irresponsible self-expression" (260). With this new understanding and definition of the arts, they could create a literature that would "help them to love generously, to work honestly, to think clearly, to fight bravely, to live nobly" (261).

In Dell's analysis, we find most of the appealing elements of 1930s radicalism—the choice for certainty over muddlement, the power of theory to correlate and explain, the chance to be responsible and disciplined, and the charge to create a new art that would help artists—and thus the masses—be generous, honest, brave, noble, and clear-thinking.

Dell did not go on to become a Marxist intellectual; his later works focused on "adult" responsibilities rather than political and social action. But he offered the critique of intellectual isolation and anomie that pervaded the period; the same critique Granville Hicks (1935) used to position radical writing against that of the humanists and what he called "the impressionists," who are called the Young American critics here.

If only, Hicks observed, there had been someone to say, "This is the situation of society today: these are the forces that have shaped that situation; here is the power that can bring change," then novelists and poets might not have "stumbled quite so blindly or taken such a precipitate flight" (249). Radical writers, artists, and critics believed they had found, in the early 1930s, a way to avoid being muddled, timid, uncertain. The Marxist analysis of history offered clear causes, known cures, and particular forms of collective action. For intellectuals, this included a vital role for art and artists in the coming revolution.

The New Masses *and the Road to Revolution*

The Great Depression offered final proof to intellectuals that the old order was in decay; Marxism offered the most captivating and thoroughgoing critique of the old order and plan for the new. While economic "muddlement" reigned at home, the Soviet Union was enacting a clear and certain version of a new order. Marxism also offered, in some version or another, a clear and certain role for artists in the struggle for revolution.

That role was, however, contradictory. Artists were important to the revolutionary process, but their exact function was unclear. Were writers, critics, intellectuals serving the cause only as they allied with the working class, or were they more useful as distinct voices of revolutionary truth in an age of capitalist lies? At the heart of the dilemma was the problem of trust in individual aesthetic insight—could and should artists trust their own aesthetic choices?

The problem, basically, had to do with ideology, although it was not addressed in those terms. Were artists of all kinds revolutionary by nature, or must they become so through some form of reeducation and insight? Once artists recognized the need for revolution and were supportive of particular routes to it, must their work reflect that commitment? The 1930s Left struggled to resolve various assumptions about how artists should participate in a revolutionary process that depended, ultimately, on the proletariat.

The issue of social location was a difficult one—where, in the class struggle, could intellectuals position themselves? How could they think, write, and act in appropriate alliance with a class they barely knew? If intellectuals formed, instead, a separate class, how could they appropriately think, write, and act toward the creation of a (predestined but still unformed) new society?

"Appropriate" alliances and "appropriate" actions suggested another aspect of the problem: that artists had to form allegiances and manifest behaviors that conformed to particular perspectives and that these perspectives were not, necessarily, "natural" ones. This became the problem that bedeviled committed Marxist intellectuals during the period—the perceived need to reeducate, discipline, and reimagine the self to play the appropriate role in ongoing change. To be more than or different from a class of dilettantes, radical intellectuals and artists felt the need to transform themselves.

One way for artists to avoid radical self-transformation while continuing to serve the cause of social change was to consider themselves "brain workers." Artists could thereby define themselves as members of an intellectual class, able (unlike the bourgeoisie) to think independent of the business class and thus free to ally themselves with their "true comrades," the working class. This was the logic of *Culture and the Crisis,* a pamphlet issued by fifty-two artists and intellectuals in 1932. The argument went like this: we as intellectuals can think for ourselves and "hence, to a degree, can think for our time and our people." All that is "orderly, sane and useful" in society has been created either by "brain workers" or "muscle workers," and thus their alliance, in the "frankly revolutionary Communist Party, the party of the workers," will reject the "lunacy spawned by grabbers, advertisers, traders, speculators, salesmen" (quoted in Rabkin 1964, 22).

By this logic, artists were members of an intellectual class that, along with workers, was responsible for all that was valuable ("orderly, sane, and useful") in society and, along with workers, was the enemy of the agents of capitalism—grabbers, advertisers, etc. Artists here did not claim to share the ideas, experiences, and values of the workers, only the same enemies and an equally vital role in the coming revolution.

The question of "right action" remained. What should the intellectual class be doing—what kinds of work, in what kinds of setting, toward what kinds of ends? Here is where the nature of the relationship to the Communist Party was at stake—should art be connected to a particular party line? Was such ideological discipline a temporary condition, necessary now, but unnecessary once the new social order was in place, when creativity could flow freely and "naturally?" If art was a revolutionary weapon, wouldn't it then be propaganda, not capable of whatever "true" art was capable of? A variety of conflicting beliefs about what art can and should do can be found in this debate over the value of revolutionary art.

The issue of allegiance to a Communist Party line was finessed by deploying such terms as *responsibility* and *discipline.* By 1937, at the second meeting of the League of American Writers, Earl Browder (the general secretary of the Communist Party) shaped his remarks to writers around the need for unity against fascism. He extended the same assurances he had made at the first congress, in 1935, that there was no official Party line, that Communists simply wanted writers to write as well as they could. This point of view was often referenced by saying that the revolutionary cause needed good writers, not bad strike leaders. The problem remained, however—what constituted "good" writing from a revolutionary vantage?

In the 1937 address, Browder claimed the revolutionary struggle as the source of all strength and value in art and emphasized the necessity of higher discipline to the whole struggle for democracy. Writers must "make their own decisions on the content and methods of their work; but they are responsible to their fellow-men that their work does in truth serve the common cause. The freedom which every writer demands cannot become irresponsibility" (49).

Browder defined culture as "the social organization of the search for an ever higher truth" (54), a definition that would please the humanists. For Browder, such a search "is the creator of organization and discipline, it is the instrument whereby the progressive and democratic forces consolidate themselves, it is the hallmark of our camp as opposed to that of the fascists" (54). In this way, then, disciplined and responsible artistic creation fought fascism. In the logic of the times, the reverse also obtained: "undisciplined" and "irresponsible" art did not fight fascism and thus could be seen as supportive of it.

A 1934 exchange between Mike Gold, the quintessential radical writer, and John Howard Lawson, a radical playwright, painfully illustrates the difficulty of personally negotiating "disciplined and responsible" creativity.[6] In this exchange we sense the dilemma of the 1930s radical artist who attempted to create the kind of work "appropriate" in its allegiances, messages, role.

Mike Gold was the prime spokesman for "proletarian realism," a form of literature that was both revolutionary in influence and representative of the new kind of literature that a revolution would allow to flourish. According to Gold, proletarian literature dealt with "real" conflicts, not "sickly, sentimental subtleties" (à la Proust) but "the suffering of the hungry, persecuted and heroic millions." Proletarian literature had to have a social theme, otherwise it was "merely confectionery." The assumption that a worker's life was dull and drab was a bourgeois notion—proletarian writers portrayed the horror but included the "revolutionary elan" that would sweep it all away. True proletarian realism did away with all "lies" about human nature; as "scientists," proletarian writers knew "what a man thinks and feels" (quoted in Aaron 1965, 225–26).[7]

This was the critical sensibility that Gold brought to the ouvre of John Howard Lawson, whose experimental and radical credentials were strong.[8] In the 1920s, Lawson had been involved in the formation of the Workers' Drama League and the New Playwrights, whose experimental social theater presaged the 1930s social drama. Yet Gold, in the *New Masses,* attacked Lawson as "A Bourgeois Hamlet of our Time," lost in his "inner conflict" "between two worlds," indulging in "adolescent self-pity," which was why Lawson's work lacked maturity and "esthetic or moral fusion" (quoted in North 1969, 199–204).

According to Gold, the problem was in the man himself—a problem that could not be solved until Lawson had "honestly faced himself, and found out what he actually believes." It was only through this process that Lawson would free himself from his prolonged adolescence and bourgeois sentimentality, because "to be a 'great' artist, one must greatly believe in something. When a man has achieved a set of principles, when he knows firmly he believes in them, he can, like the Soviet diplomats, make compromises, box office or otherwise. Until then, a man or an author is forever betraying the fundamentals. This is what Lawson and the liberals always do; he has no real base of emotion or philosophy; he has not purified his mind and heart" (quoted in North 1969, 203).

Lawson's response to Gold's attack is remarkable—respectful, apologetic, at times almost self-abasing. It began by "admitting the truth of 70% of Mike's attack" but argued that Lawson himself was painfully aware of his own faults: "I would not be worth my salt as an author if I were not acutely familiar with the problems facing me in breaking away from bourgeois romanticism and being of some genuine literary use to the revolution" (quoted in North 1969, 204).

What we see, in the exchange between Gold and Lawson, was the human cost of Browder's call for responsibility and discipline—artists could be charged with betraying the cause, even as they struggled desperately to rout out any tendencies that could be seen as reactionary, reformist, counterrevolutionary, liberal, bourgeois. Lawson and Gold agreed that these tendencies had to be eliminated if artists were to justify their existence and create the kind of art that was of genuine use to the revolution. In the Gold-Lawson exchange, we see that the social role of artists was valuable only after they achieved revolutionary clarity, after they purified their minds and hearts, disciplined themselves to a firm set of principles, and extirpated all bourgeois tendencies. Then and only then could they create work that would have social value.

This purification, discipline, and extirpation was, in Lawson's case, a process he continued long after others left Marxism behind. At the time of this exchange, Max Eastman (1934b) was criticizing such self-abasement in *Artists in Uniform* (see also 1934a). As a former editor of the *New Masses,* Eastman was incensed at the enthusiasm with which editors of the *New Masses* and a short-lived journal, *Left,* responded to "Moscow-based" criticism. He saw, in the relentless self-scrutiny of radical writers, humiliation and spinelessness: "Underneath these exaggerated acts of abnegation something serious is the matter" (27).

He called such writers "sickly and unsound" and suggested that "the American masses are quite right not to trust them," because they "do not believe either in science or art or in themselves" (27). In an memorable paragraph, Eastman administered a stinging salvo: "When the time comes to change the foundations in this country there will be suffering masses of the people looking for a leader. And they will be looking for him on the level of their own eyes. They will not expect to find him kowtowing toward Moscow in a position which leaves nothing visible to the American worker but his rump" (27–28).

Lawson's painful dilemma about the appropriate role of the artist in the class struggle became for Eastman a repellent obsequiousness to Communist Party beliefs. Such men could not possibly lead a revolution. For Gold, Lawson's dilemma was evidence of adolescent and sentimental bourgeois romanticism. For both Lawson and Gold, such muddlement could not result in literature that was an effective revolutionary weapon. What no one suggested in these endless debates on the left was that art had no direct revolutionary role—that art was *not* a socially potent weapon.

The radical artists of the 1930s were deeply committed to social change and believed that their work, somehow, could bring about a new society. Whether it did so through some kind of general alliance of artists with workers (as proposed in *Culture and the Crisis*) or through work that represented "social truth" (as in proletarian realism) was never settled. Whether it was necessary for artists to transform themselves into pure, vigorous, and creative revolutionaries (as advocated by Eastman, Gold, and Lawson, in spite of their differences) was never clear. For our purposes, the dilemma of artists committed to revolution demonstrates a particularly intense and doctrinaire version of a faith that art, somehow, is a weapon for social change, that artists are, in Dell's ironic phrase, servitors of the Future.

The New Humanists and the Search for Unity

The fervently argued dilemmas of 1930s leftist writers and artists was not the only intellectual game in town. The New Humanist position grew in certainty and strength during the 1910s and 1920s and was at the apex of its influence by 1930, when Norman Foerster ([1930] 1967) edited a collection that included essays by the two key figures in New Humanism, Irving Babbitt and Paul Elmer More.

In introducing the essays, Foerster made a clear connection between the ills of modernity and the necessity of an alternative system of belief. As with the two previous perspectives, the fundamental problem was perceived to be the modern condition. The key difference was that the solution was not in creating a new kind of society, either through a renaissance or a revolution. The solution was through personal cultivation and discipline in relation to a higher system of morals and beliefs. There were many similarities in the Marxist and Humanist belief in purification, responsibility, and disciplining the self to a concrete set of principles.

Foerster introduced the book by suggesting that "the modern temper has produced a terrible headache," that "the noise and whirl increase, the disillusion and depression deepen, the nightmare of Futility stalks before us." People, he argued, were tired of the stale skepticism of the postwar era and were "looking for a new set of controlling ideas capable of restoring value to human existence." Foerster offered humanism as the new set of "controlling ideas," ones that could "make for order and new objectives" (v–vi).

Like Marxism, New Humanism offered order and goals, through self-discipline, in relation to larger truths. The differences between the two perspectives were profound, but they shared a common response to the perceived flux, aimlessness, and chaos of modern life—the possibility of order, direction, discipline, and, finally, certainty. This is why, I believe, both Marxism and Humanism are appealing. They offer a definite version of life, one that suggests a particular mode of conduct in relation to a particular vision of a good society. In the early twentieth century, this distinguished them from the energetic pluralism of the "renewal" approach and the subdued cynicism of the "subversive" stance—neither clearly delineated how to be or what to work toward.

The easiest way to get a sense of what the New Humanism offered in relation to other perspectives is to sketch the debate between J. E. Spingarn and Irving Babbitt about the relationship between genius and taste, meaning the relationship between artistic creation and criticism. In his essay "The New Criticism," written in 1910, Spingarn ([1924] 1969) developed an argument for art as individual expression. In his response, "Genius and Taste," Babbitt ([1924] 1969) ridiculed this notion of art as "unchained emotion" and offered his alternative—art as the utilization of the "ethical imagination" in the service of a "super-sensuous truth" (169).

Spingarn wrote his essay to "clear the ground of Criticism of its dead lumber and its weeds" (26). He listed this critical detritus bit by bit: the invocation of rules, the discernment of genre, the use of abstract conceptions or rhetorical terms, and finally, the application of moral judgments to art. "We are done with these" (32–42), Spingarn repeatedly thundered, and thus we are also done with the division between genius and taste.

Spingarn argued that if we return, via Croce, to art as expression, then the critic's role is to understand what the poet tried to express and how it was expressed. That understanding involves the critic's momentarily "becoming" the creator—"taste must reproduce the work of art within itself in order to understand and judge it" (43). At this moment, genius and taste merge. This means that criticism can be finally freed of its self-contempt, because it realizes that "esthetic judgment and artistic creation are instincts with the same vital life" (44).

Babbitt's response to Spingarn's blend of naturalism, romanticism, and modernism is a classic statement of the principles of New Humanism. Babbitt began by pointing out that Spingarn's perspective, offered as "ultra-modern," could be traced to the eighteenth century, with its exaltation of spontaneity and free expression and its definition (via Diderot) of genius as calling for something "enormous, primitive and barbaric." He labeled Spingarn and his followers "primitivists" who saw genius as "purely expressive, a spontaneous temperamental overflow" (156).

According to Babbitt, this allows critics to vicariously anoint themselves with genius: "According to the primitivist . . . the genius has simply to let himself go both imaginatively and emotionally, and the whole business of the critic is to receive so keen an impression from the resulting expression that when it passes through his temperament, it issues forth as a fresh expression. By thus participating in the creative thrill of genius the critic becomes creative in turn, and in so far genius and taste are one" (156).

In contrast to this "intoxicating" view of the linked roles of artist and critic, Babbitt offered a more restrained and judicious alternative. Babbitt did not believe that genius and taste merge; rather, the critic always criticizes—the critic must always ask if the poet's aim was intrinsically worthwhile. The critic answers this question with reference to some standard that is set above both the critic's and the poet's temperament.

This was the defining element in all New Humanist criticism—the belief in the necessity for standards above and distinct from individual situation and experience. These standards could and should guide human conduct and therefore should also serve as the criteria of evaluation for both the creation and criticism of art. These standards serve, too, as the "inner check" that separates the individual from animal, because they bridle passion and, through imagination and insight, orient the individual toward the good.

The New Humanist perspective thus relied on a dual vision of the nature of human beings—they are "natural," in flux, at the mercy of their animal nature; at the same time they are "human," with an unchanging element, a higher self, a *frein vital.*[9] It is this element, the ethical will, that restrains desire and keeps the natural self "in check." Babbitt argued that "the two great traditions," the classical and the Christian, offer appropriate checks—the classical tradition offers decorum, a sense of proportion; the Christian offers humility. These checks can mitigate against what Babbitt called the two root diseases of human nature, conceit and laziness.

Babbitt predicted dire consequences if Spingarn's "expressionistic-impressionistic view" triumphed: "To repudiate the traditional Christian and classical checks and at the same time fail to work out some new and more vital control upon impulse and temperament is to be guilty of high treason to civilization" (164).

Thus the definition of New Humanism was as a standard bearer for civilization against barbarism, through the invocation of classical or traditional virtues, operating as "inner checks" in people's lives. Humanism was defined against Rousseauian romanticism, evidenced in Spingarn (and the Young American critics and the surrealists), as well as against Jamesian pragmatism and Darwinian naturalism. Against visions of life as spontaneous, in process, instinctive, chaotic, and in flux, the New Humanism offered a vision of human life as disciplined, decorous, poised, and virtuous.

Paul Elmer More ([1915] 1967), in *Aristocracy and Justice,* refuted the claim, associated with Dewey, that the cure for democracy is more democracy. His response was that the cure for democracy is *better* democracy, democracy that protects and advances the interests of the gifted few. These gifted few (like Matthew Arnold's "saving remnant") could develop and enhance institutions, laws, and processes that could offer the necessary restraints on the natural excesses of the people.

The Humanist conception of the arts as "civilizing" was connected to a belief in man's dual nature and the need for certain restraints on natural excess. These restraints are individual but also, in Humanist social theory, institutional. The arts function at the individual and social level as repositories for traditional values of wisdom and restraint. The few who know and understand these values must lead and transform a modern society at risk. The modern risk, from the humanist perspective, is unchecked, unrestrained democracy, based on a false faith in the individual's natural goodness. A society based on such false faith is at grave risk for anarchy or despotism; the barbarism of modern culture is evidence of how necessary humanistic values are to a truly civilized society.

Partisan Review *and the Tasks of the Critic*

When we compare the renewal, revolutionary, and repository perspectives on art in society, we find unexpected commonalities. The focus on art as a communal activity, demanding allegiances to other artists and to a particular social vision, characterized the *New Masses* critics and, to a lesser degree, the Young Americans. Such a communal view was the antithesis of the individualism of the New Humanists.

The unabashed elitism of the New Humanist position was tempered but not effaced in the Young American beliefs that they would create the culture that would lead to social renewal. The elitism of the *New Mass-*

es position was complex—there was belief in a necessary alliance with the working class, but that alliance involved being able to "think for our time and for our people," as claimed in *Culture and the Crisis* (quoted in Rabkin 1964, 22).

The perceived need for self-transformation was crucial in all three perspectives. The Young American critics believed they should live and work in ways that enacted the culture they were hoping to create. The *New Masses* critics demanded of themselves a discipline and purity that would allow them to create work that could serve the revolution. The New Humanists, too, sought discipline and purity to act, live, and think virtuously in concert with higher standards.

The "machine age" was the enemy of the New Humanists, one-half of the equation for the Young American critics, and the nature of the future for the *New Masses* critics. In spite of the variation in attitudes toward technology, there was virtual agreement about another of the aspects of modernity: mass culture is inadequate culture.

The predominance of new forms of mass entertainment figured in but did not orient the work of all three groups. The Young American critics, hoping for a new democratic form of culture, saw the new mass media forms as energetic but not, of course, the new democratic form they envisioned. The *New Masses* critics dismissed new commercial forms of culture as evidence of capitalism's hold on the middle classes and as forms of propaganda that kept the workers chained to their own oppression. The New Humanists found the offerings of the mass media to be antithetical to all the characteristics of true art—media fare was further evidence of civilization's corruption.

But there was not, among these critics, a developed critique of mass communication, the media, modern entertainment, or mass culture. They appeared in the argument as asides or as "obvious" examples of some larger point about the nature of modern life. A full-blown critique of mass culture did not develop until the 1950s, but American origins of the mass culture debate can be found in the critical turn, taken in the 1940s, by writers for the *Partisan Review.* We can find in them, also, an ingenious way out of the critical dilemmas posed by the previous three positions.

Legacies of 1930s Radicalism

It was much easier to believe in the inevitability of revolution, the virtues of the Communist Party, and the potential wonders of proletarian art in the early 1930s than it was by the late 1930s. By the end of the decade, the revolution seemed to be receding, the Communist Party self-serving, and proletarian art limited, even laughable. The fervent faith of various intellectuals wavered and in most cases foundered, as Stalinism and fascism loomed and factions of the Left bickered endlessly among themselves.

The classic account of intellectuals' loss of faith in radical politics is *The God That Failed* (Crossman 1949), where ex-radicals described how and why they had had faith in communism and then had lost it.[10] Each writer told the same story: the discovery of pattern, order, certainty, and the joy of being part of a larger, noble cause, then a period of uncertainty, then a period of disillusion, and, finally, a loss of faith in the Communist program.

Arthur Koestler (1949) described "the mental rapture of the convert": "The whole universe falls into pattern like the stray pieces of a jigsaw puzzle assembled by magic at one stroke. There is now an answer to every question, doubts and conflicts are a matter of the tortured past—a past already remote, when one had lived in dismal ignorance in the tasteless, colorless world of those who *don't know*" (23).

Stephen Spender (1949) noted a common vice in people: "to regard their own cause and their own supporters as real, and all other causes and their exponents as abstract examples of outmoded theoretical positions," and he argued that the Communist Party's theory of society encouraged this vice (254). The excitement of being a part of history, certain of how things work, and how it would all come out; the heady sense of being in the know when others were not, of being for the oppressed, against the oppressor—these were what drew converts and what embarrassed them after their loss of faith.

After disillusionment, these aspects of true faith became evidence of, at best, blindness and naïveté and, at worst, conscious manipulation. As Louis Fischer (1949), a journalist who lived in the Soviet Union during the period, wrote, "Hope distorted judgement. Seeing did not interfere with believing" (211).

Koestler (1949) called faith in communism "the great illusion of our time" and a "moral and intellectual debauch." In a memorable phrase, he said, "We lost the fight because we were not fisherman, but bait dangling from a hook" (44). Those who were once captivated by communism had two choices: they could either give themselves to some new, opposing addiction or suffer "lifelong hangover" (55). An opposing addiction would be manifested by intense faith in some other closed system and hatred for the one left behind—the hangover in a shift to less totalizing, fervent, and certain pronouncements.

While Koestler's two choices were surely not the only possibilities, they offer us two poles between which to locate a post-1930s sensibility. To understand how social criticism proceeded in the 1940s, we need to remember that much of it was, at some level, a reaction against the fervent social commitment of the 1930s. Even for those intellectuals who did not actively ally with the Party, the period presumed that artists could and should band together to foster radical change through their work. The reaction against that presumption, when it came, was against communism as a doctrine, against fervent belief as a critical stance, and against collective action as necessary for artists and intellectuals. It was not, however, against a faith in the power of art to change the social order.

Instead, many ex-converts developed a more personal and individual approach to social understanding. It was the "abstraction" of Marxist social theory that was critiqued. For Richard Wright (1949), 1930s radicalism offered "an organized search for the truth of the lives of the oppressed and the isolated," but it was a search, he believed, that had not yet found a language. "In their efforts to recruit masses, they had missed the meaning of the lives of the masses, had conceived of people in too abstract a manner." Wright went on to realize, after a vicious excommunication, that "in all the sprawling immensity of our mighty continent the least known factor of living was the human heart, the least sought goal of being was a way to live a human life" (120).

A return to the particular and the human characterized many of the ex-converts' understanding. Fischer (1949) argued that "all goals . . . are nothing in the abstract. They only have meaning in relation to the interests of living men, women and children, who are the means through which everything on earth is achieved" (228).

This attitude demanded a very different agenda for art and criticism. Art and criticism could not and should not demonstrate the virtues of the proletariat and the necessity of revolution. From this more personal perspective, all totalizing theories, all sweeping explanations, all doctrines were suspect. It was a position that suggested that individual lives, individual actions, and individual perceptions of particular experiences are what count. It involved, then, a mistrust of those who were most certain, most sweeping, most doctrinaire. It was this new perspective and this mistrust that characterized intellectuals in the 1940s, often those who had been most captivated by the faith of the 1930s.

The Intellectual as Subversive—Partisan Review *II*

By the end of the 1930s, intellectuals had tried and found wanting a range of possible roles for themselves and for their work. The renaissance perspective had not worked out—an energetic generation of writers and artists had not ushered in a vibrant, transformative democratic culture. New Humanist faith in certain overarching standards, based in the past, had a suspiciously totalitarian ring (although their sense of the arts as repositories of culture resonated widely as the cultural centers of Europe fell). The radical insistence on connecting art and politics had been repudiated—so how could artists, critics, writers work for the social good? By the early 1940s, past efforts seemed to many to be unsuccessful (Young American critics), reactionary (New Humanists), and misguided (*New Masses* critics). How, then, to construct and sustain a role for intellectuals, without questioning the developed faith in art and criticism as social practices?

One way out of the dilemma of past failures was to postulate a role for artists and critics that would overcome many of the perceived weaknesses, while maintaining the perceived strengths, of previous perspectives. Thus, one could imagine a social role for intellectuals that did not presume a direct positive result, which was the weak point of the Young American and the *New Masses* positions. When history had not cooperated with their predictions and neither a renaissance nor a revolution had materialized, their perspectives were undermined. A less easily disproven "effect" for art on society would withstand the possibility of disproof by history.

A new perspective on the social role of art and criticism would also have to avoid connection to organized doctrine, thus circumventing the perceived weakness of the New Humanist and *New Masses* perspectives. The authoritarian elements of both the radical and conservative approaches were now mistrusted—was there a way to be radical but not in relation to any particular political program, a way to be conservative without invoking narrow, absolute standards? Finally, a new stance would not call for collective action, would not expect artists and critics to organize for change. It would give artists, critics, and intellectuals a crucial social role, but one that would not require them to band together.

This became, I argue here, the new subversive perspective on the arts in society. It was a perspective that transcends the weaknesses of past perspectives but makes use of their strengths. It allows individual freedom, promotes critique without reference to absolutes, and requires no visible social effect. The doctrine of art/criticism as subversion is the ideal way to maintain faith in the power of artistic and intellectual practice to promote social good, while supporting any kind of creative work at all.

A key aspect of the subversion perspective was that the artist/critic has a special consciousness, a particularly gifted insight, and that the public circulation of that consciousness will always work to challenge the dominant culture. Good art, by its nature, is radical art, because good art is always in opposition to the status quo. The status quo is, of course, known to be inadequate, oppressive, and deserving of subversion. Thus the chronic critique of modernity (which characterized the previous three positions) is now wedded to a new individualist spirit. In this perspective, art and thus artists have the power (and the duty) to challenge and disrupt modern life.

Notice how this perspective was amenable to different definitions of art—art can be an inspiring, robust, invigorating force; it can be a container of standards and virtue; it can be a radical, destructive weapon. It can be all of these or something else—all that is certain is that, as art, it will be "challenging" what is. Thus, by the 1940s, intellectuals could consider themselves a force against the dominant culture and could count on being socially useful, no matter what they produced or what they believed, as long as it was nonmainstream, nondominant, non–status quo.

Philip Rahv and William Phillips are the exemplars of this new critical stance; their long editorship of the *Partisan Review* was a major means of its promulgation. In the early 1930s, both were active supporters of proletarian literature and the need for the intellectual to point the way toward a new, revolutionary art and criticism.[11] The *Partisan Review* of 1934–36 was a complement to the *New Masses;* the editors saw proletarian literature as, in the words of James Gilbert (1968), "the visible edge of the future, a projection of the time when political revolution would dramatically sweep away archaic capitalist institutions and bourgeois culture" (121).

Yet, even in this first incarnation, editorials suggested some ambivalence about art as a mere vehicle for politically expedient beliefs and suggested instead that literature has a role in reflecting the permanence of the past as well as the potentials of the new. These ideas became the rationale, two years later, for rejecting proletarian literature.

Another move away from the *New Masses* perspective was the argument that literary criticism was "a weapon of literature, not of politics" (Gilbert 1968, 136) and thus was an activity by and for intellectuals, who were most influenced by literature. This removes art and criticism from direct engagement in social struggle—it keeps it as the property of the intellectual class, whose role involves defining and maintaining cultural values instead of defining or maintaining revolutionary activities.

Such a shift in the location and purpose of art and criticism did not go unnoticed by other radical intellectuals—Mike Gold accused the *Par-*

tisan Review writers of a "terrible Mandarism." Newton Arvin characterized their writing as prosaically analytical. If the practice of criticism was for other intellectuals, not "the people," then it could take on the exclusionary characteristics so despised by those committed to proletarian art (quoted in Gilbert 1968, 143).

The *Partisan Review* folded for a year, and when it returned, it was solidly anticommunist. Rahv and Phillips had moved from skepticism to open opposition to communism as a cultural and political force. The first editorial of the new *Partisan Review* announced that it would represent "a new and dissident generation in American letters" (quoted in Gilbert 1968, 159). The revolution had become aesthetic rather than political.

This was confirmed most clearly by the importance placed on the role of the intellectual in social life—as Gilbert argued, "stripped of a dependence on a political movement, the artist, the intellectual, alone was the meeting place for radicalism in art and politics" (185). Thus the "site of struggle" was in the individual and in his or her work, written for other intellectuals and artists. This gave the intellectual a new relation to politics and the social world: "The estrangement of the intellectual was the justification for his withdrawal from real politics, but it was also an explanation for his ability to rise above the mundane and reunite art and politics into the vision of a revolutionary culture" (Gilbert 1968, 185–86). The "new generation" that the new *Partisan Review* represented was a generation whose artistic and critical activity was automatically, in itself radical.

This was an avant-garde sensibility with roots in various aesthetic modernisms. Such a stance awards to the artist a vital personal and social role: to remain pure, in the face of social contamination, so that his or her art can challenge and undermine the suffocating influences of the age.

As Rahv argued in 1939, "the dissident artist, if he understands the extremity of the age and voices what it tries to stifle will thus be saved from its sterility and delivered from its corruption" (quoted in Gilbert 1968, 159). Artistic expression thereby becomes personal salvation. By implication, those who are not dissident artists, who do not "voice what [the age] tries to stifle," are victims of it.

Phillips and Rahv thus changed the focus of their concern from intellectuals' relationship with the proletariat to the role of the intellectual in the modern age. They articulated a role that presumes an intellectual's ability to rise above the mundane, to free oneself from that which limits, constrains, deadens, and numbs others. It is a position that anoints the critic and the artist as having abilities not shared by others. It therefore offers a reassuring sense of superiority to the times and to the rest of society. It offers a stunning (if indirect) disparagement of those who are not artist/intellectuals—they are, by this definition, trapped and blind.

That artists and critics are specially gifted and thus can and should serve a special social function is a presumption in all four critical positions. Faith in the social power of art connects to assumptions about the social role of intellectuals, and, silently but inexorably, it presumes that "the people" are in need of their, of our, aesthetic and critical ministrations. This is the heritage of American cultural criticism that we need to recognize and rethink, because it has consequences for how we do our work.

Social Critics and "The People"

At stake in the debates among this band of American writers, critics, and artists was their appropriate social role—what should they be doing for the wider society? Underlying this question is a multitude of presumptions about what they *could* do for society—in dreams begin responsibility.

We can imagine a circular continuum of possible social positions: from a Babbitt/More guardian of cultural values to a more Dell-described vagabond onlooker, to a more Bourne/Brooks catalyst, to a more Gold/Hicks participant, to a more Phillips/Rahvian subverter who is also, at least in the abstract, a guardian, onlooker, and critic.

The *guardian* position presumes that cultural values are being challenged, effaced, diluted, corrupted. It is the role of the critic to point this out by maintaining scrupulous attention to the high standards available in previous cultural forms. There is an inherent conservative impulse in the guardian position, as well as an automatic respect for the works of the past. "The people" are swept up in emotionalism and greed; their barbarian traits are being catered to. Critics become spokespeople for and bearers of besieged cultural values. It is through them and their followers that the lamp of civilization is kept burning.

The *onlooker* has a far less exalted role. He or she is more of a journalistic commentator, in but not of the society being observed. "The people" are foolish and amusing, chasing after endlessly trivial delights that have little appeal for the spectator. This role has only modest responsibility for civilization—the onlooker can comment, critique, harangue. This is a social role of bemused disengagement.

The *catalyst* is more passionately connected to the society he or she is seeking to change. While the catalyst shares with the onlooker the desire to comment on the current scene, it is in connection with a more intense vision of what could and should be—the critic seeks the inchoate potential in the current situation and through his or her work tries to make it real. "The people" are unaware of the possibilities of their situation—with the critic's articulation, they can begin to imagine and work toward it.

The *participant* position inserts critics into ongoing social activity, acting in and through their beliefs and values, in concert with others. They engage, if possible, with "the people" in hopes of building a better future. This position presumes that intellectuals have an obligation to ally themselves with those less fortunate and that their mutual alliance will lead to revolution.

The *subversive* position, as noted earlier, can comfortably include any of these positions, in spite of their contradictions. It is marked by the presumption that any "good" artistic or critical work is challenging to the current situation, a situation that is unsatisfactory and oppressive and deserves undermining. As the critique of mass culture and mass society developed in the 1940s and 1950s, the role of the intellectual became a more complex kind of guardianship—involving an avant-garde as well as a traditional sensibility, protecting and defending whatever was considered a worthy alternative to the mainstream. The role of the intellectual was to know, see, and celebrate that which was increasingly unknown, unrecognized, and unappreciated in modern American life.

When we analyze various roles for American intellectuals, we find a surprising range of assumptions about "everyone else." For the *guardian*, "the people" are rude, uncivilized, and undeveloped. It is through the guardian and the art the guardian values that those who want to can become more refined, civilized, and worthy. It is a relatively straightforward form of superiority—with disciplined and rigorous aesthetic engagement, "the people" can become better.

For the *onlooker*, "the people" are a semipermanent exhibit, a tourist attraction. They are not assumed to be particularly barbaric, or misguided, or even in need of the ministrations of the critic. They are zoo animals doing things that can amuse, irritate, and surprise the onlooker. The onlooker leads an utterly different life—far more intelligent, interesting, rich, and meaningful. But the onlooker has neither pity for nor obligation toward "the people"; the onlooker's characteristic reaction is bemused disdain.

For the *catalyst*, the sense of obligation is much stronger—other people are in need of and searching for the insights the critic can offer. This position assumes that the critic is a particularly articulate and sensitive person who has an obligation to express his or her understandings in ways that can benefit others. The critic can know and see what others might only guess and glimpse. "The people" will recognize their situation through the critic's work and will thus find it easier to work toward changes.

The *participant* (as long he or she has doctrinal alliances) will already know what needs to be done; the critic's role is to get others to agree to the critic's perspective. The participants presume that they must connect with those they seek to serve, and so their job is to find a way to connect their deeper understanding with others' lived experiences. Theirs is a difficult position of having better understanding but worse credentials—their goal is to bridge the perceived gap between themselves and those for whom they seek to speak.

The *subverter* believes that "the people" are hopelessly mired in a repugnant society—evidence of their oppression is their apparent contentment with the situation. The subverter's task is to offer an alternative and a challenge to the times. Unlike the multitudes, subverters understand and appreciate the best works of the past, present, and future. They can keep the lamp of civilization burning, they can comment with amusement on the antics of others, and they can articulate an alternative world that would be better for not only themselves but also "the people." But they feel no obligation to connect with "them"—the subverters work for social change by maintaining connections to other intellectuals and various intellectual activities.

A Problematic Heritage

For our own sake, we need to consider the consequences of these positions. How do we, as scholars and students of culture, imagine our social role in relation to this American heritage of assumptions about art, intellectuals, and democracy? Should we simply continue to assume that, by virtue of our scholarly work, we offer society some salutary combination of cultural conservation, renewal, revolution, and subversion—remedies for whatever we say ails us?

Current discussion of the appropriate social role for intellectuals never questions our inherent ability to lead. Critiques center instead on a presumed historic split between academic and public life: where once there were brave voices of public truth, there are now obscure essays in scholarly journals. Where once there were manly revolutionaries, there are now timid, tenure-obsessed careerists. Russell Jacoby's (1987) account of how intellectuals abandoned public life for the secure confines of academe exemplifies this analysis. His is a model of suburbanization and failed courage: he offers such figures as Lewis Mumford and C. Wright Mills as models of heroic public thought, in stark opposition to today's professorial pedants.

A related analysis, one that is more nuanced but no less romantic, is Edward Said's (1994) exhortation to intellectuals to be marginal, exiled, on the side of the oppressed. He assumes that to be institutionally engaged is to be tamed, pandering, eager for approval, and fearful of truth. His is a paradoxical and often idiosyncratic analysis, where loyalty to doctrine is disparaged, but loyalty to causes is applauded as long as those causes are "just." The oppressed and powerless are the intellectual's natural constituency, Said argues, and the worst thing that can happen to an intellectual is to succumb to worry about being popular.

My analysis is a very different one. I do not presume that cowardice and pedantry have taken over a previously robust intellectual discourse. This means I cannot, with Jacoby, call for us to suck it up, start writing clearer prose, and find a way to re-create Bohemia. Nor can I, with Said, insist that we imagine ourselves as marginalized exiles, loyal only to our cogitations and the truths that they ostensibly tell us. I want, instead, to begin with a question that nobody seems to ask: are we, as intellectuals, really all that qualified to lead society?

I want, at least for the sake of discussion, to unpack the synthesis forged in the twentieth century among assumptions about art, intellectuals, and social change. I find it arrogant, self-serving, and guaranteed to shut off rather than promote participation in public discussion. Our heritage presumes that the arts have social power and that, since intellectuals understand, protect, and promulgate the arts, we have both the gifts and obligation to wield social power. The masses, who we think do not care about the arts, are presumed therefore not to care about the "social good" or to have what it takes to protect, defend, or enact it. *The masses need intellectuals so that the arts can save them and thereby guarantee a democracy worth living in.*

It is time to question every aspect of this formulation. Do the arts have social power? If so, by what logic? Something called "the arts" figures in twentieth-century discussions as multiply powerful and multiply beneficent, but on close examination the whole edifice crumbles. How can the arts, as process or product, do all that is claimed for them? How can they conserve civilization, purify the spirit, energize social relations, transform consciousness, and dismantle the status quo? Unless we want to define the arts so loosely as to be all forms of communication and culture and thereby make the unsurprising claim that human symbolic processes have social consequences, we are left with a hollow, magic incantation: arts are good for us.

Now, for the next part of the synthesis. Do intellectuals wield great social power because of our intimate connection to the arts? Apparently not. One way to understand the history of social criticism is as an endless lament over how ineffective our critiques are—no matter how hard we work at it, no one seems to listen. Intellectuals can be imagined as a poignant succession of disappointed Whitmans, endlessly revising our *Leaves of Grass.* We try, over and over, to find ways to be welcomed by the people we long to save. But the people stubbornly refuse our ministrations, are bored by our passions, and avoid our Whitmanesque embrace.

This lack of response from the people we so long to help exacerbates a disdain for the public that is the chronic companion of intellectual work. Our heritage is one of separateness from the public—we as artists, critics, and intellectuals are different from and better than everyone else. We have what they need, and so we continue, with increasing despair, if not cynicism and disdain, to profess, speak, and minister to people we believe are deprived of our learning, our cultivation, our wisdom, our insight.[12]

But are the people really so crude and uncultivated? And are we intellectuals really so refined and worthy? Once we imagine art as refining, uplifting, energizing, revealing, and subversive, we imagine ourselves as having those traits and imagine nonintellectuals to be crude, denigrated, enervated, blind, and hypnotized. The logic that anoints art with special power anoints us with special privileges and presumes that those without art are to be pitied and saved. This leads to the final conceit, that the masses are eager to be more like us and need only the right kinds of culture to become so.

As long as we are questioning the social power of art and the ability of intellectuals to influence social life through art-mastery, we might as well question the presumption that we are fundamentally better than the rest of the public. Are we, by virtue of our erudition, really better endowed with what democracy needs?

Considering the atmosphere of our faculty meetings, departments, colleges, universities, as well as the condition of our personal lives, I would question whether our ability to do academic work gives us any special purchase on social wisdom. We seem no better, although I hope no worse, than most everyone else in the ways we handle our work, our families, and our lives.

Maybe we should begin an analysis from a more egalitarian perspective. This means that we ask, "What can I offer the democratic process?" We can head toward an answer by considering John Dewey's accounts of art, democracy, and social intelligence. Dewey offers us a way to unhinge the historic connections between beliefs about art's social power and beliefs about intellectuals' social responsibility. He does this without sacrificing respect for aesthetic pleasure or for rational understanding and discourse and, most compelling, without disdain for "the public" he seeks to engage. A Deweyan alternative can help us find a way out of our self-serving heritage of beliefs.

In *Art as Experience,* Dewey ([1934] 1980) offers a pragmatic aesthetics, one where the arts are seen as aspects of everyday life. Mundane and daily acts are engaging, delightful, and aesthetic—art is a common quality of daily experience. This view of art presumes that all of us are artistic, responsive to color, shape, and line and that we can recognize aesthetically pleasing forms and arrangements as we garden, arrange furniture, walk the dog, wash the car. This is a democratized view of art that takes it out of the exalted, ethereal, and specialized realm of the artist, critic, and intellectual and places it in the familiar, concrete, and widely shared experience of the citizen.

If we combine Dewey's view of art with his view of democracy in *The Public and Its Problems* (1927), we have a heady alternative to prevailing notions of the intellectual's special responsibility to the arts-deprived masses. Dewey's notions of public conversation and social intelligence presume that people learn in and through community, through direct engagement with concrete experiences. This is a participatory and egalitarian model of democratic life that presumes the public is us. Dewey's is a model of social membership, not of social conservation, renewal, revolution, or subversion.[13]

If we combine these two portions of Dewey's thought, we can suggest the following: art is not social magic, a scarce and unevenly distributed commodity that can uplift, nourish, restore, or tame the masses. Intellectuals' mastery of the arts does not give them special access to social goodness. The public does not need intellectuals or the arts to participate in democracy. The social problems we as a society face are ones of access and participation—access to aesthetic variety; participation in public discussion. Democracy thrives when access and participation thrive—for Dewey, our world is better when it is inclusive, allows varieties of aesthetic experiences, and involves the freest possible circulation of ideas.

This offers a radically different role for us as intellectuals. From the Deweyan vantage, we intellectuals are fortunate people—paid to read and write and think and profess, with the leisure to cultivate aesthetic experiences and with more opportunities than most to speak in public about what we believe. But how can we make honorable use of our good fortune, how can we contribute to the common good?

As long as we assume that we alone are the bearers of wisdom and thus have an obligation to transmit that wisdom to the ignorant and deprived, we miss our chance to contribute to democracy. If we instead assume that we are fortunate members of a diverse society, with the opportunity to think and speak with others about issues that bedevil us, we are more likely to talk with rather than lecture to our fellows.

We are also more likely to assume that social experience, not just scholarly acumen, matters. We recognize that our experiences are unusually limited and incomplete—we need to know what others are going through if we are to work together toward common solutions.

This Deweyan position presumes that social truth is accessible through shared discussion; it is a particularly American position that runs counter to the theoretical legacies of Marx, Freud, structuralism, and poststructuralism. Those legacies have given intellectuals even more unwarranted license to preach to rather than to learn from other people. This is because their theories presume that there is something hidden behind appearances, something that intellectuals, artists, and critics are especially able to see.

There is a contemporary Continental gloss on the American positions I have described so far—the most recent manifestation of the dangers of the *Partisan Review* synthesis of previous positions. Theoretical sophistication is taken to be critical acumen, which, if shared with others, will help them see what is "really" going on. Intellectuals, with theory, can decode, demystify, deconstruct, and reconstruct the perceived world; we can thereby help befuddled others to escape the constraints of ideological fog.

Marxist cultural criticism is understood by practitioners to be a form of cultural and hence social intervention. The art object, like any other cultural form, can be "made to speak" through theory—as Tony Bennett (1979) argues, "It is . . . Marxist criticism which, through an active and critical intervention, so 'works' upon the texts concerned as to make them 'reveal' or 'distance' the dominant ideological forms to which they are made to allude." This is a signification, he continues, "they are made to have by the operations of Marxist criticism upon them" (156). Marxist critical intervention can proceed only through theoretical expertise; everyday interpretations of cultural forms can neither "reveal" nor "distance" dominant ideology.

One thing I especially like about the American cultural studies alternative is its potential for humility. Pragmatism offers us an alternative to the theoretical mandates that so haunt British cultural studies and have so captivated American departments of literature. With American cultural studies, we can turn away from the elitism and solipsism of elaborate theorizing and turn toward a more egalitarian and participatory discourse.

But we must realize we still operate with the same temptation—we find in our heritage, too, an assumption of intellectual privilege, manifested in the belief that we, as intellectuals, have special sight. If we can unhinge the presumed connection between the arts, intellectual activity, and social change, we can enact a less heroic but far more useful social position. In so doing, we would speak from connection with others who share our time and place, informed by what we, as intellectuals, are fortunate enough to know about other times and other places.

We would find ways to surpass our legacy. I suggest we begin by questioning our presumed obligation to use criticism to conserve, renew, transform, or subvert or to unmask or reveal. I suggest that we also question our assumption that the public has an obligation to listen and follow what we have to say. Once we let go of these conceits, we can explore ways to be members of the continuing democratic process, fully participating in already ongoing cultural, aesthetic, and social conversations. If we can get past our heritage of special power and special sight, we might find new ways to teach, write, and live, ways that work toward inclusiveness, diversity of opinion, and varieties of social possibility.

Notes

1. This essay draws on arguments developed in my book manuscript, currently entitled "Imagining the Arts: Culture and the Public in American Social Thought," forthcoming from Rowman and Littlefield.

2. This was a shift in social location but not in gender—this period, like our own, imagines intellectuals to be mostly men.

3. For the ways in which the mass culture debates of the 1950s inform current assumptions about media, culture, and society, see Jensen (1990).

4. Casey Nelson Blake (1990) locates this Puritan-philistine dichotomy in the biographies of the Young American critics. His introduction to the group and period also offers an insightful discussion of the weaknesses and potential of Young American critical perspectives.

5. Thomas Bender (1993) notes that virtually every essay in the first issue of the *Seven Arts*, including those by foreign writers, mentions Whitman (83n. 14).

6. This exchange is well worth reading in its entirety for the insight it offers into the 1930s concern with correct political thought. It can be found in North (1969).

7. The Aaron book is an essential introduction to the thought and work of radical writers of the period.

8. Biographical information on Lawson is drawn from Rabkin (1964, 127–65).

9. There is an especially good discussion of this dualistic view in Hoeveler (1977, 34–37). Hoeveler's excellent analysis of the Humanist perspective informs my discussion here.

10. See especially Koestler (1949); Silone (1949); Wright (1949); Gide (1949); Fischer (1949); and Spender (1949).

11. James Gilbert (1968) offers a particularly thoughtful account of the *Partisan Review* group.

12. Here is where an argument about university-ensconced intellectuals may have some relevance. It is easy to presume that the public is ignorant and in need of what we have to offer when we spend our working lives teaching students. It is also easy to forget that students may not really need what we have to offer and that they may not significantly benefit from our ministrations. Yet we as professors believe we have something that "does them good," and thus we enact the Whitman plea to be heard, adhered to, followed. In return we get, mostly, dutiful attention, a willingness to jump through our hoops if it results in a degree. The cynicism of our students comes to represent the whole philistine public, which ignores our attempts to seduce them into our world of ideas and instead seeks security, jobs, and the respect of their peers. Perhaps we should ask ourselves, are those such unworthy goals? Are they so different from our own? Are they necessarily antithetical to justice, knowledge, truth, creativity, kindness, and other virtues?

13. At conferences on the public and democracy, I am increasingly uncomfortable with discussions in which "our" (academic intellectuals) difference from "them" (the public) defines every analysis. As a shorthand way to reference Dewey's perspective on these issues, I suggest that every time we refer to "the public" we use the term *we.* This proves to be an impossible stumbling block—the arguments most of my colleagues want to make requires an assumption that "we" are very different from "them."

References

Aaron, D. 1965. *Writers on the Left.* New York: Avon Books.

Babbitt, I. [1924] 1969. "Genius and Taste." In *Criticism in America: Its Function and Status,* edited by I. Babbitt, 152–75. New York: Haskell House. First published in *Nation,* February 7, 1918.

Bender. T. 1993. *Intellectuals and Public Life: Essays on the Social History of Academic Intellectuals in the United States.* Baltimore: Johns Hopkins University Press.

Bennett, T. 1979. *Formalism and Marxism.* New York: Methuen.

Blake, C. N. 1990. *Beloved Community: The Cultural Criticism of Randolph Bourne, Van Wyck Brooks, Waldo Frank, and Lewis Mumford.* Chapel Hill: University of North Carolina Press.

Bourne, R. 1977. "Trans-national America." In *The Radical Will: Randolph Bourne Selected Writings, 1911–1918,* edited by O. Hansen, 248–64. New York: Urizen Books. First published in *Atlantic Monthly* 117 (April 1916): 86–97.

Brooks, V. W. 1915. *America's Coming of Age.* New York: B. W. Huebsch.
———. 1916. "Young America." *Seven Arts* 1 (December): 144–51.
———. 1917a. "The Culture of Industrialism." *Seven Arts* 1 (April): 655–66.
———. 1917b. "Our Awakeners." *Seven Arts* 2 (June): 235–48.
Browder, E. 1937. "The Writer and Politics." In *The Writer in a Changing World,* edited by H. Hart, 48–55. New York: Equinox Cooperative.
Crossman, R., ed. 1949. *The God That Failed.* New York: Harper and Brothers.
Culture and Crisis. 1932. Special Collections. University of Tulsa Library, Tulsa, Oklahoma.
Dell, F. 1926. *Intellectual Vagabondage: An Apology for the Intelligentsia.* New York: George H. Doran.
Dewey, J. 1927. *The Public and Its Problems.* New York: Henry Holt.
———. [1934] 1980. *Art as Experience.* New York: Putnam and Sons.
Eastman, M. 1934a. *Art and the Life of Action, with other Essays.* New York: Alfred A. Knopf.
———. 1934b. *Artists in Uniform: A Study of Literature and Bureaucratism.* New York: Alfred A. Knopf.
Fischer, L. 1949. "Louis Fischer." In *The God That Failed,* edited by R. Crossman, 196–228. New York: Harper and Brothers.
Foerster, N., ed. [1930] 1967. *Humanism and America: Essays on the Outlook of Modern Civilization.* Port Washington, N.Y.: Kennikat.
Frank, W. 1919. *Our America.* New York: Boni and Liveright.
Gide, A. 1949. "André Gide." In *The God That Failed,* edited by R. Crossman, 165–95. New York: Harper and Brothers.
Gilbert, J. B. 1968. *Writers and Partisans: A History of Literary Radicalism in America.* New York: John Wiley and Sons.
Hicks, G. 1935. *The Great Tradition: An Interpretation of American Literature since the Civil War.* New York: Macmillan.
Hoeveler, D., Jr. 1977. *The New Humanism: A Critique of Modern America, 1900–1940.* Charlottesville: University of Virginia Press.
Jacoby, R. 1987. *The Last Intellectuals: American Culture in the Age of Academe.* New York: Basic Books.
Jensen, J. 1990. *Redeeming Modernity: Contradictions in Media Criticism.* Newbury Park, Calif.: Sage.
Koestler, A. 1949. "A. Koestler." In *The God That Failed,* edited by R. Crossman, 15–75. New York: Harper and Brothers.
More, P. E. [1915] 1967. *Aristocracy and Justice.* New York: Phaeton.
North, J., ed. 1969. *New Masses: An Anthology of the Rebel Thirties.* New York: International.
Rabkin, G. 1964. *Drama and Commitment: Politics in the American Theatre of the Thirties.* Bloomington: Indiana University Press.
Said, E. 1994. *Representations of the Intellectual: The 1993 Reith Lectures.* New York: Pantheon Books.
Silone, I. 1949. "Ignazio Silone." In *The God That Failed,* edited by R. Crossman, 76–114. New York: Harper and Brothers.
Spender, S. 1949. "S. Spender." In *The God That Failed,* edited by R. Crossman, 229–73. New York: Harper and Brothers.

Spingarn, J. E. [1924] 1969. "The New Criticism." In *Criticism in America: Its Function and Status,* edited by I. Babbitt, 9–45. New York: Haskell House. The essay was originally published as *The New Criticism: A Lecture Delivered at Columbia University, March 9, 1910* (New York: Columbia University Press, 1911).

Wright, R. 1949. "R. Wright." In *The God That Failed,* edited by R. Crossman, 115–62. New York: Harper and Brothers.

RICK TILMAN

3 John Dewey and the American Tradition of Empirical Collectivism

John Dewey (1859–1952), America's most influential philosopher, is largely ignored in the dominant strains of cultural studies work. Even though he is, perhaps, one of the original postmodern thinkers, cultural specialists pay inadequate attention to his role in the debate over postmodernity. Outside that specific realm of inquiry, the proliferating literature on almost every other aspect of Dewey's thought threatens to become a cottage industry, if it has not already achieved that status.[1] Among contemporary social theorists, perhaps only Sigmund Freud, Antonio Gramsci, and Max Weber attract interest of such scope and intensity, and they are very different kinds of thinkers in terms of genesis and outlook. The literature on Dewey's political thought and behavior in particular examines nearly every facet of his political theory;[2] but nowhere does it fully situate him in a specific political culture with adequate historical continuity. Of course, he is labeled a "democrat," a "liberal," a "progressive," a "collectivist," and a "socialist," but he is never concretely placed in a specific historical context whose main decisional rules are explicitly outlined and whose cultural mores regarding social and institutional change are overtly stated.

Even Robert Westbrook (1991) in what is, perhaps, the finest study of Dewey's political and social philosophy fails to do this. As William Galston (1993) recently put it, "One searches Westbrook's 552 pages in vain for signs of sustained interest in the American founding, in the Constitution, in the structure of representative government or in American political history" (149). In short, Galston charges Westbrook with failing to situate Dewey adequately in the American political and constitutional tradition, and it can be stated that Westbrook is not alone in his failure. Dewey himself was occasionally guilty of it. Thus no systematic effort yet exists to examine his political theory in the context of what the political theorist Currin V. Shields (1952) called "the American tradition of empirical collectivism" in which the relationship between individualism and collectivism is uniquely delineated. The tradition is a political theory, a heuristic device, and a historical perspective on American political thought and behavior that extends back to the first English settlements in the New World. In certain respects, Shields's work on empirical collectivism reads like a tract by Dewey; in other ways, his positions clearly diverge from Dewey's, but even so the divergence is often instructive to readers. Shields states that:

> the doctrine of empirical collectivism implies an order of preferences to be observed in undertaking collective action. The three principles specifying this order can be formulated as follows: (1) *Collective action should be employed to solve only bona fide public problems.* Where a choice is possible, individual action is preferable to public action, whether governmental or non-governmental; and for solving personal problems individuals themselves are responsible. But if a problem concerns the many members of the community, it becomes a public problem, and then—but only then—collective action is warranted. (2) *Collective action should be undertaken by the agent of the community best able to dispose of the problem.* If action by a private organization can be successfully employed, well and good, for non-governmental action is preferable to action by a government. But if private action is inadequate, then government action is in order. The political agent of the community best able to dispose of the problem might be a local or state government, as well as the national action. But whenever a problem is beyond the competence of the states, the national government should act, just as a political agent of the community should act whenever a problem is beyond the competence of private organizations. (3) *Collective action should involve minimal interference in the life of the community.* Of course, the means best able to accomplish the end in view should be employed in every instance. But of the various means available, the empirical collectivist prefers voluntary to mandatory action, inducement to compulsion, restriction to prohibition. And if government action is required, he prefers public regulation of private enterprise to government operation of public enterprise. (106, emphasis added)

Shields also argues that "the empirical collectivist never propounds a pat formula for collective action; he is wedded to no doctrinaire analysis of political history or human behavior; he is hobbled by no preconceptions about political problems or their solution" (106).[3] Yet there appear to be some powerful "preconceptions" about political theory and political action in Shields's claim that collective action should "be employed to solve only bona fide public problems," "be undertaken by the agent of the community best able to dispose of the problem," and, "involve minimal interference in the life of the community." Why, then, does Shields claim the American tradition of empirical collectivism is without presuppositions?[4] Perhaps what he means is that empirical collectivism is not "unduly burdened" by preconceptions about political problems or their solution, in which case his position converges with many other political thinkers, including Dewey with his focus on "method."

Finally, the question of the relationship between American cultural studies, John Dewey, and the tradition of empirical collectivism must be raised. Simply put, can viewing Dewey through the lens of empirical collectivism provide American cultural studies with a better understanding of Dewey? This is an important question, as American cultural studies invokes Dewey and his brand of pragmatism as the richest ground for its development of a specifically American cultural studies. Dewey's pronouncements on the role of communication in creating community and his arguments for the restoration of the public and the intimate relationship between democracy and discourse are fertile ground for American cultural studies, with its concerns about creating and maintaining democracy in the age of globalization and the information society.

At the end of *The Public and Its Problems* ([1927] 1954), Dewey expresses the central concern of American cultural studies, a concern that is at once filled with darkness and with hope: "The generation of democratic communities and an articulate democratic public can be solved only in the degree in which local communal life becomes a reality. Signs, symbols, language are the means by which a fraternally shared experience is ushered in and sustained. . . . We lie, as Emerson said, in the lap of an immense intelligence. But that intelligence is dormant and its communications are broken until it possesses the local community as its medium" (217–19). This loss to the community and how to regain it are themes throughout Dewey's voluminous writings and in his actual practices. Empirical collectivism helps link Dewey into a specific historical tradition—a tradition that, as already noted, is often missing from the huge body of work on Dewey. While American cultural studies has looked at Dewey's work as a critique of positivism, it has not studied Dewey's political thought and behavior as closely. Using the device of empirical collectivism helps situate Dewey more concretely in his time, with its particular political practices and its economy.

Empirical collectivism can help articulate Dewey's understanding of what were public and what were private spheres, as well as the relationship between an increasing corporate hegemony, the government, both local and federal, and the individual. Articulating that understanding may help create new understanding of the extent of Dewey's contribution to American cultural studies.

Was Dewey an Empirical Collectivist?

The "American tradition of empirical collectivism," as Shields defines it, provides historical awareness, that is, a sense of the particular experiences that particular people have had during a particular span of time. It does this by sanctioning the right of the majority to identify the origins and nature of social problems and how shallow or deep the place of these problems in American culture. Second, it signifies some of the major conditions our society has set for reconstructing itself by specifying the most appropriate level of government for problem resolution. Third, it inventories the possibilities for change when it invokes the rule of economy, which subjects political expectations, embedded values, common memories, and institutional routine to the criterion of social parsimony. Dewey is thus placed in a tradition and context in which he has never before been fully situated. However, since Dewey's own thought regarding the American political economy went through a long period of incubation and evolution, it is essential to periodize its development over time. In this vein Gary Bullert (1983) argues:

> Four identifiable shifts of emphasis occurred: (1) Up to 1918 he advocated a capitalist system controlled by progressive governmental reforms. (2) From 1918 to 1927 he defended the orchestra leader theory of the state. In order to combat centralized political power and nationalism, the power of government should be distributed over a vast complex of economic groups (guild socialism). (3) In *The Public and Its Problems* (1927), Dewey moved from a minimal state conception toward the notion that government was a flexible instrument to provide for human wants. During the Great Depression, an expanded role for government was necessitated. At no time did Dewey justify dictatorial measures in the name of public welfare. (4) After 1936 Dewey's enthusiasms for the possibilities of social engineering waned. He still sought democratic controls in the econ-

> omy, but during this period he emphasized a mixed system with voluntary cooperation. (31–32)[5]

It thus appears that Dewey, on the whole, stayed inside the doctrinal and policy constraints of the American tradition of empirical collectivism, although in the early 1930s he approached the outer limits of government ownership and market intervention that the tradition permits. Both earlier and later in his career, however, he appears to have looked more skeptically at the use of centralized state power to achieve social engineering goals.

How, then, is Dewey's political thought and, to a lesser extent, his political behavior and social activism related to the American tradition of empirical collectivism, a term he apparently never used but seems to have understood well? These questions and the answers to them have four parts. First, how did he distinguish between the public and private spheres, and how did he think the sovereign community should make this distinction? Second, what criteria should be used to decide what level of government, local, state, or federal, should be selected to deal with public problems when they arise? Third, what did Dewey understand the rule of economy to be, and what observations can be made about the way he thought it should be applied so that the social fabric of the community would not be unduly disturbed? Finally, what did his political behavior and social activism indicate regarding his convictions about the three principles stated above?

THE RELATIONSHIP BETWEEN THE PUBLIC AND THE PRIVATE

The underlying ethos in the American tradition of empirical collectivism has been combining community service and social obligation with the pursuit of self-interest. To illustrate, when individuals on the frontier could not resolve their own problems and needs, they resorted to collective action outside the framework of formal government; in rural America, this often meant log-rolling, house-raising, corn-husking, apple-paring, quilting bees, squatter's associations, camp meetings, and vigilante movements—all these grew out of voluntary pioneer associations. In Dewey's opinion, the agrarian settlements of early America were the primary locus of not only community but democracy as well. This is so for Dewey because he considers the concepts of community and democracy—taken in their broadest sense, as social ideas—to be very similar, for community is inherently democratic, and democracy is inherently communal.[6] Dewey understood this well, yet he was also concerned in his own time with the obsolescence of voluntarism because the effects of industrialism and urbanization greatly diminished the efficacy of such action. All too often individuals were too helpless or ignorant to aid in ameliorating or solving problems clearly beyond their control. Nevertheless, as James Campbell (1995) put it:

> Dewey . . . maintains . . . that it is the indirect consequences of social interactions that give rise to the public and its efforts at control. Consequently, for him, the shape of the government at any given time should reflect the jobs that are then required of it: to serve the public in its attempts to deal with the indirect consequences of social interaction. As he notes, "at one time and place a large measure of state activity may be indicated and at another time a policy of quiescence and *laissez-faire.*" The point is adaptability to the processive nature of social interaction. (40)

Dewey was often said to be a "liberal," and "liberalism" does have some particular content in its American context: the support of a market system and private property capitalism, an emphasis on the primacy of individual freedom, an understanding of society as best when allowed to self-equilibrate, and so forth. It converges with empirical collectivism at some points, yet it is apparent that much of Dewey's political thought, during the Great Depression in particular, stresses equality and community too much to be fully congruent with the American liberal tradition. This clearly places him on the leftward fringes of empirical collectivism, particularly when it is noted that on three occasions he voted for the socialist Norman Thomas for president. Yet in 1927 he put it this way: "Just as publics and states vary with conditions of time and place, so do the concrete functions which should be carried on by states. There is no antecedent universal proposition which can be laid down because of which the functions of a state should be limited or should be expanded. The scope is something to be critically and experimentally determined" (74). To Dewey, neither political theory nor political practice suggests abandonment of "experimentalism," that is, his instrumentalist method and social value theory. Rather, it is the self-correcting method of valuation and the continuous adjustment of means to ends-in-view and ends-in-view to means that determine the size and role of government, not an a priori set of assumptions about what government can or should do. What should be left to individuals as opposed to what is the responsibility of government is thus a matter to be determined through the use of experimental method, although Dewey was often vague about how the "experiments" were to be conducted and their consequences evaluated.

Politics, to him, was not a science but an adaptive, generative process with no fixed ends or social stasis in sight.

THE APPROPRIATE LEVEL OF GOVERNMENT

Of course, to treat Dewey as an "empirical collectivist" is to acknowledge his commitment to federalism, a term he did not often use. Yet it is difficult to understand the relevance to Americans of his larger social and political philosophy outside a federalist system. Vincent Ostrom (1979) argues:

> If Dewey had been less inclined to view American constitutional development as accidental and more inclined to view it as a revolutionary and self-conscious articulation of the idea of federalism, the general thrust of his political theory might have had much greater impact upon the development of political science as an intellectual discipline. In that case he might have viewed the experimental efforts to organize first a confederation and then a federation as applications of the methods of intelligent cooperative experimentation which he made the central focus of his philosophy. The formulation of the U.S. Constitution might, then, have been viewed as a self-conscious effort to enable a public of continental proportions to find and identify itself and fashion for itself a mechanism for articulating, communicating, and experimentally coming to know its own interests. (94–95)

As Ostrom also points out, "Federalism enables concurrent and overlapping self-governing communities to function as articulate and self-conscious publics capable of regulating affairs so that indirect consequences of transactions are systematically tended to. By enabling people to participate in concurrent self-governing communities, they could apply intelligent cooperative experimentation to diverse problems and, in the course of doing so, amplify their own potentials for critical inquiry and enlightened development" (95).

Although Ostrom stresses Dewey's insensitivity to the advantages of a federal system, Dewey might be more securely placed inside the American tradition of empirical collectivism had he been more explicit about his views on federalism. Nevertheless, he was not uncomfortable most of the time with a division of labor between local, state, and federal governmental power. As Mark Mendell (1994) put it, Dewey did on occasion invoke "transformative standards" that gave evidence of his "sensitivity to the multilayered character of social reality, to the many overlapping publics that constitute the greater community" (598). Dewey was aware that federalism was part of the "multilayered character of social reality" and that it provided a more sensitive instrument than unitary or confederate systems for recognizing and dealing with the problems of publics that overlapped.

He was also cognizant of the industrial transformation of the United States and, more important, the newly emerging corporate-commercial hegemony asserting itself with all its tensions, contradictions, and accommodations. The consolidating potential of electricity, the centralizing impact of corporate mergers, and the increasing costs of machinery that caused a dramatic growth in capital-intensive production did not escape his notice. Nor did the consequence of these changes, namely, the enhanced development of corporate power that would further cement the relationship between government and the upper class. Nevertheless, as manifest in his writings on Thomas Jefferson (1940), although he did come to prefer an enhanced role for the central government, he remained well aware of the attachment many Americans had to local and state government. Dewey's respect for American federalism was more than grudging even after he came to feel that state and local organs of governmental power were often inadequate to curb and channel the now mature corporate structure.

THE RULE OF PARSIMONY IN EMPIRICAL COLLECTIVISM

As regards the use and economy of force in bringing about change, the empirical collectivist's strictures on the rule of parsimony converge with Dewey's in that both want social amelioration through government action without unduly rending or disturbing the social fabric. Although much of Dewey's writing on the use and economy of force was done during World War I and was intended primarily for the realm of politics among nations—that is, international affairs—it has implications for the use of coercion by government in domestic affairs. It suggests both the need for coercive force and the difficulty of ascertaining how much is necessary under existing circumstances to accomplish a particular course of action. Dewey's "empirical collectivism" is often evident in his sensitivity about the use of coercion to bring about social change in that he prefers the encouragement of democratic consensus rather than the employment of overt force to achieve it. Yet among empirical collectivists, he probably had fewer misgivings about the necessity of coercion than most and thus can be situated on the left-wing or radical fringe of the venerable American tradition; although skeptical of forced revolutionary upheaval, he supported radical reform.

An analysis of Dewey's proposals for socioeconomic reconstruction during the depression sheds light on the left wing of the American tradition of empirical collectivism for he supported government ownership of some basic industries and natural resources. This would involve a mixed system in which supervision and regulation of industry would be jointly administered by the government, which would represent the public interest in general and the consumer interest in particular. It would also require a role for management and one for workers through their democratically controlled trade unions. To achieve socialization, Dewey advocated heavy taxation on upper-income groups; this revenue could then be used to compensate owners of industries that were nationalized and also to redistribute wealth through subsidizing social welfare programs.[7] These are hardly the political prescriptions of a liberal ameliorist. Does it invalidate the claim that he was an empirical collectivist? Dewey (1935a) summarized the ideal relationship between radical and incremental social change:

> Liberalism must now become radical, meaning by "radical" perception of the necessity of thorough-going changes in the set-up of institutions and corresponding activity to bring the changes to pass. For the gulf between what the actual situation makes possible and the actual state itself is so great that it cannot be bridged by piecemeal policies undertaken *ad hoc.* The process of producing the changes will be, in any case, a gradual one. But "reforms" that deal now with this abuse and now with that without having a social goal based on an inclusive plan, differ entirely from effort at reforming, in its literal sense, the institutional scheme of things. The liberals of more than a century ago were denounced in their time as subversive radicals, and only when the new economic order was established did they become apologists for the *status quo,* or else content with social patchwork. If radicalism be defined as perception of the need for radical change, then today any liberalism which is not also radicalism is irrelevant and doomed. (62)

This quotation is often used by Dewey scholars to illustrate his shift toward radicalism in the 1930s, but it can mislead his readers if it is interpreted as typical of his thought during his long career. Although a fair number of such statements can be found in his writing during the early and middle years of the depression, he tended on the whole to be more parsimonious toward large-scale change induced by government.[8] Nevertheless, for some years, he was close to accepting the socialist diagnoses of problems in the United States.

Dewey did, however, prefer voluntary to mandatory action, inducement rather than compulsion, and restriction instead of prohibition; and with the exception of his "radical" phase, he preferred public regulation of private enterprise to government ownership and operation of public enterprise. To the empirical collectivist, minimal dislocation, social parsimony, and the rule of economy all meant not rending or tearing the social fabric of the community, and Dewey, for the most part, was in compliance with the tradition. However, there was no fixed standard or authoritative precedent to which to appeal to determine precisely what this meant in specific policy cases. Consequently, during much of his career, he was prone to advocate more constraint on big, especially corporate, property rights and to place more emphasis on income redistribution than did most of his peers, usually without reference to foundational principles.

However, Dewey's radicalism was inconsistent since he vacillated between advocacy of welfare-state capitalism and genuine socialism; more often than not he occupied a half-way house. Nevertheless, several years before the New Deal began, Dewey (1930) wrote prescriptively, "We are in for some kind of socialism, call it by whatever name we please, and no matter what it will be called when it is realized. Economic determinism is now a fact, not a theory. But there is a difference and a choice between a blind, chaotic and unplanned determinism, issuing from business conducted for pecuniary profit, and the determination of a socially planned and ordered development. It is the difference and the choice between socialism that is public and one that is capitalistic" (119–20).[9] Should it be thought Dewey's commitment to structural change is exaggerated, a glance at a summary of his position during the New Deal suggests otherwise. Admittedly, this is the period when Dewey moved furthest to the left, but it was the period of Dewey's work most open to question as regards his "empirical collectivism." As Edward Bordeau (1971) noted, "Dewey could not accept Roosevelt's compromise with capitalism for he saw clearly that the New Deal permitted power and rule to remain essentially in the same hands as those that brought the country to its present state—dominated as those hands are by the profit motive" (78–79). Bordeau went on to explain:

> While the New Deal was not, to Dewey's mind, radical enough in terms of his socialism, it was nonetheless greatly under the influence of his instrumentalism and pragmatism even if this pragmatism was more ad hoc and headless than his own. Dewey genuinely applauded what he, Roosevelt, had accomplished, but the New Deal was merely an attempt to save capitalism and "only a new system which destroys the profit system can banish poverty and bring the American people the economic liberation which modern science and technology is prepared to bestow upon them." (83–84)

The Far Left underestimated Dewey's commitment to radical reform, although Dewey's advocacy of radical change throughout his career was inconsistent. Dewey's sometime commitment to radicalism was more evident in the interwar period, especially in the early to mid-1930s, than earlier. Consequently, radical indictment of the liberal as opposed to the radical aspects of his work is more accurate when aimed at Dewey before 1918 than during the depression. Nevertheless, his respect for the existing social fabric made him sensitive to institutional habit and routine and strongly skeptical of Marxist proposals for command planning. It is this that enables one to argue that he never strayed very far beyond the parameters imposed by the American tradition of empirical collectivism.

DEWEY: LEFT, CENTER, AND RIGHT

In 1952, the year John Dewey died, Currin V. Shields articulated his three principles of empirical collectivism. First, when Americans encountered problems, they made judgments about whether the problem was private or public, always preferring private solutions to individual problems and thus endorsing remedial action by government only when the majority deemed a situation a bona fide public problem. Second, they decided which level of government could best deal with a public problem. The empirical collectivist preferred that level of government nearest at hand and thus preferred local action to state action and state action to federal action. Third, they adhered to the rule of parsimony, which meant that actions taken by government must not unduly disturb the social fabric of the community.

The main question, then, for Dewey scholars is one of ascertaining through textual exegesis of his work and biographical analysis the extent to which Dewey's political thought and behavior provide evidence that he consciously understood his role in the American tradition of empirical collectivism. It is also one of locating him *within* that tradition, along the ideological spectrum of left, center, and right.

Critics of the claim that "empirical collectivism" is the central tradition in the American political experience might, for example, argue that little is gained by lumping together the disparate campaign rhetoric, legislative agendas, and executive actions of Herbert Hoover and Franklin D. Roosevelt. One has only to read Hoover's *Memoirs* to see that, although occasional New Deal programs were foreshadowed in the Hoover era, Hoover himself remained a staunch, indeed bitter, opponent of most of the New Deal. He strongly disagreed with the New Deal's persistent identification of problems as public that he thought were private, what he said was its preconceived preference for national as opposed to state or local action, and its allegedly loose application of the rule of parsimony for avoiding undue disturbance of the social fabric of the community.

Although Dewey disagreed with the doctrine and the policies of both the Hoover administration and Roosevelt's New Deal, he was very interested in them. But if Hoover is interpreted as occupying the right wing of the empirical collectivist tradition, then Roosevelt occupies a position near the center, and Dewey is on the left flank. Dewey thought many of the problems the New Deal held to be individual were public; he probably preferred a more interventionist federal government than did the New Dealers; and he believed more drastic action was necessary than that endorsed by the New Deal and would undoubtedly have accepted more change in the social fabric of the community. Yet, by the late 1930s, his awareness of the totalitarian threat abroad made him increasingly skeptical about the beneficence of the centralized state power necessary to bring about structural change at home.

At times Dewey disagreed with the socialist Left's persistent identification of problems as public that he thought were private, with what he said was its preconceived preference for federal as opposed to state and local action, and with its allegedly loose application of the rule of parsimony for avoiding undue disturbance of the social fabric of the community. Clearly, if ideologies, programs, and groups can accurately be labeled "right," "center," and "left" within the tradition of empirical collectivism, a good part of Dewey's career finds him on the left of the spectrum, but he was not by any means a doctrinaire socialist. It is important to understand how this is related to his role as a political and social activist.

DEWEY'S POLITICAL AND SOCIAL ACTIVISM

Although the young Dewey shared the liberal reformist political views of his peers, his early publications did not reveal a strong focus on political issues or an overriding concern with pressing social problems.[10] Dewey did not often discuss social problems, but his University of Chicago lectures from 1894 to 1904 in such courses as "Contemporary Theories regarding Ethical Relations of the Individual and Society" and the "Sociology of Ethics" did. The public talks he gave and the discussions he led at Hull-House indicated that he considered himself a liberal.

Dewey's voting record indicates that he was an independent. Most of his votes were cast for socialist or progressive third-party candidates, although occasionally he supported a Democrat for the presidency. To illustrate, he voted for the Democrat Grover Cleveland in 1884. In 1906, he voted for Charles Evans Hughes, a progressive Republican, for governor of New York. In 1912, he voted for the Democrat Woodrow Wilson for president. In 1924, he backed Robert M. La Follette, the Progressive reformer, for the presidency and actively supported the La Follette–Wheeler ticket in the campaign of that year. On one occasion, he appeared as the principal speaker at a La Follette rally of college students in New York City (Dykhuizen 1973, 221). In the 1928 presidential campaign, which pitted Herbert Hoover against Al Smith and in which Norman Thomas ran as the Socialist Party candidate, Dewey's sympathies were with Thomas and the Socialist Party. He wrote, "If I had any special confidence in what can be accomplished by any party, with reference to our specifically political needs, I should vote for Norman Thomas, because I think those needs are connected with a much more fundamental facing of the issues of economic reconstruction than we shall obtain from the Democratic party under any conceivable circumstances" (1928, 320).

But practical politics dictated that he support Smith. Among his reasons was the "humane and sympathetic spirit" with which Smith approached social problems as contrasted with Hoover's hard "efficiency," an efficiency that "works out to strengthen the position of just those economic interests that most need weakening instead of strengthening" (1928, 321). Dewey did not foresee the time a few years later when Smith would become a Liberty Leaguer and an archconservative critic of the New Deal.

After several years of proposing radical measures through his League for Independent Political Action (LIPA), Dewey finally endorsed Norman Thomas in 1932. The explanation for his electoral support for the Socialist Party was the fact that the planks he proposed through the LIPA were almost identical to those favored by the Socialists. Only the Socialists' dogmatic insistence on the inevitability of class warfare prevented Dewey from assuming a more active role in the Socialist cause (Howlett 1977, 124–25). In view of radical strictures against Dewey, it should be kept in mind that it was during this period that Dewey wrote:

> Our entire history and experience proves that the financial and industrial leaders of the nation will not make these changes voluntarily—they will not, except under compulsion, surrender their most profitable share of a system which has concentrated four-fifths of the nation's wealth in the hands of one twenty-fifth of the people. *The federal government alone has the power to force the wealthy owners of the nation to surrender their control over the lives and destinies of the overwhelming majority of the American people and the first step is to compel them to pay taxes commensurate in sacrifice with that of people with very small incomes.* (1932b, 1, emphasis added)[11]

However, his consistent opposition to the Marxist-Leninist view that nondemocratic means can promote democratic ends should be noted.

Dewey also supported Norman Thomas in 1936 and 1940. The only other indication of his later voting record reveals that he voted for Franklin D. Roosevelt in 1944, because he admired him as war leader. On October 20, 1944, the *New York Times* ran an article in which Dewey indicated that he distrusted the "isolationism" of the Republican Party and intended to vote for President Roosevelt as the man most likely to "lead us forward" ("John Dewey" 1944, 32). Clearly, Dewey had long realized the importance of third-party pressure in offering the public real alternatives through the formulation and propagandization of progressive programs. His willingness to support the Democratic Party emerged primarily when third-party agitation seemed fruitless, as was the case during World War II. His political and social activism provide further evidence that, wittingly or not, empirical collectivism provided boundaries beyond which he did not usually go, although his votes for Norman Thomas may be an important exception to this generalization.[12]

Conclusion

The dangers of generalizing about Dewey's views on any topic are apparent when it is remembered that he wrote approximately 815 articles and 38 books over a period of about seventy years. Interpretation of his political ideas and behavior is made even more problematic when it is recognized that, in addition to the very partial and selective citation of secondary literature above, more than 750 dissertations and theses with Dewey as their central focus have been catalogued. But most Dewey scholars would probably agree that his criterion for political value was advancing the "common good," which meant individual and social "growth," a favorite term of his, and that he did not believe these could always be accurately measured by simple majorities. The voting public could have inadequate notions of the "public interest" insofar as this pertained to the size and scope of government, the level of government selected as a tool for amelioration, and the malleability as well as fragility of the social fabric of the community. Nevertheless, he remained within the American tradition of empirical collectivism in that he realized that, even within the sometimes amorphous borders of his own political theory, three principles for problem resolution existed in the political system he knew and liked best, and he seems consciously to have tried to respect these.

In summation, are Dewey's political thought and, to a lesser extent, his political behavior and social activism so related to the American tradition of empirical collectivism that it is appropriate to regard him as part of the tradition? Of course, these questions and the answers to them have four parts. First, did he distinguish between the public and private spheres in a manner befitting an empirical collectivist? Second, did he decide what level of government, local, state, or federal, would be selected to deal with public problems when they arise by focusing on the level of government nearest at hand able to accomplish the task? Third, did Dewey understand the rule of economy to be applied so as not to unduly disturb the social fabric of the community to be in keeping with the empirical collectivist tradition? Fourth, were his political behavior and social activism also within its parameters? The answer to all these questions, with qualifications, appears to be yes. We can thus conclude that the tradition contains a context of decision making, a political culture, and a historical continuity that roughly fits Dewey, provided it is not viewed as a theoretical straitjacket. He was critical of those who were nostalgic for a golden era that had never existed and utopians who sought to make a complete break with existing institutions and cultural realities;[13] thus his preference for an "empirical collectivism" that seemed to avoid both.

The usefulness of the concept of "empirical collectivism" may seem questionable since it is so inclusive that it allows Dewey, Roosevelt, and Hoover to be clustered within its span. Yet the legacy of empirical collectivism may be less a philosophical school and political tradition than a set of critical questions involving the proper functioning of democratic government. As these questions were considered by various students of politics, their solutions looked different, most obviously on the questions of how to distinguish between problems that are public and those best left to individuals, appropriate levels of government intervention, and the proper kind and amount of interference in the community. The debates between former President Clinton and his political opponents on the left and especially the right provide ample contemporary evidence of the continuing relevance of the three principles of the American tradition of empirical collectivism.

Notes

The author thanks Doug Imig, Bruce Pencek, Jerry Polinard, Hal Rhodes, Ted Putterman, Paul Goldstene, Larry Downey, and David Fott for commenting on earlier drafts of this essay.

1. See, for example, the following studies of Dewey: Sleeper ([1986] 2001); Hickman (1990); Alexander (1987); Paringer (1990); Rice (1993); Feffer (1993); Rocke-

feller (1991); Boisvert (1988); Tiles (1988); Westbrook (1991); Diggins (1994); Campbell (1992 and 1995); Burke (1994); and Ryan (1995). For the use of Dewey's ideas, see Smiley (1992); Rorty (1979 and 1982); Rosenthal (1986); Kaufman-Osborn (1991); and Carey (1992).

2. The periodical literature since the beginning of World War II is massive, but see especially Otto (1939); Cork (1949); Murphy (1960); Kent (1953); Ward (1957); H. White (1958); Lothstein (1978); Anderson (1979); Diggins (1981); Manicas (1982); Smiley (1990); Bernstein (1987); Tilman (1990); Kaufman-Osborn (1984); Callaway (1993); and Nichols (1990). See also Nathanson (1951); Geiger (1939); Bernstein (1986); Rorty (1994); Kloppenberg (1994); Damico (1978); Somjee (1968); Howlett (1977); M. White (1957); Dykhuizen (1973); and Coughlan (1963).

3. Yet Herbert Hoover (1934), whom Shields claims is an empirical collectivist, writes, "The penetration of Socialist methods even to a partial degree will demoralize the economic system, the legislative bodies, and in fact the whole system of ordered Liberty" (60–61). To further illustrate, Hoover (1922) also writes that "democracy is merely the mechanism which individualism invented as a device that would carry on the necessary political work of its social organization" (48).

4. Shields's (1958) own value commitments are revealed in his claims that "because of the mode of its development, American Democracy bears an empirical character which is still a distinguishing mark" (36). In praising the postwar Christian Democratic movements in Western Europe, Shields writes that "most impressive is the absence of any doctrinaire approach to the solution of social and economic problems" (129).

5. See also Dewey (1939, chap. 4) for an indictment of such regimes.

6. As he asserts in *The Public and Its Problems,* "Regarded as an ideal, democracy is not an alternative to other principles of associated life. It is the idea of community itself" (148).

7. Jim Cork (1949) quotes from a letter he received from Dewey in which Dewey said, "I can be classed as a democratic socialist. If I were permitted to define 'socialism' and 'socialist,' I would so classify myself today" (450). Consult the following Dewey sources: 1932a; 1932b; 1932c; 1932d; 1933; 1934; and 1935b.

8. A more characteristic expression of his doctrine can be found in Dewey (1929, 745–59).

9. Again, note the ambiguity and vagueness of the first sentence in the quotation.

10. Perhaps the strongest statement he made during this period is in his "My Pedagogic Creed" (1897, 80).

11. For a more detailed analysis of Dewey's political views during the 1930s, see Bordeau (1971, 67–84).

12. The foregoing is a brief summation of Rick Tilman's (1984) analysis of Dewey's political behavior and social activism (chaps. 7, 8, and 9).

13. James Kloppenberg (1994) has argued that Dewey believed "that all knowledge is uncertain, all claims to authority are suspect, and all candidates for truth must submit to searching investigation by democratically constituted communities of enquiry" (75). John P. Diggins (1981) adds that Dewey believed "the search for authority in immutable ideas amounted to a false and almost childish quest for certainty and security" (25).

References

Alexander, T. M. 1987. *John Dewey's Theory of Art, Experience, and Nature.* Albany: State University of New York Press.
Anderson, Q. 1979. "John Dewey's American Democrat." *Daedalus* 108:145–59.
Bernstein, R. 1986. "John Dewey on Democracy: The Task before Us." In *Philosophical Profiles: Essays in a Pragmatic Mode,* edited by R. J. Bernstein, 260–72. Philadelphia: University of Pennsylvania Press.
———. 1987. "One Step Forward, Two Steps Backward: Richard Rorty on Liberal Democracy and Philosophy." *Political Theory* 15:538–63.
Boisvert, R. D. 1988. *Dewey's Metaphysics.* New York: Fordham University Press.
Bordeau, E. J. 1971. "John Dewey's Ideas about the Great Depression." *Journal of the History of Ideas* 32:67–84.
Bullert, G. 1983. *The Politics of John Dewey.* Buffalo, N.Y.: Prometheus Books.
Burke, T. 1994. *Dewey's New Logic.* Chicago: University of Chicago Press.
Callaway, H. G. 1993. "Democracy, Value Inquiry and Dewey's Metaphysics." *Journal of Value Inquiry* 27:13–27.
Campbell, J. 1992. *The Community Reconstructs: The Meaning of Pragmatic Social Thought.* Urbana: University of Illinois Press.
———. 1995. *Understanding John Dewey.* La Salle: Open Court Publishing.
Carey, J. W. 1992. *Communication as Culture: Essays on Media and Society.* New York: Routledge.
Cork, J. 1949. "John Dewey, Karl Marx, and Democratic Socialism." *Antioch Review* 9:435–52.
Coughlan, N. 1963. *Young John Dewey: An Essay in American Intellectual History.* Chicago: University of Chicago Press.
Damico, A. J. 1978. *Individuality and Community: The Social and Political Thought of John Dewey.* Gainesville: University Presses of Florida.
Dewey, J. 1897. "My Pedagogic Creed." *School Journal* 54:77–80.
———. [1927] 1954. *The Public and Its Problems.* Chicago: Swallow.
———. 1928. "Why I Am for Smith." *New Republic,* November 7, 320–21.
———. 1929. *Character and Events.* Vol. 2. New York: Henry Holt.
———. 1930. *Individualism Old and New.* New York: Minton, Balch.
———. 1932a. "America's Public Ownership Program." *People's Lobby Bulletin* 2 (May): 1–2.
———. 1932b. "You Must Act to Get Congress to Act." *People's Lobby Bulletin* 2 (May): 1.
———. 1932c. "Voters Must Demand Congress Tax Wealth Instead of Want." *People's Lobby Bulletin* 2 (June): 1.
———. 1932d. "President's Policies Help Property Owners Chiefly." *People's Lobby Bulletin* 2 (November): 1–2.
———. 1933. "The Drive against Hunger." *New Republic,* March, 190.
———. 1934. "The Imperative Need for a New Radical Party." In *Challenge to the New Deal,* edited by A. M. Bingham and S. Rodman, 269–73. New York: Falcon.
———. 1935a. *Liberalism and Social Action.* New York: Capricorn Books.
———. 1935b. "Taxation as a Step to Socialization." *People's Lobby Bulletin* 4 (March): 1–2.

———. 1939. *Freedom and Culture.* New York: G. P. Putnam's Sons.

———. 1940. "Presenting Thomas Jefferson." In *The Living Thoughts of Thomas Jefferson,* edited by A. O. Mendel, 1–30. New York: Longmans, Green.

Diggins, J. P. 1981. "John Dewey in Peace and War." *American Scholar* 50:213–30.

———. 1994. *The Promise of Pragmatism.* Chicago: University of Chicago Press.

Dykhuizen, G. 1973. *The Life and Mind of John Dewey.* Carbondale: Southern Illinois University Press.

Feffer, A. 1993. *The Chicago Pragmatists and American Progressivism.* Ithaca, N.Y.: Cornell University Press.

Galston, W. A. 1993. "Salvation through Participation: John Dewey and the Religion of Democracy." *Raritan* 12:144–54.

Geiger, G. R. 1939. "Dewey's Social and Political Philosophy." In *The Philosophy of John Dewey,* edited by P. A. Schilpp, 335–68. Evanston: Northwestern University Press.

Hickman, L. A. 1990. *John Dewey's Pragmatic Technology.* Bloomington: Indiana University Press.

Hoover, H. 1922. *American Individualism.* Garden City, N.Y.: Doubleday.

———. 1934. *The Challenge to Liberty.* New York: Charles Scribner's Sons.

———. 1951–52. *Memoirs: The Great Depression, 1929–1941.* Vol. 3. New York: Macmillan.

Howlett, C. F. 1977. *Troubled Philosopher: John Dewey and the Struggle for World Peace.* Port Washington, N.Y.: Kennikat.

"John Dewey, at 85, Defends Doctrines." 1944. *New York Times,* October 20, 32.

Kaufman-Osborn, T. 1984. "John Dewey and the Liberal Science of Community." *Journal of Politics* 46:1142–65.

———. 1991. *Politics/Sense/Experience: A Pragmatic Inquiry into the Promise of Democracy.* Ithaca, N.Y.: Cornell University Press.

Kent, W. P. 1953. "John Dewey's Philosophical Principles and Their Political Significance." *Western Political Quarterly* 6:446–57.

Kloppenberg, J. T. 1994. "Democracy and Disenchantment: From Weber and Dewey to Habermas and Rorty." In *Modernist Impulses in the Humanist Sciences, 1870–1930,* edited by D. Ross, 69–90. Baltimore: Johns Hopkins University Press.

Lothstein, A. 1978. "Salving from the Dross: John Dewey's Anarcho-Communalism." *Philosophic Forum* 10:55–111.

Manicas, P. 1982. "John Dewey, Anarchism, and the Political State." *Transactions of the Charles S. Peirce Society* 18:133–58.

Mendell, M. 1994. "Dewey and the Logic of Legal Reasoning." *Transactions of the C. S. Pierce Society* 30:575–635.

Murphy, A. E. 1960. "John Dewey and American Liberalism." *Journal of Philosophy* 57:442–50.

Nathanson, J. 1951. *John Dewey: The Reconstruction of the Democratic Life.* New York: Charles Scribner's Sons.

Nichols, J. H., Jr. 1990. "Pragmatism and the U.S. Constitution." In *Confronting the Constitution,* edited by A. Bloom, 369–88. Washington, D.C.: AEI.

Ostrom, V. 1979. "Dewey and Federalism: So Near and Yet So Far." *Publius* 9:94–95.

Otto, M. C. 1939. "The Social Philosophy of John Dewey." *Journal of Social Philosophy* 5:43–60.
Paringer, W. 1990. *John Dewey and the Paradox of Liberal Reform.* Albany: State University of New York Press.
Rice, D. F. 1993. *Reinhold Niebuhr and John Dewey: An Intellectual Odyssey.* Albany: State University of New York Press.
Rockefeller, S. 1991. *John Dewey: Religious Faith and Democratic Humanism.* New York: Columbia University Press.
Rorty, R. 1979. *Philosophy and the Mirror of Nature.* Princeton, N.J.: Princeton University Press.
———. 1982. *Consequences of Pragmatism: Essays, 1972–1980.* Minneapolis: University of Minnesota Press.
———. 1994. "Dewey between Hegel and Darwin." In *Modernist Impulses in the Humanist Sciences, 1870–1930,* edited by D. Ross, 54–68. Baltimore: Johns Hopkins University Press.
Rosenthal, S. 1986. *Speculative Pragmatism.* Amherst: University of Massachusetts Press.
Ryan, A. 1995. *John Dewey: The High Tide of American Liberalism.* New York: W. W. Norton.
Shields, C. V. 1952. "The American Tradition of Empirical Collectivism." *American Political Science Review* 46:104–20.
———. 1958. *Democracy and Catholicism in America.* New York: McGraw-Hill.
Sleeper, R. W. [1986] 2001. *The Necessity of Pragmatism: John Dewey's Conception of Philosophy.* Urbana: University of Illinois Press.
Smiley, M. 1990. "Pragmatic Inquiry and Social Conflict: A Critical Reconstruction of Dewey's Model Of Democracy." *Praxis International* 9 (4): 365–80.
———. 1992. *Responsibility and the Boundaries of Community.* Chicago: University of Chicago Press.
Somjee, A. H. 1968. *The Political Theory of John Dewey.* New York: Teachers College Press.
Tiles, J. E. 1988. *Dewey.* London: Routledge.
Tilman, R. 1984. *C. Wright Mills: A Native Radical and His American Intellectual Roots.* University Park: Pennsylvania State University Press.
———. 1988. "The Neoinstrumental Theory of Democracy." In *Evolutionary Economics,* vol. 1, edited by M. Tool, 427–50. Armonk: Myron E. Sharpe.
———. 1990. "New Light on John Dewey, Clarence Ayres, and the Development of Evolutionary Economics." *Journal of Economic Issues* 24:963–79.
Ward, L. R. 1957. "John Dewey in Search of Himself." *Review of Politics* 19:205–13.
Westbrook, R. B. 1991. *John Dewey and American Democracy.* Ithaca, N.Y.: Cornell University Press.
White, H. B. 1958. "The Political Faith of John Dewey." *Journal of Politics* 20:353–67.
White, M. 1957. *The Revolt against Formalism: American Social Thought.* Boston: Beacon.

ROBERT W. McCHESNEY

4 Whatever Happened to Cultural Studies?

The question I ask in this essay is whatever happened to cultural studies? What happened to the cultural studies that was an explicitly politically radical enterprise? By *politically radical,* I mean anticapitalist, antimarket, pro-dispossessed, pro-democratic, and therefore pro-socialist, broadly construed. This was certainly the project of Raymond Williams and the other founders of cultural studies, yet this sentiment appears far less frequently in cultural studies today. In my view, cultural studies without explicitly radical politics is an uninteresting proposition and produces work of no greater or lesser value than, say, mainstream quantitative social science. I argue that a necessary measure to reassert the radical political project in cultural studies is for cultural studies to develop a more systematic critique of capitalism and the market and to pay closer attention to actual movements for social change. Many in cultural studies—not the least of whom are Larry Grossberg and Jim Carey—share some of these concerns, but I sense the trajectory of the field is in the other direction.

I believe an excellent place for American cultural studies scholars to begin would be the work of those writers associated with the *Monthly Review,* the New York–based socialist magazine that has been in existence since 1949. I am not alone in this assessment. Aijaz Ahmad (1993), in his germinal *In Theory,* specifically chastises U.S. cultural theorists for ignoring the *Monthly Review* tradition. No less than Raymond Williams himself commented on more than one occasion that he felt most comfortable politically and intellectually with the U.S. *Monthly Review* (Thompson 1988, 310; Thompson 1994, 243).

I do not wish to provide a polemic; many of the debates on these issues involve people talking past each, speaking in categorical terms that make dialogue impossible. These debates often strike me as so much self-indulgent showboating, with people throwing their reading lists and quips at each other. I take no pleasure in impaling cultural studies, nor does attacking it make me feel as if I am winning some important political victory. Grossberg (1995) concluded his debate with Nick Garnham (1995) in *Critical Studies in Mass Communication* by stating that while debate can be valuable, it is inappropriate to question the commitment of cultural studies to the political Left. Yet that is exactly what I will do here. I write this essay to share my honest concerns regarding what I see as basic flaws in U.S. cultural studies as it has developed over the past decade. I try to be as specific as possible. My spirit is meant to be genuinely inclusive, but without false sentiment or dishonesty. I want cultural studies back.

I should offer a couple of provisos. I do not do what is now considered cultural studies, and I stopped following the literature years ago. I am not writing this to promote history or political economy or some other field; in fact, I am not writing this as an academic. I write it as a radical intellectual who happens to work in the academy in a number of different fields. I am a radical first, and my being an intellectual developed out of my politics. I pretty much wrote off cultural studies as a political project by 1990 or 1991. To a large extent, this was because I was at the University of Wisconsin in Madison, where John Fiske and his particular version of cultural studies holds sway, but I sense I am justified in generalizing beyond Fiske. I sometimes think Fiske is subjected to more criticism than other major figures in cultural studies because he is one of the few theorists who writes clearly, something for which he is to be commended. I frankly do not understand some of the theoretical work in cultural studies, and I would be interested to know how many people do or if it possible. I would be more convinced of the notion that Fiske is an anomaly in cultural studies if I saw more criticism along the lines that follow. I suspect his role in cultural studies is that of grasping its logic and trajectory and applying reductio ad absurdum.

I remember when I began graduate work in the early 1980s, cultural studies had an air of excitement and resistance to it. It was the radical alternative to the brain-dead positivism that seemed best suited to showing "scientifically" that this was the best of all possible worlds. It was cultural studies—in communication at least—that led the way in demanding that mainstream social science explain why it assumed capitalist social relations were a given and why it was assumed that there could be no alternative and superior manner in constructing a society. Today that is long gone. In a manner similar to how Marx and Engels regarded the new German philosophers in the opening two paragraphs of *The German Ideology* (Tucker 1972, 111), cultural studies gives us much hype but little action. Unfortunately, in Madison and I suspect elsewhere, the very term *cultural studies* has become an ongoing punch line to a bad joke. It signifies half-assed research, self-congratulation, and farcical pretension. At its worst, this newfangled cultural studies is unable to defend its work, so it no longer tries, merely claiming that its critics are hung up on such outmoded notions as evidence, logic, science, and rationality. It then becomes akin to a religious sect, requiring a leap of faith to participate.

Some of cultural studies, such as the work of Julie D'Acci (1994), Richard Campbell (1991), Thomas Frank (1997), and Susan Davis (1997), is brilliant and reminds me just how important cultural studies can be. Most of what I have seen, however, is not great, nor does it aspire to greatness. My sense is that this is due primarily to the marginalization of explicitly radical politics.

In my view, there are two clear reasons for the decline of political radicalism in cultural studies. First, this is the normal consequence of becoming institutionalized in the academy. The professionalization of cultural studies implicitly encourages depoliticization, while depoliticization makes it far easier to accrue institutional resources. For those who do not espouse radical politics or who believe that radical politics must be secondary to institutional success, this depoliticization is a welcome turn of events, a sign of the field's maturation. The radical origins of cultural studies are best ignored or forgotten. Needless to say, this institutionalization is especially damaging to cultural studies, in view of its explicitly populist origins and project. It tends to produce a lifeless caricature of itself.

Second, the postmodern or poststructural turn in cultural studies has had disastrous implications for its politics. I acknowledge that postmodernism has produced some keen insights; it is quite useful for issues of identity and representation. But postmodernism is similar to mainstream quantitative social science: each is well suited for specific types of tasks, usually narrowly defined, but neither is especially useful for the "big picture." Each is good for looking at specific trees, neither at assessing the forest. Understandably, neither quantoids nor postmodernists are eager to accept that they deal with small potatoes while other scholars deal with the big issues. In the case of quantoids, they assume away the big issues, whereas in the case of postmodernists they claim that big issues do not exist or that they are impossible to understand or what have you. Familiarity with postmodern literature has now become almost mandatory for admission as a full-time participant in academic cultural studies. There is no reason why cultural studies needs more than a smidgen of postmodernism, and I would love nothing more than a quick divorce. But to the outsider's untrained eye, cultural studies has become effectively synonymous with postmodernism.

I recognize that some cultural studies scholars influenced by postmodernism remain politically active on the left. I would argue that these people tend to bring their strong politics to postmodernism; they do not get their politics from postmodernism. Alan Wald has argued that postmodernism may have the same politicizing effect on young people today that existentialism did on youth in the 1960s and early 1970s (personal conversation, n.d.). I hope he is right, but I have seen little evidence to support such a view. To the contrary, postmodernism points the way to disillusion, apathy, and inactivity. As Paul Loeb (1995) noted after his seven-year study of U.S. student activists in the late 1980s and early 1990s, what is striking is how unaffected activists are by postmodernism. I am also hopeful that such people as Doug Kellner succeed in their efforts to reconcile cultural studies, postmodernism, and critical theory. Once again, however, I am not hopeful. Whatever gems can be mined from postmodernism are small compared with what could be gained by putting the same amount of attention elsewhere.

Politically oriented postmodernists in cultural studies and elsewhere might recoil at what I have just stated. To them, postmodernism offers a basic repudiation of old-fashioned, out-of-date leftist analysis and politics and points the way to a new radical democratic future. In particular, traditional leftists have put too much emphasis on economics and class exploitation and not enough on culture and sexism and racism. There is a great deal to criticize in traditional leftist politics and theory concerning racism and sexism and much else, but in my view postmodernists are being disingenuous to leap from this to calling for a rejection of materialism and class-based politics and a move to identity-based politics. An even rudimentary study of history also shows that the Left invariably has been among the leaders in battles against racism and sexism, despite its shortcomings. Radicals are opposed to all forms of oppression, and it is ludicrous to debate which—sexism, racism, classism, or homophobia—is most terrible, as if we were in some zero-sum game. Socialists have traditionally emphasized class—and continue to do so today—because the fundamental decisions made in a capitalist society are made because of profit maximization. Moreover, it is only through class politics that human liberation can truly be reached. At times it seems that postmodernists have the notion that the U.S. working class is made up of middle-aged, overweight white men. In fact, the U.S. working class is the truly multicultural segment of our society, and that is increasingly the case. What is meaningful social change for African Americans or non-upper-middle-class women unless it includes radical changes in the political economy? Those changes will not be sufficient, but they will be the basis for the creation of a genuinely democratic society. I am still waiting to hear about a postmodern identity politics model for democracy that does not follow this course. In my view, Terry Eagleton (1995) has hit the nail on the head: although never stated directly or subjected to analysis, the politics of postmodernism are based on accepting the complete victory of capitalism and the repudiation of the possibility of socialism. In short, the politics of postmodernism are the rejection of radical politics.

I find it ironic that in the middle of the most one-sided class war in U.S. history, with business and the neoliberal Right smashing the interests of the poor and working class, there are actually people in cultural studies unconcerned about these developments or denying their importance. Yet if the intellectuals are unclear about where power lies in our society and what the real threat to it is, those who rule have no doubt whatsoever. Consider the experience of the legendary writer Amiri Baraka, who was left alone by the FBI while he espoused the "white man is the devil" jargon but was harassed unmercifully once he became a socialist. He also found that he was no longer accorded access to the mainstream media and that his speaking offers declined dramatically.

Explicit state repression is not, however, the primary enemy of the Left or of democracy today. Although we have the makings of a racist police state, this accords with the standard job of policing and terrorizing the victims of a vicious class society, something formerly found primarily in third world societies but increasingly seen as necessary in our rapidly polarizing social order. The key battle we fight is with the culture of depoliticization, which is the hallmark of monopoly capitalist society and also infects even the most oppressed elements of society, though the myths of the existing order are far less accepted the further down the social pecking order one goes. I believe C. B. Macpherson (1977) is correct to say that democracy in monopoly capitalist societies can "succeed" only when there is rampant depoliticization, when the masses do not interfere with elite control over fundamental policy decisions. As Noam Chomsky (1987) notes, it is considered a "crisis of democracy" when the dispossessed actually organize to promote their own interests. In such cases as these, as with the Black Panthers mentioned earlier, the state then works explicitly to repress the movement and have people return to their proper subservient and passive role.

In general, the social order produces profound intrinsic pressures to maintain depoliticization as the dominant and unquestioned motif. People are told in countless ways that it is not cool to be political. Our job as radical intellectuals is to constantly battle depoliticization and, as we used to say in the late 1960s and early 1970s, to "make the connections." Our job is to show that the deterioration of urban America is related to the decline of labor and the working class, which is related to the assault on the environment, which is related to the rise of racism and sexual assault and to the overall crisis of community. Our job is to show these connections—to study and comprehend this social order—so that we can understand what we must and can do to change these things. Our job is to pursue this politicization in the face of extreme pressures on people to do exactly the opposite, to think only of number one, to obey orders, to never think social change is possible or desirable, and to confine rebellion to fashion statements. The current crisis of capitalism has given the material whip to these pressures, such that college students today are under vastly greater pressure to toe the line than I felt twenty years ago. To be a radical student on a U.S. campus today is a feat of not inconsiderable courage. Cultural studies was once committed to this politicization process in very important and creative ways. But that is the case no more.

Grossberg (1992) argues, too, that cultural studies needs to maintain its commitment to leftist politics, and he also calls for cultural studies to be better versed in economics. I am delighted that in *We Gotta Get Out of This Place* Grossberg's final two chapters dealt with capitalism and the future of the Left. This is precisely the necessary agenda for cultural studies. Yet, at the same time, Grossberg's treatment of capitalism reveals a narrow reading list of Fordist and post-Fordist theorists, and it suggests little familiarity with the broader literature in radical political economy. If it is fair to say that cultural studies should not be political economy, it seems fair also to say that all political economy need not be doused in poststructuralism. So while I applaud Grossberg's spirit, I encourage him to dive deeper into the waters and into realms unexplored by cultural studies. I think by doing so, Grossberg and cultural studies will be able to make a far greater contribution to the political Left. In particular, I recommend that cultural studies make itself conversant in the political economy associated with the *Monthly Review* and the *Monthly Review* tradition. This should not be the only stop on a tour of political economy, but it should be on the itinerary.[1]

What is *Monthly Review* and the *Monthly Review* tradition? *MR* was founded as a monthly journal in 1949 by Leo Huberman and Paul Sweezy. Huberman was a journalist, activist, and popularizer of radical ideas. When he died in 1968, his place as coeditor was taken by Harry Magdoff, a self-educated economist who had been a New Deal whiz kid during World War II. Sweezy and Magdoff remain *MR*'s editors today. Sweezy is a Harvard-educated economist who worked with Joseph Schumpeter and Harold Laski. Sweezy's work has been strongly influenced by Veblen, Keynes, and the radical economists interested in the same issues that Keynes explored. Other key people include the economist Paul Baran, who came to the United States after working at the Frankfurt School, and Harry Braverman, a radical activist and working-class intellectual best known for *Labor and Monopoly Capital* (1974). Other intellectuals whose work fits comfortably within the *MR* tradition are I. F. Stone, C. Wright Mills, and Noam Chomsky. Younger scholars associated with the *MR* tradition include John Bellamy Foster, Ellen Meiksins Wood, and Cornel West. For the most part, the *MR* tradition emerged independent of the academy and has maintained that independence. Among other things, this probably accounts for the clarity of language and lack of jargon that is the hallmark of *MR*. The purpose of *MR* from its inception has been to speak intelligently to progressives about contemporary politics. In the early 1950s, the Monthly Review Press was launched; its first title was Stone's *Hidden History of the Korean War*.

Monthly Review calls itself an independent socialist magazine and would probably also be characterized as Marxist. (In my view, the term *Marxism* has been so mangled by its supporters and detractors that it has lost much of its meaning. I tend to agree with Chomsky that it would be best to just junk the term because it is treated more like a religion than a social theory or mode of social analysis. But if I am to be called a Marxist, *MR* provides the type of Marxism with which I would be proudly associated.) A core problem for U.S. Marxism has been the same for U.S. cultural studies: in reactionary times, it has become the province of intellectuals operating without any popular base in society, and it has lost its bearings. Beyond the question of Marxism per se, *Monthly Review* points the way for how radical intellectuals can maintain their principles and honesty in times that bode poorly for the Left. For most of its forty-six years, *MR* has been in a political culture where its ideas and values are marginalized and the prospects for socialism have been minuscule. *MR* has faced up to the situation by taking what Paul Baran (1969) termed "the longer view," making a hard analysis of the existing situation and working to support those elements of society that suffer the most from the status quo.

If *MR* has only one lesson for cultural studies, I hope it is this: history does not always deliver victories in your own lifetime. Do we admire the person who opposed slavery and fought it on principle in 1750 or do we dismiss that person as a fool and admire the person who knew slavery was wrong but decided that since it was entrenched it would be best to go with the flow? We understand the latter person, but we admire the former person. Who can predict if we are a hundred years away from radical change or five hundred years or twenty years? If inequality, poverty, greed, plutocracy, and exploitation are wrong in principle, they remain wrong even if the forces of darkness seem in control of society and even if their ideologues fill the air with their propaganda. In this situation, the duty of the intellectual is to analyze why we are in that situation and what we need to do to get out of it. While intellectuals may not be paying attention, material conditions for the mass of humanity are worsening, and the prospects for the future everywhere are grim. Although understandable, it is morally unconscionable for intellectuals to throw in the towel because it does not look as if there is hope for change in the foreseeable future. The victims of this system do not have the privilege of throwing in any towel, since they are already lying face down on the canvas. There are many difficult issues that need much debate and study—not the least of which is how to build a democratic socialist society—but the core principles remain in place. I will return to this point later.

Monthly Review can take a principled "longer view" of contemporary issues because of its capacity to the see "the present as history" (Sweezy 1953). This is where the *MR* tradition draws quite directly from classical Marxism. This was once also a trait of cultural studies, and it certainly permeated Williams's work. Although historical work is being done in cultural studies today—and some of it is quite good—most of it has little sense of history as a process. This is especially the case in cultural studies of U.S. television. My own work analyzed the battle to establish a nonprofit U.S. broadcasting system in the 1930s (McChesney, 1993), and I never cease to be amazed by the historically complacent and misinformed attitudes cultural studies scholars take toward U.S. commercial broadcasting. Cultural studies needs more than social history and more than histories of texts and audiences. It needs three-dimensional histories of culture industries and political fights over their control and development.

The centerpiece of the *Monthly Review* tradition has been its critique of contemporary capitalism, or what Baran and Sweezy term *monopoly capitalism,* because it is dominated by large corporations working in oligopolistic markets. It is in political economy that the brilliance of the *MR* tradition shines through. Unlike some Marxist political economy, the *MR* tradition never tries to show how existing capitalism conforms to predictions made by Marx in 1867 or Lenin in 1914. Rather, the object is to understand how contemporary capitalism works, based on its actual behavior and using tools provided by Marx, Veblen, Keynes, Steindl, Kalecki, and Hanson, among others. Unlike mainstream economists, those in the *MR* tradition do not assume the market is neutral, that class inequality is natural, and that capitalism is ahistorical. Unlike both Marxist and mainstream economists, they have refreshingly integrated the real-world capitalism of finance and corporate behavior into their theory.

Baran and Sweezy's core argument is that monopoly capitalism has a strong tendency toward economic stagnation. Unlike neo-classical theorists, who maintain that the system tends toward full employment if the market is left to its own devices, Baran and Sweezy argue that the system tends toward crisis and depression. They laid this out in a book entitled *Monopoly Capital,* published in 1966. After twenty years of historically unprecedented economic growth, *MR* argued that the tendency of modern capitalism was toward stagnation and depression. Although there is a good deal of debate over the merits of the *MR* position, its fundamental argument has proven true and provides a superior context for understanding contemporary economic policy-making. This would be political economy's magnificent lesson for cultural studies: capitalism is a flawed, irrational, and contradictory economic system with inherent problems, which must be studied and understood. The workings of the capital accumulation process profoundly influence every segment of our social existence. In dismissing everything except cultural studies as economic reductionism, too many cultural studies people have accepted an ahistorical notion of a capitalism that delivers the goods. As Ellen Meiksins Wood (1995) has pointed out, cultural studies and postmodernism often reveal a sense of capitalism as it operated during the halcyon days of the 1960s, not the actual system that is in crisis everywhere and in free-fall in some parts of the world.

Baran and Sweezy, drawing heavily on Veblen, have also provided the most penetrating analysis of the political economy of advertising. They answer the questions that mainstream commentators ignore: why does advertising become prominent in modern capitalism, and why is it so bogus? Given the importance of advertising in the creation and production of popular culture and the overall direction of the media, this alone would be valuable material for cultural studies. It is astonishing how such a central cultural institution is so commonly misunderstood. Those familiar with Raymond Williams's (1980) work on advertising as the "magic system" will find the unmistakable imprint of Baran and Sweezy on his argument (170–95). A distinguishing feature of *MR*'s political economy is its emphasis on the political economy of *consumption*, in contrast to the traditional concentration on production and distribution. This, too, recommends *MR* as particularly important to cultural studies.

Perhaps the stupidity—and there is no better word for it—of some cultural studies is best shown by its stance toward the market. John Fiske (1990) argues the market is not the top-down authoritarian mechanism that political economists claim, where bosses force the masses to swallow whatever they are fed. To the contrary, Fiske exults, the market is where the masses can contest with the bosses over economic matters; it is a fight without a predetermined outcome. Angela McRobbie echoes this view, going on to characterize the market as "an expansive popular system" (quoted in Grossberg 1995, 81). How far cultural studies has fallen from Stuart Hall's (1979) brilliant conception of the market and its relation to class inequality (323). What a grotesque and callous mischaracterization of the political economic critique of the market. *All* radical political economy recognizes that the market is based on competition and has formal voluntarism (Herman 1995). Of course people receive value for their money; otherwise they would not spend it. I am not opposed to the market per se; there may be some creative ways to use it in a postcapitalist world. But it is absurd—even vile when one considers the human toll generated by neoliberal free market policies around the world today—to extrapolate from this that the market is an "expansive popular system." The market is hardly a democratic mechanism; participation on the demand side is based on one-dollar, one-vote rather than one-person, one-vote. The rich have many votes, and the poor have very few. Is it any surprise that the market reproduces class inequality? Participation on the supply side has distinct strings attached; it is not so much "giving the people what they want" as it is "giving the people what they want within a range that is profitable and in the interests of the suppliers to produce." This is often a far narrower range than one might hope for in a democracy. I could go on and on. The point is simply that by naively accepting the market, cultural studies effectively eliminates its capacity to provide a radical critique. If the market is so wonderful, why should we want to make radical social change? The McRobbie/Fiske position also reveals a supreme ignorance of elementary social theory.

Moreover, the market is the mortal enemy of community, a term invoked widely and glowingly in cultural studies circles. Markets have no respect for community or traditions, they only understand profit and personal gain. Markets encourage some of the worst traits of humanity and discourage some of our best traits, including selflessness and compassion. This, of course, is the grand hypocrisy of the religious Right: it claims to want a combination of free market policies and a return to family and community values. In fact, markets are destroying families and communities faster than beef production is laying waste to the Amazon rainforest. This is where Marxism still provides the keenest insights into the flaws of bourgeois society; it has never been better stated than by Marx and Engels in *The Communist Manifesto* when they discuss how capitalism reduces social relations to "the cash nexus." The extent to which we value a world of caring, warmth, and community in the best sense of the term is the extent to which markets—and therefore capitalism—are our enemy.

As flawed as the McRobbie/Fiske characterization of the market is in general or for commercial entertainment, it is utter nonsense when applied to journalism or political ideas. The political marketplace of ideas is not under any circumstances an "expansive popular system." The quality of our journalism and public affairs—at the hands of the market—is abysmal, and it is deteriorating. There are volumes of studies of the news media revealing the antidemocratic biases of a corporate, commercial news media system. This is no blind marketplace servicing the needs of the citizenry; to the contrary, our journalism tends strongly to conform to elite interests and to marginalize positions critical of the existing order. One of the most impressive areas in cultural activism concerns progressive attempts to monitor and improve journalism, working through mainstream channels and working to build alternative media and networks. In the 1970s, cultural studies would have been at the forefront of such groups as Fairness and Accuracy in Reporting, but no more. Likewise, an enormous public relations industry working for corporate America has emerged with the general project of shaping our political culture to suit the interests of business (Carey 1995). It accounts for a significant percentage of our news and has played a central role in providing the ideological basis for the right-wing victories of the past two decades. Activists in labor, women's, environmental, and other progressive groups are well aware of the battle they are engaged in with this supremely well-oiled propaganda machine (Stauber and Rampton 1995). But cultural studies has little apparent interest in corporate public relations and propaganda onslaughts.

This naïveté about the market is the logical result of a culturalist reductionism now prevalent in cultural studies. As Mulhern (1995) notes, it seems to be based on the assumption that anything but culturalist reductionism is economic reductionism. Mulhern concludes that this has had the ironic effect of removing the politics of culture from cultural studies. Cultural studies has very little to say about the actual politics of culture. To the extent that it weighs in on policy issues, it seems to be on the side of the market, though it appears mostly disinterested in establishing the institutional basis for democratic communication. Consider George Gerbner's new Cultural Environment Movement, a coalition of labor, women's, environmental, religious, educational, and minority group organizations that has been organized to battle the corporate domination and commercialization of global culture. Why is cultural studies not at the center of this movement rather than nowhere to be found? If people in cultural studies disagree with Gerbner's outfit or with Fairness and Accuracy in Reporting, why don't they get involved and explain why? Work with people who are working for social change. The cultural studies work concerning the Internet tends to be utopian or dystopian and technologically determinist. It is worthless politically and often plays directly into the hands of the transnational firms striving to capitalize on the new technologies (McChesney 1996; Stallabrass 1995). The contrast between the work of current leading figures in cultural studies and the work of Williams on policy and politics is both striking and depressing.

What underscores all of my criticism goes back to Eagleton's point. In reading cultural studies, one is struck by the sense that the writers find the market and capitalism invincible and socialism either impossible or even dangerous. In short, cultural studies has accepted the primary ideological defense of the status quo. In my view, this is a critical area where the *Monthly Review* tradition can be distinguished from what reigns in cultural studies. I would go so far as to say that this is the defining issue of whether one is or is not on the political left. This issue is not whether capitalism and the market appear to be in full command for the foreseeable future; on that point there is agreement. Nor is the issue whether the humane and rational thing to do is to make the best of the situation and attempt to improve the quality of life that is adversely effected by capitalism, in other words, to work for reforms; on that point there is agreement too. The critical issue is whether one maintains a principled critique of capitalism, continues to examine capitalism thoroughly, and works to lay the foundations for a postcapitalist social order. In *MR*'s approach, capitalism, despite its power, is a fundamentally unstable, inegalitarian, irrational, and inhumane system that is recklessly driving humanity toward ecological and social disaster. This leftist position, the *Monthly Review* position, is hardly sectarian. To maintain a commitment to continue studying capitalism with the eventual goal of replacing it with a truly democratic order is hardly a narrow litmus test for admission to the Left. It just means keeping our eyes on the prize. There is room under this tent for social democrats, anarchists, liberation theologians, feminists, environmentalists, trade unionists, Moslems, Christians, Jews, atheists, punk rockers, rappers, nudists, and Marxists, and the list goes on.

Contrast this with most of postmodernism and too much of cultural studies: if capitalism is a given, then why spend much time studying it critically? As a result, much of cultural studies has a completely undeveloped or asinine notion of how capitalism actually works and with what result (see Fiske and McRobbie above). Once you stop thinking about capitalism critically, you gradually accept its dictates and eventually become as concerned with successfully managing the system as with advocating the interests of the dispossessed. Capitalism goes from being all-powerful because the system has temporarily neutralized or crushed its opposition, to being all-powerful because it must represent the natural order of things and accords to human nature, to being all-powerful because it is good. Your politics gradually move from being progressive to being regressive. You are neck deep in a pool of reaction without a paddle or a clue. This is all done without ever candidly studying and analyzing capitalism and reaching that conclusion after careful deliberation. Just the opposite is the case. Since reforms that were commonplace within capitalism twenty-five years ago seem nearly impossible nowadays, without a firm effort to understand how capitalism operates as a mode of production and as a social system, this "capitalism is off-limits" approach will almost certainly lead to cynicism and depoliticization, if not outright reaction. It is ironic that even if you regard capitalism as entrenched for all time, the radical Left approach probably has a better chance of leading to reform within the system.

Some cultural studies people want to maintain an oppositional air about them, all the while conceding the capitalist control of society and no longer questioning its propriety. Fiske (1993) has done this in the most entertaining manner, by trivializing politics beyond recognition. He points to the "tiny" victories—such as, in an extreme example, when slaves commit suicide rather than go to work on the plantation—as the true liberation politics, demonstrating the slaves' "ultimate undefeatability" (312). I suspect the slaveowners were willing to concede some "tiny" victories to the slaves as long as their system remained intact. Contrast this with the idea that the true liberation politics might also be regarded as organizing to smash slavery—a "big" victory—so people would not have to kill themselves to subvert the system. But entrenched material social relations are off-limits to Fiske, impossible to change, and now, he claims, unimportant. Fiske has grounds to be confused by all this fuss about capitalism. The market, after all, he tells us, is the weapon of the dispossessed. Fiske seems to have taken to heart the joke that the 1960s antiwar protesters made when they told the government to withdraw the troops from Vietnam and declare victory. To Fiske, the revolution is over, and we won. We can make all the "tiny" victories we want, and the best thing of all is that nobody tries to stop us. Isn't this a great country?

As for the impossibility of socialism, there are legitimate grounds for concern here, and we do need to apply all our energies to determining how to establish an egalitarian, libertarian, democratic society. It will require much experimentation and openness. Perhaps conventional wisdom and postmodernism are right, and it cannot be done. But what, exactly, is the evidence for this claim? That the Soviet Union failed? By that logic, I guess we can throw capitalism overboard, too, because it has made an even bigger mess in Russia. The failure of antidemocratic state socialism hardly establishes the excellence of capitalism; it only established the failure of antidemocratic state socialism. Or is it that the social democracies, as in Sweden, have come crashing down? There I submit the problem is more one of what reforms capitalism can and cannot permit rather than one of the inherent weakness of socialism. In the *Monthly Review* perspective, "socialism is as possible now as it ever was" (Sweezy and Magdoff 1993). At any rate, if we do not develop a democratic socialist alternative, the responses to global crises will tend to be highly reactionary. We really have no choice in the matter. As Bob Dylan put it, we are going a hundred miles an hour down a dead-end street. Paul Sweezy (1995) argues that unless we come up with something to replace the profit system, it is unlikely that civilization can survive as we know it much beyond another century. In the end, the rejection of the possibility of democratic socialism is the rejection of the possibility of democracy, because it is the rejection of the idea that people can govern their own lives in a humane manner.

Monthly Review not only continues to provide a forum for critical analysis of existing capitalism but also offers useful insights on the question of socialism. *MR* has studied leftist social movements and socialist societies to evaluate their strengths and weaknesses. It has made a Marxist analysis of socialism. It has been concerned with understanding exactly why leftist movements have failed and what needs to be done to build a popular left. These are critical questions, and they will be answered in the real world of practice as much as in the pages of a journal. These were once defining issues in cultural studies, but they are no more.

What seems clear from the Soviet experience and the experience of the Left everywhere is that any socialist society will be only as democratic as the movement that brings it into existence. Harry Magdoff has characterized the *Monthly Review* position as "if you are not part of the problem, you are part of the solution" (personal conversation, n.d.). The *MR* stance on building a democratic left movement that might be the basis for a democratic socialist society directly contrasts with the prevailing conception of left building found among the denizens of identity politics. It was best stated by L. A. Kaufman (1993), who worked at *Monthly Review* in the late 1980s before moving to Berkeley to pursue her interests in postmodernism and identity politics. She wrote a critique of *MR*'s old-fashioned politics in the *Progressive* a few years later while promoting the exciting new world of identity politics activism. In her piece, Kaufman described how *MR* holds weekly lunchtime brownbags in which progressives from around the world who might be in New York get together to discuss their work and politics. Kaufman noted how regardless of their race, gender, or nationality, these leftists invariably looked on each other as brothers and sisters and comrades. There was a great warmth and sense of community. Although Kaufman acknowledged the attraction of this political culture, she dismissed it as outdated and as irrelevant as socialism itself. Kaufman offered as a superior model, one in which various identities stake out their private turf and reveal limited trust for others based on their identities. Which of these positions is one that suggests a future of community and shared interests and which is one teeming with suspicion and fraught with contradiction? What type of new society will emerge from the success of identity politics activism? Ultimately, which world do you want to live in? What Martin Luther King said about all Americans is especially applicable to the Left and those who seek to provide a democratic socialist alternative: we will either learn to live together as brothers and sisters or perish together as fools.

I am not naive about how "integration" has suggested that identity groups sacrifice their interests at the expense of the dominant position. I also recognize that some identity politics can be quite progressive in certain contexts. But Kaufman, in my view, is making a virtue of a necessity, extolling identity politics as superior to the Left when, in fact, they exist in effective absence of a left. That we need a left is not disproven. But there is something even more fundamental at stake here. The Left's position is not to build a world of separate but equal, and it is not to abandon the cause of building a genuine community of men and women; it is the socialist position to integrate society in a revolutionary context. What distinguishes the *Monthly Review* from the identity politics crowd is the term *revolutionary context*. If you do not believe that people can ever truly live as one, then this seems wildly utopian. But then ultimately identity politics exposes itself for what it is: a nonrevolutionary movement at best, a reactionary movement at worst. I suspect that as a left reemerges, the accompanying optimism and enthusiasm will eliminate much of the current bickering that feeds off of pessimism and defeatism.

What has happened to cultural studies is that it has lost its politics and therefore its vitality. Is there any hope for cultural studies? As an academic entity in U.S. universities, cultural studies has done well and should remain in existence. As an occasional producer of superb scholarship and a frequent producer of poor scholarship, it has hope, too. But is there any hope for cultural studies as a participant in movements for radical social change? In the short term, probably not. Not only is cultural studies eschewing a critique of capitalism, but also the trajectory of cultural studies is away from leftist politics, and there is little sense that many in cultural studies are interested in participating and assisting organized left social movements. Cultural studies divorced from political activism is a recipe for decay, as the past decade shows, and it appears still to be the order of the day. We see signs, for example, of a resurgent, militant, and multicultural U.S. labor movement today. Moreover, it is a labor movement that for the first time since the 1940s understands it is in a cultural as well as a political and economic battle for survival. In the old days, cultural studies would have been present in the creation, but those days are long gone. At best, cultural studies will lag behind a resurgent popular movement and jump on the caboose well after the train gets moving. At worst, cultural studies will continue on its present course, denying the necessity and possibility of social change. In doing so, it will finally and forever repudiate its charter.

Note

1. This essay was originally written in 1995. In 2001, I became coeditor of the *Monthly Review*.

References

Ahmad, A. 1993. *In Theory*. London: Verso.
Baran, P. A. 1969. *The Longer View*. New York: Monthly Review.

Baran, P. A., and P. M. Sweezy. 1966. *Monopoly Capital.* New York: Monthly Review.

Braverman, H. 1974. *Labor and Monopoly Capital.* New York: Monthly Review.

Campbell, R. 1991. *60 Minutes and the News: A Mythology for America.* Urbana: University of Illinois Press.

Carey, A. 1995. *Taking the Risk out of Democracy.* Sydney: University of New South Wales Press.

Chomsky, N. 1987. *On Power and Ideology: The Managua Lectures.* Boston: South End.

D'Acci, J. 1994. *Defining Women: Television and the Case of Cagney and Lacey.* Chapel Hill: University of North Carolina Press.

Davis, S. G. 1997. *Spectacular Nature.* Berkeley: University of California Press.

Eagleton, T. 1995. "Where Do Postmodernists Come From?" *Monthly Review* 47 (3): 59–70.

Fiske, J. 1990. Comments to Graduate Colloquium, Department of Communication Arts, University of Wisconsin–Madison.

———. 1993. *Power Plays Power Works.* New York: Verso.

Frank, T. 1997. *The Conquest of Cool.* Chicago: University of Chicago Press.

Garnham, N. 1995. "Political Economy and Cultural Studies: Reconciliation or Divorce?" *Critical Studies in Mass Communication* 12 (1): 62–71.

Grossberg, L. 1992. *We Gotta Get Out of This Place: Popular Conservatism and Postmodern Culture.* New York: Routledge.

———. 1995. "Cultural Studies vs. Political Economy: Is Anyone Else Bored with This Debate?" *Critical Studies in Mass Communication* 12 (1): 72–81.

Hall, S. 1979. "Culture, Media, and the Ideological Effect." In *Mass Communication and Society,* edited by J. Curran, M. Gurevitch, J. Woollacott, assisted by J. Marriott and C. Roberts, 315–48. Beverly Hills, Calif.: Sage.

Herman, E. S. 1995. *Triumph of the Market.* Boston: South End.

Kaufman, L. A. 1993. "What's Left? Socialism No." *Progressive,* April, 27–29.

Loeb, P. R. 1995. *Generation at the Crossroads.* New Brunswick, N.J.: Rutgers University Press.

Macpherson, C. B. 1977. *The Life and Times of Liberal Democracy.* New York: Oxford University Press.

McChesney, R. W. 1993. *Telecommunications, Mass Media, and Democracy: The Battle for the Control of U.S. Broadcasting, 1928–1935.* New York: Oxford University Press.

———. 1996. "The Internet and U.S. Communication Policymaking in Historical and Critical Perspective." *Journal of Communication* 46 (1): 98–124.

Mulhern, F. 1995. "The Politics of Cultural Studies." *Monthly Review* 47 (3): 31–40.

Stallabrass, J. 1995. "Empowering Technology: The Exploration of Cyberspace." *New Left Review,* no. 211: 3–32.

Stauber, J., and S. Rampton. 1995. *Toxic Sludge Is Good for You: Lies, Damn Lies, and the Public Relations Industry.* Monroe, Maine: Common Courage.

Stone, I. F. 1952. *The Hidden History of the Korean War.* New York: Monthly Review.

Sweezy, P. M. 1953. *The Present as History.* New York: Monthly Review.

———. 1995. Personal correspondence to author, 15 August.

Sweezy, P., and H. Magdoff. 1993. Personal correspondence to author, June 1.
Thompson, E. P. 1988. "Last Dispatches from the Border Country." *Nation,* March 5, 310.
———. 1994. *Making History: Writings on History and Culture.* New York: New Press.
Tucker, R. C., ed. 1972. *The Marx-Engels Reader.* New York: W. W. Norton.
Williams, R. 1980. *Problems in Materialism and Culture.* London: Verso.
Wood, E. M. 1995. "What Is the 'Postmodern' Agenda? An Introduction." *Monthly Review* 47 (3): 1–12.

LINDA M. BLUM AND
ANDREA L. PRESS

5 What Can We Hear after Postmodernism? Doing Feminist Field Research in the Age of Cultural Studies

We start this essay with a personal yet professional observation. As feminist sociologists and qualitative field researchers, we each have experienced the fractured or split identities and lack of stable communities so aptly described by postmodern philosophers as characteristic of our era. For both of us, seeking "homes" in our discipline proved problematic (as each of our career trajectories attests).[1] The qualitative tradition has long been important in American sociology, as the discipline lacks a unified paradigm and has had, in each generation, its share of critical practitioners. But resources and institutional power have been dominated by the quantitative core at least since the mid-twentieth century. Many employ qualitative approaches and do feminist research, though they (together with us) tend to be assigned to the "periphery" of the disciplinary terrain.

Ironically, seeking interdisciplinary "homes" can also be problematic. As feminist ethnographers, we have each often found ourselves the sole representative of the social sciences in interdisciplinary locations dominated by humanists and their linguistic and textual approaches to cultural studies. We have also often been seen as throwbacks, theoretically naive, for continuing to engage in dialogue with human subjects.

To humanists unaware of sociology's arcane intradisciplinary politics, the social sciences can reek of their overarching postwar positivism. Postmodernism, a significant if diffuse influence in contemporary cultural studies, has challenged the basis of such modernist projects and has posed instead the ubiquity of power lying behind modern science's quest for shared human truths.[2] Though we are also influenced by postmodern insights, it is odd, even painful to be so dismissed when we have been so effectively marginalized in our own discipline. In this essay, we thus focus on the divide between feminist field research and cultural studies, share our hesitations about the devaluing of fieldwork with the postmodern discursive or textual turn, and touch on some of the important insights that the ethnographer and the textual critic can offer each other. We specifically ask what value talking with others can still have in the face of postmodern challenges.

Feminist Fieldwork

With enthusiasm sparked by the resurgent women's movement, feminist sociologists over a quarter-century ago embraced qualitative interviewing and fieldwork techniques as "feminist methods" (e.g., Oakley 1981). Such techniques were embraced as less objectifying and more egalitarian and reciprocal than quantitative approaches, though paradoxically, early in the century the gendered knowledge hierarchy had been reversed, with the surveys of women reformers seen as "soft" and biased because they were value-engaged and the ethnographies of the Chicago sociologists viewed as "hard" and scientific in their detachment. In fact, however, the persisting gendered dichotomy with numbers dominant solidified as American sociologists struggled to legitimate the discipline and ensure professional, manly career structures (Laslett 1992).[3] Qualitative work has been poised, since that time, on the critical margin between science and the humanities, between objectivist causal models and humanistic models of *verstehen* (or understanding), and in the political gulf between value neutrality and value engagement. Second-wave feminist method discussions therefore had strong kinship ties to other critical approaches outside the quantitative positivist core. These included the value engagement of the first-wave women reformers, Marxism's emphasis on perspectival or class consciousness, and humanistic or phenomenological strands' focus on the subjective meaning orientations of social actors. Because feminist researchers were less interested in tracing such kinship or in metatheoretical "theorizing about theory," we inherited a weakly justified framework somewhere between the humanists' proclivity to side with the "underdog" and Marxism's standpoint epistemology. This tacit framework led to an ever-growing, rich empirical literature "giving voice to the voiceless."[4]

Dorothy Smith has been the rare feminist sociologist to work on the metatheoretical level. Smith strove to tie insights from the discipline's critical traditions into a "sociology for women" to strengthen the justification for feminist research as an alternative knowledge project. For Smith, this project would illuminate the social organization within which women's lives were embedded, lives and features of social organization that ostensibly objective social scientists ignored. Though she did little empirical research herself, Smith (1990) later observed that she aimed to create "an umbrella" under which her students could work. Smith's metatheory has since been cast by the philosopher Sandra Harding (1991) as *the* exemplar of a feminist standpoint epistemology. Standpoint theories argue that all knowledge is affected by social location and the conditions under which it is produced and that subordinate locations provide better, more accurate angles of vision on social conditions. For Smith, alternative knowledge should therefore begin from women's experience, from the social locations to which women are assigned. Like other feminist standpoint theories, Smith's alternative knowledge is, in Donna Haraway's words, a "cognitive-emotional-political achievement, crafted out of located social-historical-bodily experience" (Haraway 1997, 304n. 32).

Smith's key points of critique were positivist sociology's abstract, genderless knowers and its unacknowledged involvement in the relations of ruling. She drew an explicit analogy from Marx:[5] the bifurcated consciousness of the proletariat, whose lived experience of alienated labor and exploitation contradicts bourgeois ideology, was similar to that of women, whose lived experience in everyday life, reproducing everyday life, contradicts the abstracted power relations of patriarchal corporate capitalism. It also contradicts the abstracted forms of social and scientific thought that represent and codify these structural relations (D. Smith [1977] 1987). As Smith ([1977] 1987) explained, "women are outside the extralocal relations of ruling, for the most part located in work processes that sustain it and are essential to its existence. There are parallels then between the claims Marx makes for knowledge based in the class whose labor produces the conditions of existence, indeed the very existence of a ruling class, and the claims that can be made for a knowledge of society from the standpoint of women" (79).

It is important to note, as Smith (1993) has herself (with some irritation), that her sociology for women is *not* simply an identity politics in which "one has to be one to know one" (Harding 1993 concurs). Knowledge, in Smith's framework, does not spring up spontaneously and immediately from the experiences or subjectivities of the oppressed; rather, the material, practical activities of daily life, lived in that social location, provide a starting point. Alternative or critical knowledge is then possible by scrutinizing the "line of fault" or "the point of rupture" that lived experiences of marginality open up, from the "bifurcated consciousness" of women reproducing everyday life within and against dominant ideologies. The starting point, women's standpoint, Smith emphasizes, must then be theoretically reconstructed to be "named" and "actionable," particularly as structures of oppression often are obscured in everyday life (Gorelick 1996, 26). To Smith ([1977] 1987), feminist sociology should provide women with analyses "of their situation, of their everyday world, and of its determinations in the larger socio-economic organization" (50) and of "the way in which it passes beyond what is immediately and directly known" (88–89).

Just as Western Marxism grappled to appreciate the complexities of working-class consciousness that were not (or rarely) fully revolutionary, Smith (1993) rejects flattened readings of her work contending that women have a "purely" oppositional view. Such flattened misreadings have been part of the unfair dismissal of feminist sociology. But, at the same time, Smith's irritation and our rush to defend her important contributions can close feminist sociologists to instructive aspects of postmodern challenges (e.g., Mann and Kelley 1997).

Postmoderns, for instance, point out that the standpoint perspective places too much emphasis on being "outside the relations of ruling." Such a dichotomized notion of ruling and of the workings of dominant ideologies may have been important in the 1970s as a corrective to androcentric social science. Yet contemporary cultural studies has been better served by the postmodern insight that all "subjects" are discursively constructed and live within dominant discourses; though they may have different responses or negotiations, no woman can be wholly "outside."[6]

Postmoderns also question the modernist goal of "giving voice" in feminist sociology. As Patricia Clough (1992) writes, the project of making the subordinates' standpoint intelligible implies an arrogant imposition of authority, a power move, which ought to inspire greater wariness on our parts. While such wariness has influenced and indeed reenergized anthropology as a discipline, sociologists have been less prone to ask who we are to be "giving voice" or why it is our language that is intelligible. We have, for the most part, taken for granted that our academic locations and access to professional language are wholly positive resources.[7]

Marjorie DeVault, a student of Smith (who may be less familiar outside sociology), has written about and used feminist methods, and her work illuminates the strengths and limitations of working under Smith's "umbrella." DeVault's ethnographic study, *Feeding the Family* (1991), aimed to make visible women's invisible caregiving in the home and to name women's activities that are not captured in the masculine social sciences. She develops a critique of language as a key "line of fault" (this is a materialist rather than poststructuralist critique: language is embedded in material relations of power, constituted by and constitutive of these relations, so that some voices are louder than others). Because women's caregiving is unrepresented in the dichotomized categories of work and leisure, women's lived experience contradicts dominant ideology and provides a better, less partial starting point. Moreover, in the standpoint formulation, it is not impossible for women to name the unnamed or to create new categories, as it very nearly is for the postmodern. DeVault argues that "communities of women can both expose gaps in social knowledge and begin to develop alternative forms of expression" (6). She therefore concludes, "My strategy . . . has been to focus on difficulties of expression as women talk. . . . This strategy relies on informants' human capacity for creativity of expression as well as their willingness to engage with me in a 'search' for adequate description of their experience" (229). She adds, "With [such descriptions] we are better prepared to insist that the work of producing connection and sociability . . . figure much more centrally in public debate about families and caring" (243). For DeVault, dialogues between researcher and researched that are "driven by respect" are valuable for feminist politics (29). But, the postmoderns will unrelentingly remind us, this creation of "voice" and "visibility" for women is never so seamless or so positive, nor is women's experience itself. Although we share DeVault's political objectives and stubbornly attempt to maintain them in this essay, we can also see that the provocations of postmodernism can improve feminist fieldwork. DeVault writes, for example, that women are the "expert practitioners" of family life whose ongoing, effortful activity produces meals, sociability, group and community connectedness, and central cultural rituals of everyday life. Yet while she does acknowledge the "dark side" of female caregiving (i.e., its subordination), DeVault gives too much coherence and an overly positive gloss to women's experiences. Driven by respect, her desire to counter masculine devaluation leads to a flattened account in which the dialogic elements so important to feminist methods do not end up in the text. DeVault's own ambivalence toward caregiving is mentioned only in the introduction—and, as readers, we do not know if this foreclosed dialogue in the interviews themselves or only in our access to those dialogues. In either case, this flattens the very concept of gender and misses the postmodern insight that subjectivities are fractured and multiple and that ambivalence may be at the center of the accomplishment of gender.

In its first decade at least, interdisciplinary women's studies was animated by inspirations of finding female voice and identity similar to those DeVault so well demonstrates. Since at least the mid-1980s, however, women's studies or interdisciplinary feminist scholarship has increasingly diverged from this "voice giving" tradition of field research. The divergence was fueled largely by the postmodern challenges we have touched on briefly so far, insights that led to the growth and ascendance of cultural studies. The remainder of our essay takes up and recapitulates three closely interrelated points in this divergence for greater scrutiny: the notion of difference, of experience, and of the text (not as our "data," or input, but as our research product, or output).

Difference

By now multiracial feminists' criticism of the feminist standpoint approach is familiar: the approach ignores, obscures, or diminishes the importance of differences among women (e.g., Collins 1990). Some women obviously have more access to power and privilege than others do, and women represent a complex array of locations. Gender has therefore been "decentered" as the key "line of fault" and as the center of analytic attention. Although this decentering is now widely espoused, interdisciplinary feminist scholars have dealt very differently with "difference." Qualitative sociologists have delved into empirical research on experiences of the "simultaneity" of race, class, gender, sexual orientation, and other oppressions. Women's studies scholars, in contrast, have moved into discursive and theoretical analysis as the critique of multiracial feminists ran into the postmodern challenge.

DIFFERENCE WITHIN SOCIOLOGY

Patricia Hill Collins's (1990) metalevel writing on black feminist epistemology has been very influential in feminist sociology, key to revising standpoint approaches to include multiple dimensions of marginality. Collins seems to draw from Smith and similarly rejects flattened readings of her work that would see it as merely advocating identity politics; she writes that it does not work to add together race, gender, and class as if the *most* oppressed have the privileged, best view. Rather, she argues that when scholars struggle to *rearticulate* the standpoint of a specific marginalized location, to clarify and theoretically interpret from and for their particular "line of fault," then better, more liberatory knowledge is generated—that is, knowledge that enhances antiracist and feminist politics (21–22, 207). She differs from Smith, however, in emphasizing that this work must be done in dialogue with communities of African American women.[8]

Most feminist sociologists in field research now rely on such "enriched" or plural standpoint perspectives. Most still typically leave the "meta" level unexamined while empirically examining differences, which ones have mattered when and why, or what experiences of simultaneous oppressions are like (e.g., Glenn, Chang, and Forcey 1994); but a few have begun attempts at greater reflexivity.[9] DeVault (1995), for example, analyzed how race difference was encoded in her dialogue with an African American working-class woman. To put this in context, she reexamined the qualitative tradition's history of attention to difference and the preoccupation with whether researchers were "insiders" or "outsiders" in the groups they studied. Sensitivity to difference has been long present, according to DeVault, though limited by sociology's overarching positivism. Difference, in other words, was attended to only if it hampered access or the establishment of rapport and thus the researcher's data collection. Difference was *not* thought to affect the social scientist's hearing or ability to interpret the "data" of the researched's voice and words.

In these reflections, DeVault comes close to questioning the "giving voice" project in the same way Clough, the postmodern critic, does. DeVault does not, however, recall that a stronger, value-engaged attack against researching across difference emerged in the 1970s from black activist scholars. Such scholars argued for their epistemic privilege in understanding and studying racial oppression (e.g., Ladner 1973), thus embracing an identity politics appropriate for that controversial era. But black activist scholars' attention to the saturation of any research endeavor with societal power relations and to the way research *on* black communities could end up pathologizing or disciplining them while building prestigious careers for white professionals is closer to the current postmodern critique. DeVault thus does not question the naively colonizing potential of the feminist method, "voice giving" project.

How might we respond to such criticism? On the one hand, it seems unfair. The ideal of "giving voice" has a less naive aspect, acknowledging the privilege that we have in the academy however tenuous our positions there. Moreover, the tradition of respect that drives most qualitative work tempers the worst sorts of exploitation of the researched that critics imagine. This respect has long pushed feminist sociologists to struggle with problems of listening effectively across differences of culture, identity, and power (e.g., Oakley 1981; Riessman 1987), and it now promotes the reflexive willingness to stand back and stand corrected (which can actually illuminate much about the workings of dominant discourses) (e.g., Blum and Deussen 1996; DeVault 1995).

Postmodern criticism, on the other hand, should not be too quickly dismissed because it has contributed greatly to this reflexive tendency, which DeVault calls "tentativeness." The unrelenting postmodern challenge might be seen as energizing, in other words, rather than debilitating. We can clearly learn more about difference with greater sensitivity to the effects of our positionality and categories of analysis; and perhaps we can do this better if we are on edge and worried about, in each context, whether we are respectfully taking up others' voices without taking over (summarized from DuCille 1994). In short, we accept aspects of the postmodern challenge and think feminist sociologists can use it to establish a basis for "good enough" dialogues across and about differences.[10]

DIFFERENCE IN THE INTERDISCIPLINARY ARENA

Women's studies scholars, in contrast to feminist sociologists, have taken a different path in dealing with difference, though the considerable overlap between the two that we find is often ignored or misunderstood. From postmodernism and cultural studies, the fracturing of the female subject takes center stage, with women internally and externally split and multiple subjectivities rather than the "subject-active" and reasonably coherent identities that they appear as in sociology. To paraphrase the philosopher Christina Crosby (1992), while some years ago everyone in women's studies was talking about "women's identity," it now seems no one is; everyone is talking about "differences" (130). This focus has had two somewhat contradictory effects in interdisciplinary work: to encourage the extremes of theoretical abstraction and of concrete autobiography, while sociology is lost in the middle.[11]

Western European intellectual traditions have assigned great prestige to "high theory," the ability to speak in global and abstract terms about how culture works (P. Smith 1998). This no doubt influences how interdisciplinary feminist scholarship grapples with difference. From the sociologist's perspective, difference (ironically) becomes nearly homogeneous in abstracted treatments, as it is removed from any particular historical, political, economic, or cultural context. The philosopher Crosby (1992), however, advocates the need for just such treatments when she writes that "specifying differences and 'describing minority experiences' [are] not going to transform women's studies at the level of theory, that is, enable it to break through the circle of ideology" (136). Crosby maintains that what we really need is to ask how "difference" is constituted *as a concept*—with the opposite of the social scientist's perspective, she writes that to do other than that would be to assume we know what the "incommensurate triumvirate" of race, class, and gender really means substantively or as "something in themselves" (137).[12] From our perspective, in contrast, differences have "real meaning" only in specific contexts.

The abstract "high theories" that Crosby prefers can eschew the careful but narrow research for the bold, the innovative, or the virtuoso realm of speculative interpretation (P. Smith 1998, 11) and can, at the same time, seem more optimistic about the possibilities of social change. What sociology offers is perhaps less appealing: mapping differences of greater and lesser fixity, always pointing out that some differences have a stubborn and substantive obduracy even as meanings (of race, class, gender, categories of sexuality, etc.) can vary historically. The abstract project of high theory casts difference as superficial in its very choice of terms and metaphors: play, disrupt, dodge, travel, traverse, perform (e.g., Butler 1990). While we find it instructive to envision multiple forms of resistance and new bases for community and coalition, it seems unfortunate to ignore the more sociological questions of why some differences make fluidity, easy disruption, and "passing" more difficult than others and why some identities appear so static and essential. To be fair, not all those engaged in high theory dismiss such questions outright. Most, however, only call for this lowly work to be done by others, failing truly to engage with us or, at worst, even to note that research like ours already exists (e.g., Felski 1997; Martin 1994, 1996; Phelan 1991). Interdisciplinary scholars should appreciate that to engage in, rather than to simply call for, such empirical work would unavoidably lower them into the flaws, compromises, and messy relations of power and authority involved in research with human subjects.

The other direction in which interdisciplinary women's studies has moved contrasts notably with this flux of abstract differences. Memoirs and autobiographies from the margins speak of actual lives and specific experiences of difference and have long been valued in women's studies. Originally such personal writing shared the spirit of "giving voice" with the middle-range standpoint perspective of sociology. Although the margins are now viewed as multiple, autobiography and personal narrative have come to be viewed with much less suspicion than such middle-range research.[13] "Outsider" approaches that speak about experiences or life events not based on the author's own life, identity, or social location have become ethically and politically questionable and may be "speaking FOR others." As mentioned in the previous section, such speaking is seen as appropriating subjugated voices for the speaker's professional gain (Alcoff 1991–92) and perhaps for her unconscious desires for mastery and omnipotence (Clough 1992). Interdisciplinary critics ignore emerging efforts (or grapplings) for a feminist ethics for speaking across differences, for establishing respectful, "good enough" dialogues, efforts they might instead encourage and participate in.

Though we always have some interests distinct from those we study, to foreclose research across differences also imposes a "tyranny of experience" that brings back the identity politics problem.[14] As the philosopher Sandra Harding (1993) notes, privileging the direct experience of oppression has been an epistemology tempting to many feminists and members of liberatory movements; yet it is ultimately an untenable position that (among other problems) falsely effaces diversity and fragmentation within identity groups (whether of women, black women, black lesbian women, etc.). It poses this paradox: just at the theoretical moment when subject position was supposed to matter less because we are all fragmented, multiple, and constructed by discourse, why should subject position become the only basis for authentic speaking about experience and particularity?

These developments in women's studies as it faces the problem of difference—veering between high theory and autobiographical writing—have placed sociology and field research, typically at the mezzo-level between such generality and particularity, in disfavor compared with the humanist disciplines and cultural studies. As the British theorist Michelle Barrett (1992) notes, "Academically the social sciences have lost their purchase within feminism and the rising star lies with the arts, humanities, and philosophy" (204).

Experience

The discussion to this point has circled around another key divergence between interdisciplinary women's studies and feminist sociology: the concept or category of experience itself. As we just began to discuss, it is ironic that in women's studies a new "tyranny of experience" has snuck in—where the "subaltern's" experience becomes the basis for authorial voice—just as the category of "experience" had been challenged by postmodern critics. Standpoint perspectives have been castigated for seeking a purity in experience, a pure point of opposition and agency in the consciousness of daily material activity. For the postmodern critic, such a notion is mythical because (to reiterate) subjectivity is fragmented and never coherently "real" or outside the dominant culture.

In a particularly rancorous exchange, Dorothy Smith (1993) defended her standpoint perspective from this attack on "experience," in this case by Patricia Clough (1993). Just as standpoint epistemologies are not simply identity politics, Smith's concept of experience is not one of direct access to external reality or the truth of oppression. In Smith's words, "experience" is "a transition between what is lived and what is spoken," a potentially creative moment (184). Smith counterattacks by pointing out that Clough and other postmodern critics have implicitly located themselves outside discourse, for as other defenders of standpoint frameworks ask, "Who is the *I* [of the postmodern theorist] that is so certain of its fragmented and discursively constructed nature[?]" (Barrett 1992, 208). A less rancorous exchange, however, might find that each treatment of experience faces the danger of self-contradiction. While there may be little basis for the omniscient voice of the postmodern critic, for the assumption of Clough and others of the better angle of vision, work from a feminist standpoint does struggle against giving too much reality and too much coherence to women's experience.

How can feminist fieldwork escape this epistemological conundrum—stuck between slippage into empiricism, the reliance on experience as a reflection of reality, and the floating voice-from-nowhere/everywhere of the omniscient metatheorist? According to Dorothy Smith (1993), fieldwork creates a site in which subjects can speak back, where women can speak for themselves (184). She contends that "we've learned in practice that women speaking as such have things to tell us of their lives, of how things happen to them, of their work and struggles, that we don't already know . . ." (189). This is also key in Patricia Hill Collins's (1990) black feminist epistemology: one begins from black women's experiences as "[o]nly African-American women occupy this center and can 'feel the iron' that enters Black women's souls . . ." (33–34). Yet, at other points, both Smith and Collins back off from or complicate such empiricist treatments of experience and its coherence, grappling toward what we would term a critical realism that can complement current interdisciplinary work.[15]

There are many respects in which fieldwork, being inherently dialogical, is ideal to investigate the political questions motivating cultural and women's studies: the relations between representation, hegemonic ideologies and identities, and social practices. Fieldwork does not just make "hearable" other voices beyond that of the lone theorist's, voices of those who may have something new or different to say (although what people say is often not purely oppositional or coherent, it is often different from the lone critic's or high theorist's readings). This is at least partly because the process of studying others promotes the reflexivity needed to "deconstruct" the voice and identity of the researcher/critic. Talking to subjects who talk back and doing this with respect always mean risking such provocation. This potential has motivated much of the flourishing "critical ethnography" debate in anthropology.[16]

Qualitative researchers bank on this dialogical aspect of their work. When they enter into discussion with participants/informants and later repeatedly reflect back on the conversation, identities on both sides of the researcher/researched divide are expanded, challenged, changed—or at least, that is the objective of the research. It may be a goal seldom fully realized; nevertheless, a goal of such mutual reflexivity between subjects remains.[17] In my own research (the first author, Blum, 1999), for example, on discourses of maternalism and breast-feeding, I had not realized how captive I was to the dominant moralism of "natural" mothering until confronted with its ironic rejection by the African American working-class mothers I was interviewing. I confronted a new angle of vision on myself and the privilege of white middle-class mothers like me, who valiantly struggle to "do the right thing" and receive cultural esteem for doing what is "best" for our babies. But such cumbersome practices as combining breast-feeding and full-time employment look quite different and less valiant to women facing a legacy of embodied exploitation that was legitimated by their ostensibly primitive closeness to nature. If we, feminist researchers, did not attempt such "good enough" dialogues, with all their dangers and limitations, we would surely miss many such insights.

Those in cultural studies doing audience reception studies, such as Andrea Press (the second author, 1991, 1999), strive to combine the strengths of textual criticism and ethnographic research.[18] But some have moved further to conflate the two by treating ethnographic data as "text." Janice Radway, for example, has moved in this direction (personal communication with Press); and Liesbet van Zoonen (1994), in a comprehensive review of feminist media research, advocates this stance. According to van Zoonen, cultural studies moved from the analysis of the "textual audience" in textual criticism, to the "actual audience" of reception studies, and then, more recently, to the "audience-as-text" (105–7). Of course, in one sense it is obvious that people's talk in interviews is not transparent but a kind of text, since we have just said that experience cannot be treated as an uninflected picture of external reality. To the extent that this "turn" leads to more nuanced and respectful "readings," it can be a very useful insight. In another sense, however, this argument might obscure what is different (though no more or less valuable) from textual criticism: the dialogic, reflexive potential of talk with people who can talk back and engage with us in deconstructing their multiply-layered "experiences" as they negotiate cultural texts.[19] The communications scholar Bruce Williams generously offered this example: in a focus group giving African American women the chance to talk back to media researchers in the mid-1990s, the researchers expected talk of the O. J. Simpson trial to dominate. Instead, the women wanted to talk about the Susan Smith trial (convicted of killing her two young children by driving her car into a lake) and compare her life sentence with the lighter sentence a black woman convicted of killing her children had received. What mattered most to them was the message of how little black children were valued, how lightly their murder was taken.[20]

Perhaps, as scholars interested in enlarging the voices and movements for social justice, we must always weigh the risks of giving too much versus too little coherence, reality, and agency to others' lived experience. As Donna Haraway (1997) writes, though, this should encourage a greater inclusivity of approaches: "Textual analysis must be articulated with many kinds of sustained scholarly interaction among living people in living situations. . . . These different studies need each other . . . [in the] contentious search for what accountability to freedom projects for women might mean, and how such meanings are crafted and sustained in a polyglot world of men and women . . ." (191).

THE TEXT AS THE RESEARCHER'S PRODUCT

Although ethnographic research is prone to the several problems or dangers that we have just discussed, we argue it is also uniquely suited to discovering the "unsaid" embedded in everyday life. The intersubjective dialogic context, like the clinical psychodynamic context, can uncover or discover the absences, the taken-for-granted, the seemingly "natural" aspects that are so much a part of social and political life in American society. Ruth Frankenberg's (1993) study of the social construction of whiteness, *White Women, Race Matters,* is an interesting example of such a project. Frankenberg actually came out of a cultural/textual studies background, but she attempts to combine these insights with a dialogic interview method. In the analysis of her intensive interviews with white women, she claims to listen for silences, inversions, contradictions, gaps, and ambivalence, because race privilege is unspoken; in fact, its unspokenness is one basis of the privilege itself, of how it works, with the white self the unmarked, the raceless, universal individual. Thus, Frankenberg writes, the interviews generated "memory lapse, silence, shame, and evasion" (23). The challenge of eliciting dialogue about such an unspoken required, according to Frankenberg, a certain inventiveness; she writes that she looked for clues and metaphors in long digressions, elicited stories and life histories, and shared aspects of her own life history as a strategy as well as an ethical stance (30–33).

An earlier classic in women's cultural or media studies, Radway's (1984) ethnographic project, *Reading the Romance,* also combined textual and dialogic research—and its strength was also in its ability to articulate the unsaid. Radway was able to listen respectfully and engage in dialogue with women romance consumers/readers and then articulate the activity of romance reading. This had remained invisible or unheard in previous studies based on the readings of omniscient cultural studies critics; such critics "read" women consumers as acquiescing to passivity and conformity with traditional femininity. Radway recast this submission because the consumers she spoke with had a sophisticated knowledge of the genre and, she maintained, actively used romance reading to negotiate the oppressive structures of daily life.

But there are other levels of what is "unsaid" in which the feminist ethnographer and cultural studies critic both fare less well. This involves the reflexive scrutiny of our own practices—both feminist ethnographers and discursive analysts produce texts as products and themselves (ourselves), make choices of what to say and leave unsaid in these texts. (In this sense, power relations pervade not only the research interaction but the writing itself.) Reflexivity may be a more explicitly placed and agreed upon objective in the discursive perspective, but both the feminist fieldworker and the cultural studies critic tend to fall short in representing this reflexive level in the final research product. We see this as a shared problem or limitation, where we may learn valuable lessons from each other.

Radway, for example, has been rightly criticized for filling in the silence of women romance readers with her own feminism, that is, for maintaining that these women do not fully recognize their own dissatisfaction with patriarchy (Modleski cited in van Zoonen 1994, 107–17). Angela McRobbie (1994) makes a similar point, maintaining that many feminist ethnographers try to reproduce their own feminist selves in this manner (9, 73). In constructing such critical arguments, the feminist ethnographer also tends to fall back into the omniscient, nonreflexive voice, foreclosing further dialogue or, at least, its representation in the text that is her product (as in DeVault's silence after an introductory admission of ambivalence about domesticity). Here the postmodern point is well taken: more might be gained by resisting the desire for coherence and closure and by allowing conflicting voices and interpretations into the text.

Frankenberg, for example, after writing a telling example of her own incoherence and entrapment in racialized discourse in her methods chapter (39–40), represents herself as seamless, coherent, omniscient critic through much of the rest of the text.

Many field-workers have grappled with the tension between respect and critique, that is, with how to treat subjects and their words respectfully but also critically, with their own voice as author/ity. Some have pointed out that it is far easier to be respectful and to give agency and voice to the subversive minority than it is to study members of dominant groups—although this can lead to the problem of writing about resistance everywhere.[21] Certainly cultural studies has been accused of this tendency to do better when "celebrating" cultures of resistance. Within qualitative sociology, we find instructive examples of studying dominant groups and a willingness to grapple with, as Arlene Kaplan Daniels (1988) has written, studying people you do not like. In the introduction to her study of upper-class women's "invisible careers" in philanthropic activity (1988), she acknowledged rewriting the manuscript in the attempt to balance respect and critique. Compared with Susan Ostrander's (1984) far more critical *Women of the Upper Class,* however, Daniels's work still might be seen as erring on the side of respect. Although these studies predate the current wave of concern with reflexivity, they illustrate the value of later postmodern insights: as with Frankenberg, it might have been most productive to let the tension of conflicting interpretations and voices be apparent in the finished product.[22]

Briefly, we return to the qualitative sociological tradition for one last insight about the text-as-product: the feminist methods conversations of the 1970s promoted the objective of producing more accessible texts, intelligible to nonacademics, and they had had many formidable examples from earlier sociological field studies to inspire them (Riesman's *Lonely Crowd,* Whyte's *Organization Man,* the Lynds' *Middletown* series, Rubin's *Worlds of Pain,* to mention just a few). Feminist ethnographers, in our view, have done far better in pursuing this objective than of representing reflexive, multiple voices. Here discursive research seems to fall sadly short and might reflect on the power relations implicit in its modes of writing. Ultimately, however, we would not want to overdraw such differences; feminist ethnographers may resist fracturing their authoritative voice and discursive analysts may resist writing more accessibly for similar reasons and from a shared social location. In other words, a large "unsaid" for all of us may be the constitutive pressures of university career structures and life in the now-crowded margins of the academy.[23]

Conclusion

Though inevitably incomplete, these points of epistemological debate, where theory and method collide, may be some of the most productive points for cultural studies in the next decade. Of course, those of us doing field research can hardly ignore the problems, biases, and blindnesses that have been challenged by postmodernist cultural theory. We remain committed to confronting, arguing over, and struggling with these insights, in the continued belief that qualitative research, with all its flaws and inadequacies, creates valuable opportunities for people to talk back to us, to talk with us, and to help us uncover the large areas of social life taken for granted or unspoken.

On the other side of the divide, we fear the direction of influence is not symmetric. Those in the forefront of interdisciplinary cultural studies today may call for research on local or specific subjectivities, but this objective is typically posed abstractly, from high theory, with no attention paid to "the ground" that feminist qualitative research on local subjectivities continually produces. We hope that increased respect can develop from those on either side of the experiential/discursive divide. If debate remains fragmented and hostile, we have less hope for better self-conscious research and grounded and knowledgeable theory.

Notes

1. Blum, after serious professional setbacks, moved further into women's studies, and Press, to avoid such experiences, moved into communications.

2. Postmodern philosophy has had less influence on contemporary U.S. sociology, though it is taken seriously by those involved with social theory (e.g., Lemert 1993). It includes a range of positions, but generally it is based on the work of the French theorists Michel Foucault and Jacque Derrida. Key tenets include the critique of modern science as a socially situated process of "power-knowledge" and the critique of Western "master narratives" of progress as "power moves" (see Lemert 1993). Postmodern philosophers take as their project the "deconstruction" of these modernist "myths" to uncover the power in claims to truth and knowledge, along with the "myth" of the unified, reasoning, autonomous subject. But these positions break with earlier perspectives (such as Marxism) in that no truth undistorted by power can truly exist (as in the Marxist critique of ideology), only a multiplicity of knowledge practices, subject positions, and truth claims. Postmodernism has an important affinity with cultural studies, legitimating its academic presence, as subjects are created within and are "subject to" discourses, and it is the place of the cultural critic or scholar to analyze or interpret these.

Postmodern also refers to our particular epoch in Western culture. After the modern, global capitalism, advanced technologies, and the many postcolonial movements and voices have led to greater fluidity or hybridity of once stable identities and communities.

3. In late-nineteenth-century European universities, some social scientists (most notably Max Weber) distinguished the project of *verstehen,* of achieving cross-cultural understanding or shared human intelligibility, from the goal of prediction in the natural sciences emphasized by many others (notably, Emile Durkheim). As Barbara Laslett and others argue, the status problems this led to, with the scientific model valued over the cultural, were exacerbated in the context of academic professionalization in the United States. More recently, the margins of the American university, in which both feminist research and interdisciplinary cultural studies have been contained, have become crowded sites, and efforts for professional status and legitimacy have been undermined by institutional efforts to get "lean and mean" (e.g., Honan 1998).

4. In the first rush of enthusiasm, second-wave feminist sociology simply reversed the "hard" and "soft" labels instead of rejecting the dichotomy or considering the ways in which feminist methods might fail to live up to their (many) claims. Such issues have been taken up more recently and represent a growing subfield (e.g., Gottfried 1996; Reinharz 1992; and Stacey 1988; see also Burawoy 1998).

5. D. Smith's ([1977] 1987) reading of Marx's *German Ideology* was closest to Hegelian interpretations.

6. Many have contributed to this line of thought, for example, the film theorist Teresa de Lauretis (1990), who argues that even the lesbian is not wholly "outside" dominant discourses of gender and sexuality.

7. The philosopher Linda Nicholson (1990) argues similarly that such totalizing moves lead feminist researchers to unknowingly replicate the problematic traditions out of which they came.

8. Patricia Hill Collins's work is itself complex and somewhat contradictory and, comparing it with D. Smith's, warrants more attention than we can give (see Mann and Kelley 1997; and D. Smith 1997).

9. These atypical attempts at reflexivity (such as Blum and Deussen 1996) tend to emerge from those influenced by postmodernism and interdisciplinary cultural and feminist studies. Though this contradicts a major thesis of our essay, it remains a small and tangential trend in sociology—one we would like to see grow.

10. See Nancy Scheper-Hughes's (1992) discussion of the "good enough" ethnography and similar postmodern challenges in anthropology (28).

11. This may also characterize the divide between intradisciplinary cultural sociology and interdisciplinary cultural studies (see P. Smith 1998, who sees American cultural sociology engaged in substantive, middle-level empirical research, while interdisciplinarians prefer the prestige of "high" theory).

12. The abstracted treatment of difference in this sense also contradicts the multiracial feminist critique that provoked or inspired it. This is evident in the resounding criticism directed at the one anomalous attempt by sociologists to write such a treatment. Candace West and Sarah Fenstermaker (1995), both ethnomethodologists, wrote the piece "Doing Difference" for *Gender and Society.* The article was reviewed in a symposium by six sociologists of race, class, and gender, including Patricia Hill Collins (1995), who argued, "One by one, race, gender, and even class were erased. As a result, an article that claims to retheo-

rize [their] interconnectedness . . . said remarkably little about racism, patriarchy, and capitalism as systems of power" (491). She maintains that their article "strips the very categories of race, class, and gender of meaning and then recasts the problems of institutional power in the apolitical framework of how we might 'do difference.' . . . [But] it is hard to discuss global capitalist markets as performances and representations" (493).

13. For one provocative exception to the embrace of personal narrative, see Kauffman (1993).

14. We adapt this phrase from Betty Bell, coined in the Differences among Women Project, University of Michigan, 1995.

15. Some interpret Patricia Hill Collins as more contradictory and different from D. Smith than we do (see Mann and Kelley 1997).

16. We cannot explore this burgeoning literature here, but see Scheper-Hughes (1992) for a stunning example.

17. See, however, Jane Roland Martin's (1996) provocative criticism of such "compulsory verstehenism" (593–96). From the realm of high theory, Martin has much to contribute; however, she seems, as we mentioned earlier, to find no actual fieldwork that satisfies her many criteria for adequate research. Our position is closer to that of Donna Haraway's (1997) ethnographic attitude (190–91).

18. Following the research design of others, such as Sharon Hays (1996), Blum (1999) attempts this as well by reading thirty years of popular advice on infant feeding.

19. Our perspective here is similar to that of Jacqueline Bobo (1995). Comparing the Bakhtinian frame of textual analysis, in which the critic engages in intertextual dialogue (Stam 1988), with ethnographic approaches to dialogue with living human subjects would (and should) be a topic for another essay.

20. Bruce Williams, personal communication, University of Illinois at Urbana-Champaign, November 1995. There may have been other troubling aspects of the Susan Smith story for African American women: notably, Smith had originally charged that a black male "carjacker" was responsible for drowning her sons.

21. It may be too easy to "go overboard" for those studying "down," and DeVault's book can be criticized on similar grounds. Tania Modleski contends that Radway fell in love with her participants and thus ended up apologizing for mass culture (cited in van Zoonen 1994, 117); and Blum's students felt that DeVault ended up silencing any conflict her interviewees must have felt about their exclusive responsibility for caregiving.

22. Press and her collaborator Elizabeth Cole have also grappled with the issue of studying people you do not like. In a study of media abortion rhetoric, Press and Cole (1999) conducted focus group interviews with right-to-life or anti-abortion women. They are currently attempting to write a more explicit text/product about their varied reactions and how this affected their collaboration across race and disciplinary divides.

23. The British sociologist Ann Oakley (1992) and the black feminist legal scholar Patricia Williams (1991) are fascinating, important exceptions. Each attempts, in very different ways, to pay reflexive attention to the influence of institutional pressures on the texts they produce. Exploring such issues warrants yet another essay.

References

Alcoff, L. 1991–92. "The Problem of Speaking for Others." *Cultural Critique* 20:5–32.

Barrett, M. 1992. "Words and Things: Materialism and Method in Contemporary Feminist Analysis." In *Destabilizing Theory,* edited by M. Barrett and A. Phillips, 201–19. Stanford, Calif.: Stanford University Press.

Blum, L. M. 1999. *At the Breast: Ideologies of Breastfeeding and Motherhood in the Contemporary U.S.* Boston: Beacon.

Blum, L. M., and T. Deussen. 1996. "Negotiating Independent Motherhood: Working-Class African-American Women Talk about Marriage and Motherhood." *Gender and Society* 10 (2): 199–211.

Bobo, J. 1995. *Black Women as Cultural Readers.* New York: Columbia University Press.

Burawoy, M. 1998. "The Extended Case Method." *Sociological Theory* 16:4–33.

Butler, J. 1990. *Gender Trouble.* New York: Routledge.

Clough, P. T. 1992. *The End(s) of Ethnography.* New York: Sage.

———. 1993. "On the Brink of Deconstructing Sociology: Critical Reading of Dorothy Smith's Standpoint Epistemology." *Sociological Quarterly* 34 (1): 169–82.

Collins, P. H. 1990. *Black Feminist Thought.* New York: Routledge.

———. 1995. Symposium: On West and Fenstermaker's "Doing Difference." *Gender and Society* 9 (4): 491–94.

Crosby, C. 1992. "Dealing with Differences." In *Feminists Theorize the Political,* edited by J. Butler and J. Scott, 130–43. New York: Routledge.

Daniels, A. K. 1988. *Invisible Careers.* Chicago: University of Chicago Press.

de Lauretis, T. 1990. "Eccentric Subjects." *Feminist Studies* 16 (1): 115–50.

DeVault, M. 1991. *Feeding the Family.* Chicago: University of Chicago Press.

———. 1995. "Ethnicity and Expertise: Racial-Ethnic Knowledge in Sociological Research." *Gender and Society* 9 (5): 612–31.

DuCille, A. 1994. "The Occult of True Black Womanhood: Critical Demeanor and Black Feminist Studies." *Signs* 19 (3): 591–629.

Felski, R. 1997. "The Doxa of Difference." *Signs* 23 (1): 1–21.

Frankenberg, R. 1993. *White Women, Race Matters.* Minneapolis: University of Minnesota.

Glenn, E., G. Chang, and L. R. Forcey, eds. 1994. *Mothering: Ideology, Experience, and Agency.* New York: Routledge.

Gorelick, S. 1996. "Contradictions of Feminist Methodology." In *Feminism and Social Change: Bridging Theory and Practice,* edited by H. Gottfried, 23–45. Urbana: University of Illinois Press.

Gottfried, H., ed. 1996. *Feminism and Social Change: Bridging Theory and Practice.* Urbana: University of Illinois Press.

Haraway, D. 1997. *Modest-Witness@Second-Millenium.* New York: Routledge.

Harding, S. 1991. *Whose Science? Whose Knowledge?* Ithaca, N.Y.: Cornell University Press.

———. 1993. "Rethinking Standpoint Epistemology." In *Feminist Epistemologies,* edited by L. Alcoff and E. Potter, 49–82. New York: Routledge.

Hays, S. 1996. *The Cultural Contradictions of Motherhood.* New Haven, Conn.: Yale University Press.

Honan, W. H. 1998. "The Ivory Tower under Siege? Everyone Else Downsized; Why Not the Academy?" *New York Times,* Education Life Supplement, January 4, 33+.

Kauffman, L. 1993. "The Long Goodbye." In *American Feminist Thought at Century's End: A Reader,* 258–77. Cambridge, Mass.: Blackwell, 1993.

Ladner, J., ed. 1973. *The Death of White Sociology.* New York: Vintage.

Laslett, B. 1992. "Gender in/and Social Science History." *Social Science History* 16 (2): 177–95.

Lemert, C. 1993. *Sociology after the Crisis.* Boulder, Colo.: Westview.

Lynd, R. S., and H. M. Lynd. 1956. *Middletown.* New York: Harcourt, Brace.

Mann, S., and L. Kelley. 1997. "Standing at the Crossroads of Modernist Thought: Collins, Smith, and the New Feminist Epistemologies." *Gender and Society* 11 (4): 391–408.

Martin, J. R. 1994. "Methodological Essentialism, False Difference, and Other Dangerous Traps." *Signs* 19 (3): 630–57.

———. 1996. "Aerial Distance, Esotericism, and Other Closely Related Traps." *Signs* 21 (3): 584–614.

McRobbie, A. 1994. *Postmodernism and Popular Culture.* New York: Routledge.

Nicholson, L. 1990. *Feminism/Postmodernism.* New York: Routledge.

Oakley, A. 1981. "Interviewing Women: A Contradiction in Terms?" In *Doing Feminist Research,* edited by H. Roberts, 30–61. London: Routledge and Kegan Paul.

———. 1992. *Social Support and Motherhood.* Oxford: Blackwell.

Ostrander, S. 1984. *Women of the Upper Class.* Philadelphia: Temple University Press.

Phelan, S. 1991. "Specificity: Beyond Equality and Difference." *Differences* 3 (1): 145–60.

Press, A. L. 1991. *Women Watching Television.* Philadelphia: University of Pennsylvania Press.

Press, A. L., and E. Cole. 1999. *Speaking of Abortion: Television and Authority in the Lives of Women.* Chicago: University of Chicago Press.

Radway, J. 1984. *Reading the Romance.* Chapel Hill: University of North Carolina Press.

Reinharz, S. 1992. *Feminist Methods in Social Research.* New York: Oxford University Press.

Riesman, D. 1950. *The Lonely Crowd.* New Haven, Conn.: Yale University Press.

Riessman, C. K. 1987. "When Gender Is Not Enough: Women Interviewing Women." *Gender and Society* 1 (2): 172–207.

Rubin, L. 1976. *Worlds of Pain.* New York: Basic Books.

Scheper-Hughes, N. 1992. *Death without Weeping.* Berkeley: University of California Press.

Smith, D. [1977] 1987. *The Everyday World as Problematic.* Boston: Northeastern University Press.

———. 1990. Personal communication with the first author. University of Michigan, Ann Arbor.

———. 1993. "High Noon in Textland: A Critique of Clough." *Sociological Quarterly* 34 (1): 183–92.

———. 1997. "Response to Mann and Kelley." *Gender and Society* 11 (6): 819–21.

Smith, P. 1998. *The New American Cultural Sociology.* Cambridge: Cambridge University Press.

Stacey, J. 1988. "Can There Be a Feminist Ethnography?" *Women's Studies International Forum* 11:21–27.

Stam, R. 1988. "Bakhtin and Left Cultural Critique." In *Postmodernism and Its Discontents,* edited by E. Ann Kaplan, 118–43. London: Verso.

van Zoonen, L. 1994. *Feminist Media Studies.* London: Sage.

West, C., and S. Fenstermaker. 1995. "Doing Difference." *Gender and Society* 9 (1): 8–37.

Whyte, W. H. 1956. *The Organization Man.* New York: Simon and Schuster.

Williams, P. J. 1991. *The Alchemy of Race and Rights.* Cambridge, Mass.: Harvard University Press.

LINDA STEINER

6 *The Uses of Autobiography*

A 1982 documentary included the following dialogue between Simone de Beauvoir and Jean-Paul Sartre:

> de Beauvoir: When I started writing—it wasn't exactly memoirs, but an essay on myself—I realized that I needed first of all to situate myself as a woman. So first I studied what it meant to be a woman in the eyes of others, and that's why I talked about the myths of woman as seen by men; then I realized it was necessary to go deeper to the heart of reality. . . .
>
> Sartre: It's rather odd. You began as a non-feminist, as a woman in this sense like any other woman that would have simply liked to know what it meant to be a woman. And in writing this book you became a feminist. You recognized your enemies and attacked them, and you specified what being a woman was like. . . . You became a feminist in writing this book.
>
> de Beauvoir: . . . But I became a feminist especially after the book was read, and started to exist for other women. (Quoted in Felman 1993, 11)

Others agree that, in writing our lives, we come to know ourselves with a particular social-political identity. Writing her autobiography in 1814, Margaret Cavendish, Duchess of Newcastle, answered the question she imagined others would ask: "Why hath this Lady writ her own life . . . [I]t is to no purpose to the Readers, but it is to the Authoress, because I write for my own sake, not theirs . . ." (quoted in Stanton 1984, 15). Nearly two centuries later, bell hooks (1989) explained that telling her story "was intimately connected with the longing to kill the self I was without really having to die." But even in confessing that she wanted to erase that "other" self and "more easily become the me of me," hooks speaks to the way we become ourselves in autobiography (155). She, too, acknowledges that such processes of "becoming" depend on interaction, albeit an implied or tacit interaction, with an audience. De Beauvoir directly corrected Sartre's simplistic notion of how de Beauvoir became a feminist in the process of examining womanhood. She clarified: she became a feminist in addressing herself to readers. Making a different point with this interchange, Shoshana Felman (1993) notes that de Beauvoir's book engenders its own readers. These readers simultaneously en-gender the author's knowledge of herself. The reading of lives, then, by both autobiographer and audience is a useful and signifying political act.

I suggest that life stories can enrich our understanding of cultural problems, including those inhering in media practices. If autobiographies are, as Mary Jo Maynes (1992) would have it, "causal arguments about the forces that made a particular life turn out the way that it did" (522), life stories can reintroduce into our calculus a subject—specific persons—that has been strangely missing. Autobiographies are social-cultural tales about narrators' relations—close and distant, intimate and strained—with their own multiply intersecting communities as well as with "Others." For all its attention to audiences, recent cultural studies work often reads off cultural practices without reference to the people involved in cultural work. Imbedded in such research agendas is a dubiousness about people's self-assertions. Given the commitment of cultural studies to speak on behalf of resisting and oppressed people, this suspiciousness is surprising, because self-writing represents people's refusal to let their stories be forgotten or appropriated by others. The field's intellectual foundations, to which my title alludes, were personal, autobiographical works that spoke directly to and on behalf of people. This depersonalized approach to cultural studies is all the more ironic because common understandings of human cultures often begin with storytelling. Clifford Geertz (1973), to take one famous example, defines culture as the ensemble of stories we tell ourselves about ourselves (448).

What I want to do here, then, is supply some warrants for using autobiography in cultural studies. The initial references to specific autobiographies are fairly general and random; at the end, I briefly turn to patterns in autobiographies written in the early twentieth century by women journalists. Despite my methodological focus, the point is twofold. First, grappling with autobiography and its claims about identity, representation, truth, and reality provides entrée into some thorny and as yet unresolved theoretical problems at the heart of cultural studies. Second, while media work clearly involves collaboration and interaction, more complex understandings of media practices and the political economy of media can be accessed through the lives of individual workers, at least once those lives are read collectively. Although autobiographies are typically dismissed as mere navel-gazing by individuals, their goal often is situating narrators in a social or professional context. Even those attempts to distance the self from context often bespeak an important problem for the group. As Sidonie Smith and Julia Watson (1996) point out, "Autobiography is contextually marked, collaboratively mediated, provisional. . . . [A]utobiographical telling is implicated in the microbial operations of power in contemporary everyday life" (9). The evidence is flawed and messy. Nonetheless, autobiography offers comparative sociological and historical depth unavailable with such discursive methods as interviews and textual analysis.

As the opening quote from de Beauvoir attests, we come to be in dialogic self-narratives. People offer up narratives of a certain way of being. It is the linguistic turn to an extreme, but plausible. In particular, women autobiographers underline this point. The writer bell hooks (1989), for example, notes that "the longing to tell one's story and the process of telling is symbolically a gesture of longing to recover the past in such a way that one experiences both a sense of reunion and a sense of release" (158). Moreover, this is a double reunion. It is a kind of remembering, involving a joining of fragments of old selves, as well as "relating" oneself to others. Since the self here is a social self, autobiography is social and interactive. As Janet Varner Gunn (1981) suggested in looking at how Henry David Thoreau became a "Faithful Reader" not merely of nature but also of himself, autobiography represents an act of reading the self rather than a private act of writing the self. That reading is cultural, since self-knowledge is not transcendent but "always grounded in the signs of one's existence that are received from others, as well as from the works of culture by which one is . . . interpreted" (82).

Claims about the cultural uses of autobiography do require a different kind of reading of these texts. Psychological knowledge of the "*auto*" is not the point. Nor is the issue merely "*bio*," facts provided readers about individuals. Although historical knowledge is at stake and a cultural history of the genre would be useful, reproducing historians' search for facts about a singular "worthy" is insufficient, if not unproductive. Meanwhile, although the literary scholars who otherwise monopolize the study of autobiography have provocatively theorized the "*graphy*" (to reveal either authors' aesthetic intentions or the genre's principles per se), cultural studies need not treat autobiography merely as literature or popular culture. While publication and sales figures suggest that many readers find the genre as engaging as fiction, the value of autobiography is not its status as popular culture.[1] Instead, the call here is to reunite these dimensions and refocus on textual artifacts, as a cultural anthropologist might, as a way of understanding cultural politics and "author-ity." Among other things, autobiographies reveal responses to workplace structures, process, and changes, from ideological changes, such as the emergence of professionalism, to personnel changes. As complex, overdetermined documents, they offer crucial—if not entirely reliable—insights about how people work together or do not in such sites as the newsroom and about the scripts culturally in stock for professional interaction.

More specifically, women reporters' autobiographies may be particularly useful for their testimony regarding how or whether women understood themselves as females practicing journalism. Gender is not necessarily the "hermeneutic key" to either authorial intention or textual production (Peterson 1993; Gilmore 1994). Granted, many feminist literary theorists claim that critical theory is based on a male canon, particularly Saint Augustine's dramatic story of conversion and spiritual victory and Jean-Jacques Rousseau's secular story of self-discovery. As a result, they argue, such theorizing misreads how women's autobiographies highlight different themes than men's (Friedman 1988). Estelle Jelinek (1980) contrasts men, who tend to make their lives into a coherent whole, and women, whose narratives are "disconnected, fragmentary or organizing into self-sustained units" (17). Such criteria as orderliness and harmonious shaping, imported from the male tradition, not only are irrelevant to women's autobiographies but also misrepresent their value, Jelinek adds. They are, in Sidonie Smith's (1987) words, "outside the dominant culture's boundaries in a spatial, experiential, and metaphysical 'no-man's-land'" (9).[2]

This binarism is problematic on several grounds, beginning with its reification of the public-private polarity that has been applied to so many communication forms. The stubborn insistence on male-female difference essentially manufactures a gender opposition that, among others, women journalists have described as frustrating. To take just one example, Marie Manning (1944), who in 1898 began a highly successful advice column under the pseudonym Beatrice Fairfax, complained that she and her sister reporters had to exercise considerable ingenuity to "horn in" on interesting assignments: "The only course open to us to get away from our chores was to invoke that abracadabra, 'the Woman's Angle'" (71). Manning acknowledged that, for women, journalistic success required a certain kind of subversive collaboration with female subjects. Manning explained, "As for Mrs. [William Jennings] Bryan, she was a graduate in law, and probably a suffragist. . . . But I understood perfectly, of course, the silly questions they expected me to ask her" (80).

Certainly, plots come and go in biography and autobiography. Generic conventions change over time. Various plots—conversion, education, self-criticism—also vary by gender. I suspect that women journalists have been (and still are) more mindful of the rules of the autobiographical "pact" (the term is Philippe Lejeune's [1975]) than have "writerly" women—poets and novelists—on whom literary critics have based the feminist/autobiographical canon. However, as I eventually show in greater detail, my own reading of women journalists' autobiographies suggests that most of these writers, especially most of the white women, have conformed to the expectation that women be modest and even self-deprecating. In telling their stories of work and workplace, they ascribe to themselves no particular talent, no particular intellectual or moral virtue. In any case, whether narrative content or performative styles are idiosyncratic should be a matter of investigation. More to the point, autobiographies are a rare resource for examining the extent to which writers are conscious of being propelled into a gendered consciousness or a gendered style.

Before suggesting what can be learned about work from studying people's lives, I will anticipate some probable objections to autobiographies: first, that they rely on a disreputable concept, that is, the individual or, worse, the liberal bourgeois individual; second, that even if individual authors putatively exist, their works are mediated in hidden ways, that authors are unrepresentative, and that writing as a form is particularly suspect; and third, that even if autobiographies represent what authors wrote, the content is false or at least misleading. These objections raise valid questions about the usefulness of autobiography to cultural studies. Susan Geiger (1986) comments that the accusation that life histories are not representative "assumes we already have knowledge about the culture in general against which individuals can be evaluated" (337). Moreover, as Geiger notes, precisely because traditional social scientists often fail to consider women's experiences, their methods produce invalid claims. Only by including women's lives—by accepting data that would allow for such inclusion—can the issue of typicality begin to be addressed. No resource is perfect. One must recognize the blind spots of any method. These issues should be regarded not as fatally undermining the status of autobiography but as challenges to thoroughly contextualized cultural analyses. This essay suggests how autobiographic issues test the theoretical musculature of cultural studies. In combination with other resources and methods, autobiographical documents help address questions of agency, power, representation, and truth and the mediation of these by cultural institutions.

Cultural studies itself has avoided conceptualizing the individual—perhaps for some of the reasons that James Carey suggests in this volume. It acknowledges how humans are socially embodied and how collective/mutual responsibility makes impossible an atomist notion of the rational individual. Beyond this, however, it has not yet theorized human activity. Meanwhile, autobiography and individuality are intimately connected, as the classic theorist of autobiography Georg Misch first noted. Friedrich Schlegel commented already in 1798 that pure autobiographies are written by neurotics fascinated by their own egos; authors of "a robust artistic or adventuresome self-love"; born historians; pedants who refuse to leave the world without commentary; and "women who also coquette with posterity" (quoted in Folkenflik 1993, 3). True or not, at least in the American context and in the interests of a peculiarly American cultural studies, the stories individuals tell about themselves reveal their responses to democracy and to the American romance with individualism, sometimes critiquing the American mythology but sometimes celebrating it. Autobiography is not uniquely American, but as Thomas Doherty (1981) points out, "it does seem to be a form peculiarly suited to the traditional American self-image: individualistic and optimistic" (95). "Writing autobiography testified to arrival in 'America' and the achievement of an 'American' identity," say Sidonie Smith and Julia Watson (1996, 5), who regard the telling and consuming of autobiography as a "defining condition of postmodernity in America" (7).

Yet simply because autobiographies purport to offer personal stories does not mean that they must be read separately or as stories of bourgeois individuals working in isolation. Quite the reverse. At least some autobiographers actively engage in politics and conflict in a particular social-historical context. Women journalists use autobiographies to examine how, as individuals bound up in a tangle of social threads, they become implicated in a complex work fabric. There is less about management and interaction of domestic and work lives than researchers might like; likewise, women journalists wrote less about domesticity than the stereotype of women's lives—emphasizing family and friends—would predict. But there is rich detail about management of personal and professional relationships; about self-perceptions and perceptions of others; about negotiating among available models for identity.

Furthermore, autobiography is useful in studying media organizations precisely because workers are not autonomous in their activities in newsrooms, film sets, and broadcast studios. Of course, the way that workers either try or refuse to try to take responsibility for their individual actions is a part of what they do. The use here of the language of ethics is intentional. Although individualism and egoism are typically blamed for weakening the hold of community as a moral telos, the very notion of individual agency may activate a sense of moral responsibility and action. Fred Inglis's (1993) proposition about the explanatory value of biography is relevant here. In treating cultural studies as centrally concerned with moral value and the way to lead a good life, Inglis says life histories, referring to biography, are not merely examples—prescriptive models as well as counterexamples—but theories with real explanatory value: "[T]he stories we tell ourselves about ourselves are not just a help to moral education; they comprise the only moral education which can gain purchase on the modern world" (214). Unfortunately, his argument echoes now unpopular nineteenth-century literary and social critics who unself-consciously evaluated autobiographies on moral terms that invariably regarded masculinity as normative. We may resist Wilhelm Dilthey's (1962) assertion that autobiography is "the highest and most instructive form in which the understanding of life confronts us" (85). As it turns out, autobiographies were long measured against precisely that Enlightenment notion of accomplishment, a standard that marginalized women's stories—both as lived and as written. Yet, hypothetically, one could try to inspire moral responsibility in people's lives without valorizing exaggerated individualism. As Mary Jo Maynes (1992) points out, "Focusing on life stories does not entail a retreat into methodological individualism or a return to great-man history" (534).

Self-narrative is not equally available to all persons at all times in all places (Gilmore 1994). Compared with other forms of published writing, however, autobiography has resisted monopolization by extraordinary figures and remains accessible to diverse voices. With respect to media workers, autobiography is not the purview of the elite, in marked contrast to such resources as archival repositories. William Dean Howells (1909) commented that autobiography is not restricted to "any age or sex, creed, class, or color," thus constituting the most "democratic province in the republic of letters" (798). This remains the case.

Ironically, the genre's accessibility—to women as well as men—is protected in part by its low status relative to such literary genres as epic poetry and drama, which make grand claims to divine creativity. Although autobiography has been a somewhat positive term when applied to the male canon—Jean-Jacques Rousseau, Saint Augustine, Henry Adams—when applied to women's writing, it regularly references the assumption that women only record, but cannot transcend, their private concerns (Stanton 1984). Quite possibly, autobiography's marginalization, at least until recently, has resulted from its access to women, especially when the genre is defined as including diaries, memoirs, and letters. Again, the advantage of this marginality is that it leaves the medium available for people the literary elite assumed were unable to write for public audiences (Marcus 1988). Leigh Gilmore (1994) and others emphasize that the literary canon excludes women's self-writing such that women autobiographers see themselves as trespassing on the genre. Nonetheless, all sorts of little-known figures have publicly announced their claim to authority for their lives. Margery Brunham Kempe, the first woman to compose her life story in English, drafted her account in 1432–36, although it was not actually published until 1940 (Glenn 1992).[3]

Notably, autobiography is also an accessible Afro-American literary tradition. Nineteenth-century black women wrote two types of autobiographical narratives. They used accounts of their spiritual lives to challenge the male church officials who tried to prevent women from preaching (McKay 1989). Slave narratives, such as Harriet Jacobs's 1861 *Incidents in the Life of a Slave Girl,* were openly political documents that emphasized the secular humanity and rights of blacks (Blackburn 1980; Fox-Genovese 1988). Thus while African American women's autobiographies may tend to highlight different themes (such as the tension between race and gender), this genre is no less important to cultural studies for its access to crucial arguments.

Assumptions about marketability change from publisher to publisher and from time to time. Again, they vary by gender and race, although not in some consistent or pure way. Notably, most women reporters seemed to have preferred chronologically arranged memoirs rather than more formal, full-scale autobiography that begins with family ancestry. It is difficult to tell whether this preference for memoirs expresses women's modesty—it was apparently enough of a public declaration to reveal oneself at all—or it represents what publishers would accept from women. Elizabeth Banks, probably the first woman journalist to publish her life story, seems typical of women journalists. That is, although Banks provided rich anecdotes about the evolution of her career, her *Autobiography of a "Newspaper Girl"* (1902) was quite coy about several major details. For example, she never named certain people and papers for whom she worked.

Analogously, what was written in narratives that were never published is an open question. The scholar with access to unpublished drafts (never completed, never submitted, never accepted) can consider the social and cultural assumptions behind the industrial process along several dimensions. Those are the drafts that allow for speculation on why manuscripts get published or rejected: what accomplishments or violations of literary/aesthetic or political/personal conventions; what choices of narrative devices; what combination of contacts, friendships, and serendipity. More specifically, investigating which women had the toughest time getting their autobiographies published says much about "powerful" conceptions about gender (i.e., what publishing executives find acceptable from a marketing point of view) as well as assumptions about what readers will find plausible and interesting.

Furthermore, since autobiographies get edited, blessed indeed is the researcher who can either compare serial drafts of published manuscripts or consult publishers' correspondence. The recently discovered draft of the poet Zora Neale Hurston's autobiography exposes several instances where her publisher had demanded deletions and changes, especially her references to politics and her more "extreme" expressions of love and hatred (Raynaud 1992). Claudine Raynaud sees the controversial passages as "pockets of resistance" to the publisher, although Hurston's voice—erotic and black—was eventually suppressed and brought under control.[4] The substantial editing of Raymond Carver's work, only recently brought to public attention, also brings to the fore rather dramatically the collaborative nature of "authorship"—a process that journalists have always acknowledged, albeit with varying degrees of bitterness or tolerance. Notably, some of Carver's fellow writers, who do not necessarily dispute that the changes represented improvements, oppose any open discussion of editing (Max 1998).[5] Such cases remind scholars of the difficulty of studying the impact of the expectations, rules, and outright actions of publishers and editors. Changes to ideas and drafts as well as to manuscripts over the course of production are amazingly (again, from a researcher's vantage, regrettably) invisible.[6]

Autobiographers also "police" their accounts in anticipation of readers' concerns and mindful of their obligations to family members, friends, and future generations.[7] Despite the stereotype that self-narratives are introspective and intimate, male and female autobiographers seem to avoid emotional life, especially painful memories. Women reporters' refusal to mention sex, for example, not only accommodates the false dichotomy between public and private spheres but also prevents readers from understanding how reporters believed that sex (that is, sexual harassment or sexual relationships with colleagues or sources) did or did not interfere with their work. The erasure is understandable, given the mythic self-representation of journalists as disembodied professionals, but unfortunate.

Meanwhile, it is precisely because media work is not controlled by autonomous authors that newsworkers' autobiographies can be used to understand editing and publishing processes. Female reporters have been very specific about mediation of their newspaper work, if not about the transformations of their published autobiographies. Women regularly described how their journalistic work was altered by editors, publishers, and colleagues. They recall battles lost, battles won, and battles avoided. Sometimes they lied to editors, saying that they had failed to get a story when in fact they were trying to protect innocent sources. Sometimes, in anticipation of controversy, they censored themselves. Usually, their agonizing over such decisions was kept private until the autobiography's publication. Since newsroom dynamics and the ways that news stories get changed are so difficult to study, autobiographers' reflections on arguments with editors, colleagues, publishers, sources, and advertisers are consistently and possibly uniquely insightful.

Even admitting the distorting effects of production processes, one need not necessarily assume that an autobiographer's first draft is significantly more authentic than the redrafted one. That a narrative has been altered involuntarily, self-consciously, or without informing readers does not automatically undo its truth value.[8] Take, for example, Florence Finch Kelly, the self-professed dean of American newswomen who wrote for papers across the country before settling down for thirty years at the *New York Times Review of Books*. In her autobiography, which appeared shortly before her death at age eighty-one, Kelly (1939) excoriated the men who discriminated against her and other members of "the skirted sex." But, she claimed, the reliving she experienced while drafting her story was more satisfactory than the actual living, since it brought "ampler and serene tolerance of events and conditions and personalities that formerly had deeply disturbed and perhaps irritated" (xv). Kelly herself did not privilege the angry, albeit more passionate version over the rewritten version. Nor are there empirical or theoretical grounds for implying that oral discourse, even "spontaneous" talk, is more truthful or correct than what appears in writing. In any case, since evidence of self-censorship may itself point to something important, different accounts of events and different accounts of causality should be compared instead of being taken as invalidating the documents. Again, cultural studies analysts must locate autobiographies in historically, ideologically, and materially specific contexts that take cognizance of culture as well as social rules, publishers' expectations, and production dynamics.

One early study of the genre warned readers to reconcile themselves to being deceived by autobiographers (Bates 1937), and fidelity remains a major issue. The ways that authors manipulate the events of their lives are covered over in self-narratives no less than the convention-laden selection and organization of events are covered over in news narratives. Autobiography is not transparent recitation of fact. Many women warned readers that they would occasionally be coy about personal information. For example, Adela St. Johns (1969), the Hearst reporter famous for her coverage of Hollywood and crime, admitted at one point, "I am inclined to embellish, to twist to suit my purposes or prove my point, and we all forget some" (146). Ellen Tarry (1955), who wrote for the African American and Catholic press, announced, "I have omitted the telling of certain events because their inclusion might have infringed upon good taste and in no way would they contribute to the total effect of this volume. Some of these omissions were necessary to safeguard the welfare of innocent persons" (viii).

It is not surprising, however, that professional reporters—even those who disdained "tell-all soul-baring"—would promise fidelity per se. After mocking the "regurgitation school of writing," Edna Ferber (1939) declared, "Imagination has no chance here: fancy is not free but shackled. The plump and determined seventeen-year-old reporter on the Appleton, Wisconsin, *Crescent* will not be permitted to turn into a thing of lithe loveliness at the sight of whose beauty strong men turn pale and women bite their handkerchiefs and faint" (13).

Never one to mince words, Alice Allison Dunnigan (1974), who worked for the Associated Negro Press, insisted, "[This autobiography] is based on raw facts, uninhibited, unembellished and unvarnished. No punches are pulled, no rough stones left unturned, no skeletons pushed into the closet, no shady incidents shoved under the bed, no hideous ogres hidden behind the door and no ugly blemishes eradicated or shellacked" (i).

Fidelity was an important theme for women reporters, who apparently felt compelled to account for career decisions in ways that implied, if not explicitly provided, useful advice. Tarry (1955), for example, said, "This story is . . . told so that future generations may avoid the mistakes of our time; so that they may know the price we have paid for tomorrow" (viii). Dunnigan (1974) declared even more emphatically, "It is my fondest hope that this story of my life and work will, by interpretation, investigation, information and inspiration, encourage more young writers to use their talents as a moving force in the forward march of progress" (iii).

The accusation of deceitfulness has been both charged to and admitted by women in disproportionate numbers. Virginia Woolf (1980) speculated that "chastity and modesty" prevented women from writing truthful autobiographies" (453). Woolf's friend, the writer Vita Sackville-West, called her life "a deceitful country," to which one feminist scholar responds, what woman's life is *not* a deceitful country (Felman 1993, 15). Yet Leigh Gilmore (1994) suggests that such accusations of historical infidelity in autobiography are downright sexist. At the least, it could be argued that women are simply more willing to bring into question their truthfulness.

Timothy Dow Adams (1990) resolves the apparent fallibility of memory and unreliability of self-constructions by saying:

> All autobiographers are unreliable narrators, all humans are liars, and yet . . . to be a successful liar in one's own life story is especially difficult. Because what we choose to misrepresent is as telling as what really happened, because the shape of our lives often distorts who we really are, and because, as Roy Pascal reminds us, "consistent misrepresentation of oneself is not easy, even those authors with the most problematic approach to lying should be valued for telling the truth of their lives." (x)

Adams's suggestion that autobiographers' reasons for telling lies are more important than absolute accuracy, of course, wholly erases the already blurred distinction between fiction and nonfiction. What is more problematic, in challenging scholars to determine reasons for autobiographical lies, Adams forces analysts into anticulturalist, mechanistic accounts of psychology.

This tendency to psychologize and thereby censure emerges in critical treatment of several women autobiographers, including Joan Lowell, "Gal Reporter" for the *Boston Daily Record.* Granted, Lowell had already attracted controversy with her 1929 best-seller, which described her upbringing aboard a schooner captained by her father. The Book-of-the-Month Club ultimately offered subscribers the chance to return *The Cradle of the Deep* after skeptics alleged that Lowell had spent her childhood largely in California, not sailing through the South Seas. Lowell herself was quoted as saying "truth is contained as much in the dreams and legends of people as in the factual chronicle of their lives" ("Joan Lowell Is Dead" 1967, 47). In her 1933 autobiography, *Gal Reporter,* Lowell described finding adventure, pay, and "regeneration" as a reporter, despite her misgivings about the press (presumably a reference to *The Cradle*). One chapter recounted how a notorious criminal, who was eventually convicted, literally attacked her during an undercover investigation. Of Lowell's gory prose about this "white slaver," Howard Good (1993), one of the few journalism historians to take autobiography seriously, comments, "Sex gave her power over sources and readers, or at least the illusion of it, but power . . . tends to corrupt. Lowell was so corrupted—so lost in tabloidism—that even when she described herself being assaulted . . . she was tempted to titillate" (92).

Instead, cultural scholars need to consider how women's autobiographies have arisen and continue to be judged in terms of particular—if controversial—constructions of womanhood and of particular—if changing—notions about what is appropriate for female narrative. Leigh Gilmore (1994) puts this bluntly: "This gendered vision of the autobiographer affects the production and reception of women's self-representational texts" (2). After all, the legitimate focus is how these women wrote about themselves, not "facts" about individuals. Furthermore, the fact that narratives are not reducible to historical reality does not mean that they are incommensurable with it. As Janet Varner Gunn (1981) notes, the surface is a real clue, not merely a false scent to what is beneath or hidden in the self's narrative (10). The self displayed in autobiography is a true self, albeit not the only one. One need not assume that autobiographers significantly, consistently, or intentionally distort their accounts, although this position would be undermined if many autobiographies were as "fantastic" as Lowell's *Cradle of the Deep.* Lowell was an exception, however; I would argue that women journalists rarely adopt the more experimental or playful writing styles that characterize the literary figures upon whom most autobiographic theorizing and psychologizing are based.

Virginia Woolf provides another useful escape hatch in her 1929 *A Room of One's Own:* "When a subject is highly controversial—and any question about sex is that—one cannot hope to tell the truth. One can only show how one came to hold whatever opinion one does hold. One can only give one's readers a chance to draw their own conclusions as they observe the limitations, the prejudices, the idiosyncrasies of the speaker (4).

She added, "For in a question like this truth is only to be had by laying together many varieties of error" (105). It is a crucial point: notions of what matters to media workers cannot be based on the experiences of a few. Even having cautiously studied the autobiographies of several people working in a field at a particular time and place, scholars must proceed slowly and tentatively, piecing together mosaics of discourse taken from a variety of sources, and they must be ever humble in the face of the duplicity of self-writing and of language itself. But if a single autobiography represents retrospective imposition of coherence, then looking at several should reveal patterns of patterns.

One productive use of autobiography regards how gender politics are constructed in and at work. Autobiographies of women writing for U.S. papers in the early twentieth century offer considerable insight into journalism as a gendered practice. They had much to say about highly gendered conventions and professional codes and about the controversial, if not marginal, status of women in the profession. Several women publishing autobiographies from 1900 to 1950 acknowledged how individual men helped them in their careers, generously giving them opportunities to work despite their immaturity or inexperience and offering advice and consolation. Yet women also underscored their resentment of the stubbornly overriding pattern that men doubted women's abilities, even if they did not actively erect barriers. Indeed, several women described being driven out of the profession.

Estelle C. Jelinek (1980) asserts that women's autobiographies rarely mirror the establishment's history of the times; they deemphasize the public aspects of their lives, concentrating instead on domestic details, family difficulties, close friends, and people who influenced them: "This emphasis by women on the personal, especially on other people, rather than on their work life, their professional success, or their connectedness to current political or intellectual history clearly contradicts the established criterion about the content of autonomy" (10). Jane Marcus (1988) says the autobiographies of certain privileged, successful women at the turn of the century represent a "re/signing" of their names in women's history: "Enacting a deliberate resignation from the public world and patriarchal history, which had already erased or was expected to erase their names and their works, they re/signed their private lives into domestic discourse" (114). Carolyn Heilbrun (1988) accuses female autobiographers of refusing to acknowledge their anger, their desire for control over their own lives, and their interest in public power (see also Spacks 1976). Passivity and sentimentality taint even the stories of some twentieth-century heroines, who accepted responsibility for failure but avoided claims of ambition (Spacks 1980).

This emphasis on the personal does not seem true of women reporting for mainstream papers in the first half of the twentieth century. They all put newsworthy adventures—who, what, where, when, and how—at the center. For the most part, they ruthlessly excised their personal life or emphasized that work required them to do so. They barely mentioned occasions that might otherwise be assumed to be important to women, such as marriage and pregnancy. Florence Kelly's (1939) 571-page narrative, complete with index and tables of content for each chapter, was exceptional in that she covered so much. Kelly included not only detailed accounts of her life but also extensive sermonizing on sundry topics, from the value of college education to the problems of youth, as well as chapters on the history and status of women in journalism. Yet, after conceding that she had agonized over a colleague's marriage proposal because it might damage her career, Kelly never described her marriage. Most of the other married women did the same. They barely named their husbands and skipped over critical events in the life cycles of their families. As reporters, these women focused on their careers and measured themselves by male standards. They underlined their ambition and, in that context, announced their sense of injustice and inequity.

It should also be noted that these journalists seemed to have walked the same tightrope challenging most women of the period who tried to describe their professional work. Men have usually legitimized their autobiographies with the assumption that their lives are exemplary yet representative. In contrast, women who achieved eminence apparently wanted to avoid both claims to specialness and claims to representativeness (Lane 1991). Women who wrote professionally had long been the targets of criticism on the grounds that women are uniquely "sexed" but that they "unsex" themselves through writing. No wonder their lives betray some unease at having violated cultural expectations about women. Certainly, the journalists described here were well aware that their profession was seen as antifeminine and that memorializing their achievements in the public domain was seen as unfeminine.

One obvious strategy for negotiating this tension and winning over readers' sympathy (in some sense this also worked in reporting per se) was to exploit stories about women already in currency. In particular, except for Alice Dunnigan, journalists emphasized their modesty, as if self-mockery might deflect criticism of their public and private lives. The self-deprecation may have eased the prescriptive implications of self-descriptions, thus weakening the accusation that they spoke exclusively to and about a special female breed. Elizabeth Jordan (1938) provided an almost paradigmatic example of the self-effacement that literary scholars regard as characterizing women's autobiography. Jordan began her autobiography, *Three Rousing Cheers,* by hastening to deny that her title was "the offspring of any delusion as to my individual importance" (vii). Jordan went on to add, "I have been pianiste, reporter, newspaper editor, magazine editor, public speaker, playwright, dramatic critic, and novelist, which helps to explain why I have never done any one thing superlatively well" (11). Even the Pulitzer Prize–winning war reporter Marguerite Higgins (1952) repeatedly referred to good luck, as well as hard work (that is, not "natural" talent). Higgins said, "I've always found that when the breaks finally came it was either through such accident or through the kind of luck that defies all formula" (17).

Many women journalists writing in the early twentieth century were well aware of their special place as "the" female reporter. This is not identity politics in the contemporary sense, for their autobiographies betray not pride but frustration at being pushed into this role. At least in the 1900–1950 period, few of them explicitly identified themselves as feminists; Kelly was a prominent exception. Rather, women autobiographers expressed clear unhappiness over the conflation of reporting by/for/on women. Elizabeth Jordan (1938), who loved working for the *New York World,* underscored her distaste for her first job, editing a Milwaukee newspaper's women's page: "It is a miracle that the stuff I had to carry in 'Sunshine' did not permanently destroy my interest in newspaper work" (14). Perhaps this near-unanimous distaste for supplying, as Jordan put it, "light and warmth to the women of the universe" (13) was, as a matter of fact, exaggerated. Such discourse delivered a clear message, however: women were unwilling to concede their lesser status as reporters.

The autobiographies suggested that just as these women were aware of their gender (having been forced into this awareness), they sensed how their autobiographies were being read by women readers. These women were clearly struggling to be heard on their own terms, as reporters who understood their cultural positioning as women. Yet they marked their sense of responsibility to women subjects and to women readers. In the tradition of Margaret Cavendish—who, despite (or through) her denial, addressed readers directly—these autobiographers more or less explicitly offered women readers warning, encouragement, and a sense that things could be done another way. The reiteration of common problems seems to bear witness to not only the stubbornness of gender politics in the newsroom but also the possibility of change. Finally, that women reporters might have self-consciously—whether from choice or market factors—avoided what otherwise would be identified as a "female" literary tradition in autobiography suggests the value of that methodological preference in cultural studies for beginning with specific texts rather than assuming the existence of such a gender/genre tradition and then seeking it out in texts. By attending to their stories in the context of critical reaction from editors, critics, and readers, we enliven cultural studies work.

Notes

1. Using a narrow definition of the genre that excluded such artifacts as journals and slave narratives, Louis Kaplan (1962) listed 6,377 titles published before 1945. Notably, he categorized authors by profession, which may imply agreement that the genre is helpful in understanding various professions.

2. Some critics of biography analogously propose that the linear form of biography is unsuited to women's lives.

3. In 1786, Ann Yearley, the so-called milkmaid poet, wrote something she called "autobiographical narrative" (Folkenflik 1993).

4. Hurston herself corrected her grammar and punctuation and marked some passages as possibly irrelevant or libelous.

5. Illuminating testimony to editor/publisher-ordered change also occurs in Piers Anthony's novel *But What of Earth?* (1989), subtitled *A Novel Rendered into a Bad Example.* Anthony, the curmudgeonly science fiction novelist, provided the entire history of how his original manuscript was changed, without his permission, by a series of copy editors and a hired writer. Ultimately he took back the manuscript and republished it. His 1989 version includes 168 long and detailed footnotes indicating exactly where and how the others intended to change his draft. In my view, many, if not most, of those changes would have improved Anthony's clumsy and often sexist writing.

6. With materials transferred on disk or over modems, evidence of change is likely to be totally lost.

7. Mindful of just such concerns, my mother felt compelled to publish two versions of her memoirs herself.

8. No one invalidates academic scholarship because the researcher received help or responded to referees' or editors' comments; a researcher may even self-censor in the face of tenure worries. Just as we as scholars may come to know our academic points in the process of writing papers, we may learn more in rewriting, with the subsequent drafts embodying useful corrections. Only a few academic stars can "get away with" inserting themselves into their published work; the rest are not allowed autobiographical excursions.

References

Adams, T. D. 1990. *Telling Lies in Modern Autobiography.* Chapel Hill: University of North Carolina Press.

Anthony, Piers. 1989. *But What of Earth? A Novel Rendered into a Bad Example.* New York: T. Doherty Associates.

Banks, E. L. 1902. *The Autobiography of a "Newspaper Girl."* New York: Dodd, Mead.

Bates, E. S. 1937. *Inside Out: An Introduction to Autobiography.* New York: Sheridan House.

Blackburn, R. 1980. "In Search of the Black Female Self: African-American Women's Autobiographies and Ethnicity." In *Women's Autobiography: Essays in Criticism,* edited by E. C. Jelinek, 133–48. Bloomington: Indiana University Press.

Dilthey, W. 1962. *Pattern and Meaning in History.* Edited by H. P. Rickman. New York: Harper and Brothers.

Doherty, T. 1981. "American Autobiography and Ideology." In *The American Autobiography,* edited by A. E. Stone, 95–108. Englewood Cliffs, N.J.: Prentice-Hall.

Dunnigan, A. A. 1974. *A Black Woman's Experience—From Schoolhouse to White House.* Philadelphia: Dorrance.

Felman, S. 1993. *What Does a Woman Want?* Baltimore: Johns Hopkins University Press.

Ferber, E. 1939. *A Peculiar Treasure.* New York: Doubleday, Doran.
Folkenflik, R., ed. 1993. *The Culture of Autobiography: Constructions of Self-Representation.* Stanford, Calif.: Stanford University Press.
Fox-Genovese, E. 1988. "My Statue, My Self: Autobiographical Writings of Afro-American Women." In *The Private Self: Theory and Practice of Women's Autobiographical Writings,* edited by S. Benstock, 63–89. Chapel Hill: University of North Carolina Press.
Friedman, S. S. 1988. "Women's Autobiographical Selves: Theory and Practice." In *The Private Self: Theory and Practice of Women's Autobiographical Writings,* edited by S. Benstock, 34–62. Chapel Hill: University of North Carolina Press.
Geertz, C. 1973. *The Interpretation of Cultures: Selected Essays.* New York: Basic Books.
Geiger, S. N. G. 1986. "Women's Life Histories: Method and Content. *Signs* 11 (12): 334–51.
Gilmore, L. 1994. *Autobiographics: A Feminist Theory of Women's Self-Representation.* Ithaca, N.Y.: Cornell University Press.
Glenn, C. 1992. "Author, Audience, and Autobiography: Rhetorical Technique in the Book of Margery Kempe." *College English* 54:540–53.
Good, H. 1993. *The Journalist as Autobiographer.* Metuchen, N.J.: Scarecrow.
Gunn, J. V. 1981. "Walden and the Temporal Mode of Autobiographical Narrative." In *The American Autobiography,* edited by A. E. Stone, 80–94. Englewood Cliffs, N.J.: Prentice-Hall.
Heilbrun, C. G. 1988. *Writing a Woman's Life.* New York: W. W. Norton.
Higgins, M. 1952. *News Is a Singular Thing.* Garden City, N.Y.: Doubleday.
hooks, b. 1989. *Talking Back.* Boston: South End.
Howells, W. D. 1909. "Editor's Easy Chair." *Harper's Monthly Magazine,* October, 795–99.
Inglis, F. 1993. *Cultural Studies.* Oxford: Blackwell.
Jacobs, H. A. [1861] 1988. *Incidents in the Life of a Slave Girl.* New York: Oxford University Press.
Jelinek, E. C. 1980. "Introduction: Women's Autobiography and the Male Tradition." In *Women's Autobiography: Essays in Criticism,* edited by E. C. Jelinek, 1–20. Bloomington: Indiana University Press.
"Joan Lowell Is Dead in Brazil: Author and Adventure Seeker." 1967. *New York Times,* November 15, 47.
Jordan, E. 1938. *Three Rousing Cheers.* New York: D. Appleton-Century.
Kaplan, L. 1962. *A Bibliography of American Autobiographies.* Madison: University of Wisconsin Press.
Kelly, F. F. 1939. *Flowing Stream: The Story of Fifty-Six Years in American Newspaper Life.* New York: E. P. Dutton.
Lane, A. J. 1991. Introduction to *The Living of Charlotte Perkins Gilman: An Autobiography,* by C. P. Gilman. Madison: University of Wisconsin Press.
Lejeune, P. 1975. *Le pacte autobiographique.* Paris: Editions du Seuil.
Lowell, J. 1929. *The Cradle of the Deep.* New York: Simon and Schuster.
———. 1933. *Gal Reporter.* New York: Farrar and Rinehart.
Manning, M. [Beatrice Fairfax]. 1944. *Ladies Now and Then.* New York: E. P. Dutton.

Marcus, J. 1988. "Invincible Mediocrity: The Private Selves of Public Women." In *The Private Self: Theory and Practice of Women's Autobiographical Writings,* edited by S. Benstock, 114–46. Chapel Hill: University of North Carolina Press.

Max, D. T. 1998. "The Carver Chronicles." *New York Times Magazine,* August 9, 34–40, 51, 56–57.

Maynes, M. J. 1992. "Autobiography and Class Formation in Nineteenth-Century Europe: Methodological Considerations." *Social Science History* 16:517–37.

McKay, N. Y. 1989. "Nineteenth-Century Black Women's Spiritual Autobiographies: Religious Faith and Self-Empowerment." In *Interpreting Women's Lives: Feminist Theory and Personal Narratives,* edited by the Personal Narratives Group, 139–54. Bloomington: Indiana University Press.

Peterson, L. J. 1993. "Institutionalizing Women's Autobiography: Nineteenth-Century Editors and the Shaping of an Autobiographical Tradition." In *The Culture of Autobiography: Constructions of Self-Representation,* edited by R. Folkenflik, 80–103. Stanford, Calif.: Stanford University Press.

Raynaud, C. 1992. "Rubbing a Paragraph with a Soft Cloth? Muted Voices and Editorial Constraints in Dust Tracks on a Road." In *De/colonizing the Subject,* edited by S. Smith and J. Watson, 34–62. Minneapolis: University of Minnesota Press.

———. 1980. "Selves in Hiding." In *Women's Autobiography: Essays in Criticism,* edited by E. C. Jelinek, 112–32. Bloomington: Indiana University Press.

Smith, S. 1987. *A Poetics of Women's Autobiography.* Bloomington: Indiana University Press.

Smith, S., and J. Watson. 1996. Introduction to *Getting a Life: Everyday Uses of Autobiography,* edited by S. Smith and J. Watson, 1–26. Minneapolis: University of Minnesota Press.

Spacks, P. M. 1976. *Imagining a Self.* Cambridge, Mass.: Harvard University Press.

Stanton, D. C. 1984. "Autogynography: Is the Subject Different?" In *The Female Autograph,* edited by D. Stanton, 5–22. New York: New York Literary Forum.

St. Johns, A. R. 1969. *The Honeycomb.* Garden City, N.Y.: Doubleday.

Tarry, E. 1955. *The Third Door: The Autobiography of an American Negro Woman.* New York: David McKay.

Woolf, V. 1929. *A Room of One's Own.* New York: Harcourt, Brace.

———. 1980. *Leave the Letters till We're Dead: The Letters of Virginia Woolf.* Vol. 6, *1936–1941.* London: Hogarth.

NORMAN K. DENZIN

7 Cultural Studies, the New Journalism, and the Narrative Turn in Ethnography

None of this was made up.
—John Hersey

Reality is not what it is. It consists of the many realities which it can be made into.
—Wallace Stevens

My topics are facts, fictions, the new and old journalism, the nonfiction novel, the new and old ethnography, the facts of fiction, fictionalized facts, the narrative turn in the human disciplines, and what this turn means for doing cultural studies and writing a critical, performative ethnography in the twenty-first century. My argument moves in three directions at the same time. Experimental ethnographic writing, the doing of poems, stories, plays, performances, requires that the cultural studies project simultaneously question and establish the credibility of its use of facts and fictions in the stories that are told and performed.

Ethnographers and those in cultural studies have much to learn from journalists in this regard, for it is in journalism that the arguments over factually accurate literary and nonliterary texts have been most hotly debated (see Wolfe 1973; Carey 1986, 1997b, 156; and Christians, Ferre, and Fackler 1993, 32–58, 113–22). I will, accordingly, discuss the history of new journalism, while examining select celebrated journalistic cases where the accuracy of the journalist's text has been challenged (see Eason 1986; Fishkin 1985, 209–17; and Christians, Ferre, and Fackler 1993).

I have no desire to reproduce arguments that maintain distinctions between fictional (literary) and nonfictional (journalism, ethnography) texts (see Frus 1994, xi; and Zavarzadeh 1976, 50–67).[1] Such efforts invariably resort to canon-pointing and the use of essentializing categories.[2] With Phyllis Frus (1994, xi), I oppose all hierarchical categories, including those that distinguish literary and nonliterary, fictional and nonfictional textual forms. These categories, which are socially and politically constructed, work against the creation of an expansive, complex public discourse wherein multiple narrative forms circulate and inform one another (see Frus 1994, xi; and Ellis 1995, 317). If all is narrative, then it can be argued that narrative techniques are neither fictional nor factual; they are merely formal "methods used in making sense of all kinds of situations" (Eason 1982, 143). Invoking and paraphrasing Stephen A. Tyler (1986, 123), the discourses of the postmodern world involve the constant comingling of literary, journalistic, fictional, factual, and ethnographic writing.[3] No form is privileged over another. Truth is socially established by the norms that operate for each form or genre.[4]

As ethnographers engage experimental writing forms, a parallel movement has occurred, namely, the emergence of a critical, communication- and postpragmatist-based cultural studies project (Carey 1989; Denzin 1995). The central problem of this project is meaning (Carey 1989, 85), how people bring meaning to their lives in a cinematic society where, to quote David Eason (1984) paraphrasing Norman Mailer, "reality is now negotiated in terms of a media aesthetic" (60).

The purpose of cultural studies is clear: to tell and perform critical stories about this society and the ways people make meaning in it. This shifts from a spectator theory of the news and story making to a participative, interactional, and conversation-based view of culture, communication, ethnography, and newsmaking (Carey 1989, 82; Carey 1997a).

This movement in cultural studies has been accompanied by a third turn, namely, the full-scale embrace of methods of narrative analysis, methods that have too often produced the obvious and the banal in the name of a politically correct cultural studies analysis (Morris 1990). This move by the social sciences has produced an embarrassment of riches. Multiple strategies for analyzing narrative texts now exist, including semiotic, rhetorical, tropological, structural, feminist, content-based, microlevel, dramaturgical, thematic, and functional-based models of interpretation (for reviews, see Polkinghorne 1988; Riessman 1993; Feldman 1994; Manning and Cullum-Swan 1994; Allen 1992; and Hay 1992). These models are pivotal because they authorize the turn to narrative, offering methods that ensure the truth and accuracy of a text and its interpretation (but see Trinh 1989, 142–43).

The above issues frame the story I want to tell, another chapter in the story about the narrative turn in the human disciplines, the story about facts, fictions, and how fictions become facts. I ask what an American cultural studies can learn from the new journalists about storytelling and cultural performances.[5] I begin with the facts of fiction.

From Facts To Fiction

Shelley Fisher Fishkin (1985), in her epilogue to *From Fact to Fiction: Journalism and Imaginative Writing in America,* observes that "during the last two decades the line between fact and fiction has grown more and more blurred" (207). A decade later, Richard G. Mitchell and Kathy Charmaz (1995) argue that "ethnographers and fiction writers rely on similar writing practices to tell their tales" (1). William Foote Whyte (1993), referring to an earlier age when these distinctions were not blurred, notes, "When I began my SCS research [1936], I wanted to contribute to building a science of society. . . . I based my own framework on a basic distinction between the objective (what is out there to be observed), and the subjective (how the observer or others interpret the observed phenomena) (366). . . . [if social realism is but one narrative strategy for telling stories] then the critic can only depend on the persuasive power of the author. Scientific arguments are thus transformed into literary criticism" (371).[6] For Whyte, there is a clear difference between fact and fiction. The differences are not to be minimized, for when they are, we left with only rhetoric. This argument, of course, ignores the fact that science writing is a form of rhetorical persuasion (Agger 1989; Brown 1989).

Fact and fiction have not always been so confused. Fishkin (1985) argues that from the middle of the nineteenth century through the 1920s, the journalist and the imaginative writer were held to different standards (207). Journalists worked with verifiable facts, and readers could expect stories to be factually accurate. Imaginative writers, novelists, told truths that were not necessarily factually accurate, but they adhered to aesthetic standards of good storytelling. Ethnography enters this same terrain, and ethnographers like William Foote Whyte learned how to report objectively the facts of the social situations they studied. Like good journalism, good ethnography reported the facts of life to a scientific and, at times, public community. The duties and practices of sociologists and journalists were thus separated.

All of this held steady from the 1920s through the 1960s. There were three different professional groups, each producing different but often parallel tellings about society: journalists, novelists, and social science ethnographers. Then the lines between journalism, imaginative writing, and ethnography began to again blur (see Wolfe 1973; Sims 1984, 1990; Connery 1992; Frus 1994; and Eason 1984). Impatient with the rigid conventions of objective journalism, the new journalists, Fishkin (1985) notes, "started to borrow technical devices from the novel . . . [and] novelists . . . began to borrow research methods and subjects from journalism (207).

By the mid-1970s, this situation had solidified. Tom Wolfe (1973) codified the epistemology of the new journalists and offered a rich sampling of works by representative writers (Gay Talese, Richard Goldstein, Michael Herr, Truman Capote, Hunter S. Thompson, Norman Mailer, John Gregory Dunn, Joan Didion). In 1976, Mas'ud Zavarzadeh introduced the term *nonfictional novel,* or true-life novel, to describe the works of Capote, Mailer, and Oscar Lewis. He suggested that there were three generic nonfiction writing forms (exegetical, testimonial, and notational). David Eason (1981, 1982, 1984) would soon offer paradigmatic readings of the new journalists and the nonfiction novelists, dividing them into two camps: the ethnographic realists (Wolfe, Capote) and the cultural phenomenologists (Mailer, Didion).

This situation was disturbed by a series of journalistic scandals that rocked the nation's leading newspapers in the 1980s, leading to serious challenges to the so-called new journalism (Eason 1986, 1984; Van Maanen 1988, 131–36; Christians, Ferre, and Fackler 1993, 118; Agar 1990).[7] At the same time, increasing numbers of social scientists were turning to imaginative forms of ethnographic reporting, including poems, short stories, and nonfictional novels (see Marcus and Fischer 1986, 73–76; and Richardson 1994). Like those who attacked the journalists in the 1980s, a new generation of critics is charging that the new ethnography produces fiction, not scientific truth (see Agar 1990; Fine 1993; Whyte 1993, 371; Kunda 1993; and Snow and Morrill 1993, 1995).

Nonfiction Texts and the New Journalism

Seven understandings shaped this new work. The new writers treated facts as social constructions; blurred writing genres, combining literary and investigative journalism with the realist novel, the confession, the travel report, and the autobiography (Hollowell 1977, 15);[8] used the scenic method to show rather than tell (Agar 1990, 77; Wolfe 1973, 50); wrote about real people and created composite characters (Hollowell 1977, 30);[9] used multiple points of view to establish authorial presence; deployed multiple narrative strategies (flashbacks, foreshadowing, interior monologues, parallel plots) to build dramatic tension (Agar 1990, 78); and positioned themselves as moral witnesses to the radical changes occurring in American society (Hollowell 1977, 13).

The cinematic society, the society that knows itself through cinema's eye, was the point of departure for all of these writers (Denzin 1995).[10] Social life and the report about life were both understood to be social constructions (Eason 1984, 61). Norman Mailer (1966) captured this position best, arguing that the technology of the media, in Eason's (1984) words, "disengages subjects from their own expressions . . . individuals become observers of their own acts . . . both actor and spectator live a reality arbitrated by the assumptions of media technicians" (60).

The media created facts shaped into narrative accounts of newsworthy happenings that could be inserted into predetermined news slots on the evening news or in the evening newspaper. These understandings challenged the epistemology of the totalizing, fictive novel and the objective news account (Zavarzadeh 1976, 26).

Since its origins in the nineteenth century, informational, commercial journalism had operated under two imperatives (Eason 1981, 128). A report should be a valid accounting of the events it describes, and the account should be written in a way that engages the audience. Such accounts were to be written in an objective fashion. The reporter was not a biographically specific person. He or she gathered and reported facts. The report would be written in a concrete fashion, answering to the who, what, when, where, why, and how of the events in question. The account would be emotionally neutral, given to understatement, and written in a straightforward syntax. The narrator and the processes of textual production would be invisible, just as documentary cinema was. The production of the text was never at issue; the problem was to explain (and order) the facts at hand. The facts were visible events, taken as givens, objectively known and knowable by the scientific reporter. This unquestioning acceptance of the facts creates, as Dorothy Smith notes, a situation where "what ought to be explained is treated as fact or as assumption" (quoted in Frus 1994, 113). In this model, facts are reified (Frus 1994, 112). The validity of the text is self-evident; it is grounded in the objectively reported facts.

Validity thus became, as it was for positivistic social science, the key legitimating device that authorized the journalistic text's claims to truth.

So conceptualized, validity operated as a marketing device. Newspapers sold to consuming publics valid accounts of newsworthy events. Readers, as an abstract yet concrete market category, could count on their newspapers to print not only all the news that was fit to print but also only news that was truthful. The nonfiction writers and the new journalists questioned this equation. Empirical validity was a social construct, and there was no objective news reporting.

By focusing on the tension between the real and its hyperreal, larger-than-life media representations, nonfiction writers documented Hayden White's (1973) argument that the formal techniques of history and fiction are the same (Eason 1982, 143). In both forms of writing, writers use narrative strategies (characterization, motif repetition, point of view, different descriptive strategies) to bring coherence to their materials (Eason 1982, 143). The nonfiction writer uses modernist and postmodern narrative strategies to make sense of real (and imagined) situations. The historian uses narrative to bring meaning to situations perceived to be real (Eason 1982, 143). For the historian and the fiction and nonfiction writer, facts become symbolic representations to be interpreted. Narrative techniques are interpretive practices that allow the writer to make sense of the world being described (Eason 1982, 143). In this way, the nonfiction writers turned narrative on its head. They erased the distinction between fact and fiction. They produced true-life accounts of real events.

The New Writers

The basic unit of analysis for the new writers was not the fact but the scene, the situation where the event in question occurred or would happen (Wolfe 1973, 50). The distinguishing feature of this work is not empirical data, for the naturalistic and realistic novel also uses empirical materials. The new writers refused to use facts to support a totalizing reading of reality. The nonfiction text, as Mas'ud Zavarzadeh (1976) points out, "is written not *about* facts but *in* facts" (219). These facts are treated as extensions of real life, which has been interpreted (or presented) by the writer. These writers used the methods of journalistic reporting and ethnographic participant observation to gather the facts and meanings of a particular situation or experience (see Mailer 1979, 1020–21). They then fashioned these details into stories and novels. Some called it reality fiction (Zavarzadeh 1976, 226–27).

On the basis of their careful attention to status details, Wolfe and the other new writers developed a theory of life in contemporary America.

Fragmented American culture produces subcultures and enclaves (stock-cars, Las Vegas, radical chic). These social worlds have created their own authentic, bizarre lifestyles and status rituals. Generally ignored by American observers, these enclaves deserve careful study. They are the site of the "true" America, the places where we now live, and in them are displayed a basic cultural truth: in the words of Joe David Bellamy (1982) "human nature follows the same barbaric patterns regardless of class, region or circumstance" (xiii). The rapid fragmentation of America has produced status confusions, leading to the production of status drop-outs and bewildering lifestyles (Bellamy 1982, xiii).

The new writer chronicles these lifestyles, mocks them, pokes fun at them, brings them alive, and in so doing suggests that we are not unlike those written about. And so history goes on behind people's backs, as they continually struggle for social recognition and social domination over one another. By focusing on the symbolism of such events, the new writers attempt to probe and reveal a deeper level of cultural experience. At this deeper level, reality and text have become deeply entangled; life imitates art, and art imitates life (Eason 1984, 52).

The Legacies of the New Writers

The legacies of these arguments were multiple (see Eason 1986, 437–44). The new journalists and the nonfiction writers changed the way reality was represented and interpreted. They described scenes, not facts; created composite characters; and manipulated point of view and temporality in the stories they told. They reasserted the primacy of realism as a major literary style and worked from underlying interpretive theories about the postmodern culture. They generated enormous skepticism about the government as a source of trustworthy information and had no hesitation about locating themselves in the stories they told. They were part of the movement that undermined the authority of the white middle-class reporter. In so doing, they were part of the process that opened the door for minority and women reporters. They thrived on the notion of the celebrity journalist, the star literary and investigative reporter. This diminished the cultural authority of the traditional, informational journalist.

The Critics

Five criticisms, connected to the defining features of this genre discussed above, were directed against the new writers (see Eason 1986, 437–

42; Frus 1994, 155–56; Fishkin 1985, 210–17; Van Maanen 1988, 134–36; Agar 1990; and Hollowell 1977, 13, 33, 38, 53, 73–75, 148). First, the critics were unanimous on the fact-fiction issue: "The *bastards* are making it up" (Wolfe 1973, 11). The critics could not accept the argument that facts are social constructions and that all writing is narrative. It was as if the use of narrative were an option, when in fact, to paraphrase Wayne Booth ([1961] 1983), authors cannot choose whether to use rhetorical narrative strategies, including fictional accounts, the only choice is which ones will be used (116).

The critics held that a journalist should produce an accurate, balanced news story (Christians, Ferre, and Fackler 1993, 55). This story should be based on carefully researched facts, information gathered from credible sources (hopefully eyewitnesses), and quotes spoken by real people (Agar 1990, 80). The critics were unified on this point: "While wrong truths are always correctable, with facts, fictional facts are forever counterfeit" ("The Fiction of Truth" 1984, 13). Facts were facts, and fictions were fictions, and the two could not be intermingled. The new writers were producing fabrifacts (Fishkin 1985, 216), and fabrifacts cannot be disproven. These writers were sacrificing journalistic truth for dramatic effect (Agar 1990, 78). Hence, the new writers were not producing objective news accounts or objective stories about what was really going on in society.

Second, the new writers had no agreed upon method for validating their assertions.[11] Readers contended that it was not possible to determine if the writers had gotten the story right. Furthermore, writers' presence in the tale could well have disturbed and distorted the very scenes they were studying (Van Maanen 1988, 135). Since they made up quotes, fabricated events, and quoted fictitious sources, the credibility of their texts was constantly in doubt (Agar 1990, 80). The critics were most disturbed by the use of composite characters (Fishkin 1985, 212). They felt that the new writers were being dishonest with the reader, who might believe they were reading about a real person (Hollowell 1977, 30). Such writers as Gail Sheehy (1973) defended the use of this method, contending that it had a long and distinguished history in the *New Yorker* and that its use allowed them to "protect the privacy of perfectly decent people" (16). The method also allowed the writer to, in John Hollowell's (1977) words, "compress considerable amounts of documentary evidence from a variety of sources into a vivid and unified telling of the story" (31).

Third, the writer's place in the new fiction was challenged. Some felt that too much of the writer was in the prose. Others felt too little was there (Van Maanen 1988, 134), claiming that the writer's moral stance was hidden from view. These so-called neutral or objective texts were actually neither neutral nor objective (Hollowell 1977, 73). Still others felt that the writer's place in society had gotten out of hand. These people had become celebrities, larger than the stories they were writing, and they were making pretensions about doing something that was really not new at all (Hollowell 1977, 40–41, 49–50, 118).[12]

Fourth, these writers were doing "scoop ethnography . . . self-serving, pandering . . . tales [about] inconsequential topics" (Van Maanen 1988, 135). When they wrote about important things, they did not connect their work to the scholarly literature on the topic, which meant the work had the feel of something new, when the findings were not really new at all (Van Maanen 1988, 135). At the same time, much of their work was topical in nature and perhaps too close to the news of the day. This raised doubts about its durability (Hollowell 1977, 148).

Fifth, these writers eroded the public's trust in the media and the government (Eason 1986, 442). By making celebrities out of themselves, they became bad models for a new generation of journalists. Their use of literary techniques violated journalistic norms concerning objective storytelling (Eason 1986, 439). They contributed to the disorder journalism was experiencing in the 1970s and 1980s as large numbers of women and minority group members entered the news-making labor force (Eason 1986, 441).

What to Make of It All

Let us return to the basic unit of analysis for the new writers. To paraphrase Zavarzadeh, the nonfiction text is written not about facts but in facticities. These facticities are treated as extensions of real life in its multiple forms and in its many realities. These many versions of reality are then made visible and interpreted by the writer.

The new writers refused to locate reality in events per se. Rather the real, in its multiple forms, was anchored in the experience of the text itself. This called for a new form of reading. They produced texts that challenged readers to read reflexively, to read between the lines, to erase the distinction between fact and fiction, to reread experiences, altering prior understandings based on new information (Frus 1994, xx). This new information was contained in the reflexive text that disrupted temporal sequence, rearranged events and their chronology, constantly altered the past in the light of new understandings (Frus 1994, 209–10). The reality of the text could not be verified in external experience or in concrete external facts (see Frus 1994, xx). The facts were reconstituted in the telling, in the experience of reading.

As Frus (1994) points out, the appeal of the new journalism and the new writing was not that it offered "the certainty of the factual." The appeal was more complicated. The new journalists resisted the call to facts. They wrote, instead, in a way that questioned the "natural relationship between narratives and the 'reality' they appear to represent." They created reflexive texts requiring self-conscious readers. With their readers, these writers shared the view that the world outside was filled with "pseudoevents and precreated experiences" (233). The new writing produced texts and textual experiences that closely corresponded to this view of the world.

These works mirrored the reader's process of self-formation and self-understanding. They did this in their structured ambiguity and internal complexity. They did it in their hesitations and certain uncertainties, in the way they called attention to language and its use. They did it by challenging journalistic representations of truth, even as they challenged their own ability to represent reality. In these ways, these works created readers who shared the same uncertainties, who doubted the truths they were given by the media, the government, and science. These works undid old dichotomies, such as fact and fiction, journalism and science, literature and ethnography. It is doubtful that we can go back to the age where such easy distinctions so automatically operated.

The critics, of course, would have none of this. Recall James W. Carey's (1989) analysis of the two views of newsmaking: the informational, spectator model and the storytelling, participative model. Traditional journalism (and ethnography) relies on a spectator, ocular, visual epistemology. This is a representational model, in which communication (and ethnography) is "a way of seeing things aright" (77). Journalists secure accurate representations of reality, and these representations shape the formation of a correct, accurate, and well-informed public opinion (81). The storytelling framework rejects the visual model of communication. It emphasizes conversation, hearing, and listening as the chief participatory modes of knowing and learning about the world (80). In this view, public opinion is formed through discussion, conversation, and storytelling. The "purpose of news is not to represent and inform but to signal, tell a story, and activate inquiry . . . we lack . . . the vital means through which this conversation can be carried on: institutions of public life through which a public can be formed and can form an opinion" (82). To elaborate, we lack a communitarian journalism that treats communication and newsmaking as value-laden activities, as forms of social narrative rooted in the community, not in some atomized public (Christians, Ferre, and Fackler 1993, xii, 113, 121).

The new writers attempted to create a new community of discourse in America, a community critical of what was happening in the cinematic society. They turned newsmaking and ethnography into storytelling. As performers, they brought good and bad news to the American public and attempted to open a conversation that would bring this country back to its senses. Seeing themselves as moral compasses, the new writers used narrative in new ways to tell new stories about themselves and their relationships to American society. They argued for a new way of telling things about society. As Stephen Spender (1965) so aptly puts it, they used their life stories, their auto-ethnographies as "the dial of an Instrument that records the effects of a particular stage of civilization upon a civilized individual" (ix).

Their legacies are multiple and have yet to be built upon. Ethnography and cultural studies have not embraced, let alone learned from, the many narrative turns taken by these new writers. The preferred strategy, instead, has been to stand outside, as critics, or to take up the structural approach to narrative, learning how to dissect rather than how to write stories that make a difference in the lives of those we study.

Notes

1. If, as E. L. Doctorow asserts (quoted in Fishkin 1985, 207), there is no longer any such thing as a distinction between fiction and nonfiction, only narrative, then all narratives assemble their respective versions of fact, fiction, and truth. In this context, a fact refers to events that are believed to have occurred (Denzin 1989, 23). A facticity describes how facts were lived and experienced. A fiction is a narrative, a story that deals with real and imagined facts and facticities. Fictions are made up, fashioned out of real and imagined happenings (Clifford 1986, 6). Truth references statements that are in agreement with facts and facticities as known and commonly understood within a community of knowers (Peirce 1905). Ethnographic writings are narratives. Every work constructs its version of what is truthful and factual, what could have happened, what did happen, or what will happen here. In contrast, John Pauly (1990), drawing on Eric Heyne (1987), preserves the distinction between fictional and factual texts. Fictional texts make no claim to factual status or factual accuracy. Factual texts claim to be factual, and their facts can be checked and are subject to public debate. After making this distinction, Pauly then states that "all narratives are fictions." He conflates matters by invoking but not naming Peirce (1905), arguing that "to say a report is true is to affirm that it speaks the consensus of some actual community of interpreters. In turn, disagreements over truth signal appeals to different communities of interpretation, with their own standards of evidence, significance, and style" (122).

So truth is a social construct, and narratives about the world are judged, in Phyllis Frus's (1994) words, "according to their coherence and correspondence to a world we recognize . . . they do not correspond to the events themselves but to other narratives" (xiv).

2. For example, serious American novelists (e.g., William Faulkner, Ernest Hemingway, Scott Fitzgerald, Erle Stanley Gardner, John Updike, Bobbie Ann Mason, Philip Roth, E. L. Doctorow, Joyce Carol Oates, and Kay Boyle) write fiction, while Norman Mailer and Truman Capote (in their nonfictional novels) are not doing great literature, and the new journalists (e.g., Wolfe 1969; Talese 1972; Didion 1968; and Thompson 1967, 1973) were dismissed for writing "zippy prose about inconsequential people" (Wolfe 1973, 38; see also Pauly 1990, 113; and Frus 1994, 151–52).

3. Another form of representation, advertising, must be added to this list of postmodern discursive forms. Henry A. Giroux (1994) argues that advertising texts have "become the site of representational politics" (4). These multimedia, performance texts constantly redefine the connections between public culture, everyday life, "the politics of representation and the representation of politics," according to Giroux (5). Of course these texts, as a form of collective, public fantasy, totally disregard the issues of fact and fiction, instead stressing the emotional power of the story that is told, the emotional identification of the viewer with the issues (and personalities) at hand. We thus have real people, Larry Bird and Michael Jordan, doing imaginary things, making baskets by bouncing basketballs over highways, above tall buildings, and through narrow windows, and the winner gets the Big Mac.

4. Thus traditional journalism (in the information mode) invokes the norms of objectivity and impartiality and deploys a writing style that makes the narrator invisible, while privileging the visual and honoring brevity (Frus 1994, 58). In contrast, the new journalism emphasizes the production of compelling stories that convince readers of the truth of a situation (Eason 1984, 127). These works locate the narrator in the events being reported. There are important differences (see below) between those new journalists who work in the ethnographic realist mode and those who follow a cultural phenomenology (see Eason 1984).

5. At least three approaches to storytelling can be taken: the modernist, totalizing novel or ethnographic text that imposes a narrative (and theoretical) framework on the events being reported (note 1 above); the postmodern, nonfiction novel that refuses to impose a modernist narrative framework on the events described; and the critical approach, which attempts to unravel the ideological foundations of the narrative itself, that is, how it functions to bring order and meaning out of chaos. On this, Frank Lentricchia (1990) observes, "The storyteller's most powerful effect comes when he [she] convinces us that what is particular, integrated, and different in a cultural practice. . . . is part of a cultural plot that makes coherent sense of all cultural practices as a totality; not a totality that is there, waiting for us to acknowledge its presence, but a totality fashioned when the storyteller convinces us to see it his [her] way" (335).

6. Here Whyte is referring to and answering criticisms of his previous work (see Whyte 1992; and "Street Corner Society Revisited" 1992).

7. Another series of scandals would appear in the late 1990s (see "Why Did CNN, *Time* Push Gaseous Lies," 1998).

8. John Hollowell (1977) notes that the African American writers Malcolm X, Claude Brown, James Baldwin, and Elridge Cleaver were also taking a lead in this discourse through the use of the autobiography, the confessional, and the personal essay (12).

9. This often led to the use of the technique called compression, "combining quotations spoken at different times and different places into a single monologue" (Gross 1993, A12).

10. When did the new journalism and the writing of nonfiction texts start? Maybe it all started in 1957, the "year the Soviet Union's Sputnik shook America" (Zavarzadeh 1976, 38). It might have started in 1963, when John F. Kennedy was murdered. Or it might have started in 1968, when the political assassinations increased, ghettos went up in flames, students fought on American college campuses, an aging Hollywood idol was governor of California, and a new generation ran away from home in search of a new frontier. The novelistic drama of the Watergate hearings (1972–74) further eroded the public's confidence in what a fact was (Zavarzadeh 1976, 38). The center no longer held firm.

11. This criticism persisted, even though these writers invariably referenced public documents and the interviews they conducted. Tom Wolfe (1973) called this saturation reporting (52).

12. In Hunter S. Thompson's (1979) brand of the new journalism, the gonzo journalist is a performer, a film director, the main character in the films he writes, directs, films, and produces (120). On this point I thank Richard Bradley.

References

Agar, M. 1990. "Exploring the Excluded Middle." *Journal of Contemporary Ethnography* 19:73–88.

Agger, B. 1989. *Reading Science.* Dix Hills, N.Y.: General Hall.

Allen, R. C., ed. 1992. "Introduction to the Second Edition: More Talk about TV." In *Channels of Discourse, Reassembled,* edited by R. C. Allen, 1–30. Chapel Hill: University of North Carolina Press.

Bellamy, J. D. 1982. Introduction to *The Purple Decades: A Reader Selected by Tom Wolfe,* edited by T. Wolfe, vii–xv. New York: Farrar, Straus, Giroux.

Booth, W. C. [1961] 1983. *The Rhetoric of Fiction.* Chicago: University of Chicago Press.

Brown, R. H. 1989. *Society as Text.* Chicago: University of Chicago Press.

Carey, J. W. 1986. "The Dark Continent of American Journalism." In *Reading the News,* edited by R. K. Manoff and M. Schudson, 146–96. New York: Pantheon Books.

———. 1989. *Communication as Culture.* Boston: Unwin Hyman.

———. 1997a. "The Communications Revolution and the Professional Communicator." In *James Carey: A Critical Reader,* edited by E. S. Munson and C. A. Warren, 128–43. Minneapolis: University of Minnesota Press.

———. 1997b. "The Dark Continent of American Journalism." In *James Carey: A Critical Reader,* edited by E. S. Munson and C. A. Warren, 144–88. Minneapolis: University of Minnesota Press.

Christians, C. G., J. P. Ferre, and M. Fackler. 1993. *Good News: Social Ethics and the Press.* New York: Oxford.

Clifford, J. 1986. "Introduction: Partial Truths." In *Writing Culture,* edited by J. Clifford and G. E. Marcus, 1–26. Berkeley: University of California Press.
Connery, T. B., ed. 1992. *A Sourcebook of American Literary Journalism.* New York: Greenwood.
Denzin, N. K. 1989. *Interpretive Biography.* Newbury Park, Calif.: Sage.
———. 1995. *The Cinematic Society: The Voyeur's Gaze.* London: Sage.
Didion. J. 1968. *Slouching towards Bethlehem.* New York: Farrar.
Eason, D. 1981. "Telling Stories and Making Sense." *Journal of Popular Culture* 15:125–29.
———. 1982. "New Journalism, Metaphor and Culture." *Journal of Popular Culture* 16:142–49.
———. 1984. "The New Journalism and the Image-World: Two Modes of Organizing Experience." *Critical Studies in Mass Communication* 3:51–65.
———. 1986. "On Journalistic Authority: The Janet Cooke Scandal." *Critical Studies in Mass Communication* 3:429–47.
Ellis, C. 1995. *Final Negotiations.* Philadelphia: Temple University Press.
Feldman, M. 1994. *Interpreting Qualitative Data.* Thousand Oaks, Calif.: Sage.
"The Fiction of Truth" (editorial). 1984. *New York Times,* June 20, 13.
Fine, G. A. 1993. "Ten Lies of Ethnography." *Journal of Contemporary Ethnogaphy* 22:267–94.
Fishkin, S. F. 1985. *From Fact to Fiction: Journalism and Imaginative Writing in America.* Baltimore: Johns Hopkins University Press.
Frus, P. 1994. *The Politics and Poetics of Journalistic Narrative.* New York: Cambridge University Press.
Giroux, H. A. 1994. *Disturbing Pleasures.* New York: Routledge.
Gross, J. 1993. "In New Yorker Libel Trial the Analyst Is Examined." *New York Times,* May 11, A12.
Hay, J. 1992. "Afterword." In *Channels of Discourse, Reassembled,* edited by R. C. Allen, 354–85. Chapel Hill: University of North Carolina Press.
Hersey, J. 1980. "The Legend on the License." *Yale Review* 70:1–25.
Heyne, E. 1987. "Toward a Theory of Literary Nonfiction." *Modern Fiction Studies* 33:479–90.
Hollowell, J. 1977. *Fact and Fiction: The New Journalism and the Nonfiction Novel.* Chapel Hill: University of North Carolina Press.
Kunda, G. 1993. "Writing about Reading" [Review of *Reading Ethnographic Research,* by Martyn Hammersley, and *Reading Ethnography,* by David Johnson]. *Contemporary Sociology* 22:13–15.
Lentricchia, F. 1990. "In Place of an Afterword—Someone Reading." In *Critical Terms for Literary Study,* edited by F. Lentricchia and T. McLaughlin, 321–38. Chicago: University of Chicago Press.
Mailer, N. 1966. *The Armies of the Night: History as a Novel, the Novel as History.* New York: New American Library.
———. 1979. *The Executioner's Song: A True Life Novel.* New York: Warner Books.
Manning, P. K., and B. Cullum-Swan. 1994. "Narrative, Content, and Semiotic Analysis." In *The Handbook of Qualitative Research,* edited by N. K. Denzin and Y. S. Lincoln, 463–77. Newbury Park, Calif.: Sage.
Marcus, G., and Fischer, M. 1986. *Anthropology as Cultural Critique.* Chicago: University of Chicago Press.

Mitchell, R. G., Jr., and K. Charmaz. 1995. "Telling Tales, Writing Stories." *Journal of Contemporary Ethnography* 24:144–66.

Morris, M. 1990. "Banality in Cultural Studies." In *Logics of Television: Essays in Cultural Criticism,* edited by P. Mellencamp, 14–43. Bloomington: Indiana University Press.

Pauly, J. J. 1990. "The Politics of the New Journalism." In *Literary Journalism in the Twentieth Century,* edited by N. Sims, 110–29. New York: Oxford University Press.

Peirce, C. S. 1905. "What Pragmatism Is." *Monist* 15 (April): 161–81.

Polkinghorne, D. E. 1988. *Narrative Knowing in the Human Sciences.* Albany: State University of New York Press.

Richardson, L. 1994. "Writing as a Method of Inquiry." In *The Handbook of Qualitative Research,* edited by N. K. Denzin and Y. S. Lincoln, 516–29. Newbury Park, Calif.: Sage.

Riessman, C. K. 1993. *Narrative Analysis.* Newbury Park, Calif.: Sage.

Sheehy, G. 1973. *Hustling: Prostitution in Our Wide-Open Society.* New York: Dell Books.

Sims, N., ed. 1984. *The Literary Journalists.* New York: Ballantine Books.

———. 1990. *Literary Journalism in the Twentieth Century.* New York: Oxford University Press.

Snow, D., and C. Morrill. 1993. "Reflections on Anthropology's Ethnographic Crisis of Faith" [Review of *Culture and Anomie* by Christopher Herbert, *The Savage Witches* by Henrika Kuklick, *Romantic Motives* by George Stocking Jr., and *Colonial Situations* by George Stocking Jr.]. *Contemporary Sociology* 22:8–11.

———. 1995. "A Revolution?" [Review of *Handbook of Qualitative Research,* edited by Norman K. Denzin and Yvonna S. Lincoln]. *Journal of Contemporary Ethnography* 22:341–49.

Spender, S. 1965. Introduction to *Under the Volcano,* by Malcolm Lowry, vii–xxvi. New York: J. B. Lippincott.

"Street Corner Society Revisited." 1992. *Journal of Contemporary Ethnography,* special issue, 21 (1).

Talese, G. 1972. *Honor Thy Father.* New York: Fawcett.

Thompson, H. S. 1967. *Hell's Angels: A Strange and Terrible Saga.* New York: Ballantine.

———. 1973. *Fear and Loathing: On the Campaign Trail of '72.* San Francisco: Straight Arrow.

———. 1979. *The Great Shark Hunt.* New York: Summit Books.

Trinh, T. M. 1989. *Woman, Native, Other: Writing Postcoloniality and Feminism.* Bloomington: Indiana University Press.

Tyler, S. A. 1986. "Post-Modern Ethnography: From Document of the Occult to Occult Document." In *Writing Culture,* edited by J. Clifford and G. E. Marcus, 122–40. Berkeley: University of California Press.

Updike, J. 1995. "Hopper's Polluted Silence." *New York Review of Books,* August 10, 19–21.

Van Maanen, J. 1988. *Tales of the Field.* Chicago: University of Chicago Press.

White, H. V. 1973. *Metahistory.* Baltimore: Johns Hopkins University Press.

"Why Did CNN, *Time* Push Gaseous Lies." 1998. *Media Watch,* July 13, 1.

Whyte, W. F. 1992. "In Defense of *Street Corner Society.*" *Journal of Contemporary Ethnography* 21:52–68.

———. 1993. *Street Corner Society: The Social Structure of an Italian Slum.* 4th ed. Chicago: University of Chicago Press.

Wolfe, T. 1969. *The Electric Kool-Aid Acid Test.* New York: Bantam.

———. 1973. "The New Journalism." In *The New Journalism: An Anthology,* edited by T. Wolfe and E. W. Johnson, 3–52. New York: Harper and Row.

Zavarzadeh, M. 1976. *The Mythopoetic Reality: The Postwar American Nonfiction Novel.* Urbana: University of Illinois Press.

LANA RAKOW

8 The Return to Community in Cultural Studies

This essay contains a dual argument. The first argument is that U.S. cultural studies scholars need to turn their attention to the concept of community in a sustained and self-reflective way, setting aside preconceived notions of the history of community in the United States while challenging the ways that it has become acceptable to use the concept in our field. The second argument is that cultural studies scholars themselves need to return to their communities, to bring their intellectual work to the table in the nonacademic localities in which they live.

Why do we need this return to community? Cultural studies scholars in communication succeeded in recent years in turning our attention to questions of content and meaning, questions whose ideological implications had been ignored or explained away by most of the rest of the field. As important as this shift has been, the results have not been as productive as one might have expected. We have reached a political stalemate. We have been done in by our own awareness of the contradictions and complexities of explaining the coercive effects of dominant ideologies in the face of the human capacity for creativity and resistance. Rather than focus our attention on the next great question, "What should be done?" we have faltered over the question, "Do we have a right to do anything?"

Aside from Marxism and American pragmatism, cultural studies has been bereft of alternative social theories (though not social critiques) that can point the past and present into a preferred future course of action. Feminism, for all its insights into what is wrong with American culture, has not been able to produce a coherent alternative, in part because we are continuously sidetracked by a cultural studies agenda we have not set (for example, debates over the virility and paternity of cultural studies reflected in some of these essays) and in part because of the consequences of a selection process whereby certain feminists and feminist work are legitimated and allowed into the accepted self-referential cultural studies canon.

Those who propose any course of action soon realize how fraught with political and theoretical pitfalls any proposal is, as someone is always quick to point out. In the midst of our debates about the postmodern fragmentation of the self and our social narratives, and the feminist recognition of the dangers of universalizing experience and totalizing solutions, we are leery of any course of action save critique—not only critique of cultural phenomena but also critiques of one another's critiques. However, we cannot afford this luxury of debate any longer. The world is being made and remade—to all of our detriment—while we are arguing on the sidelines. Despite the important efforts of some individual scholars and strands of scholarship to engage in these larger issues of structure and processes, the usefulness of cultural studies to the project of change to produce a better world for all inhabitants, which I believe is its purpose, can be accomplished only by a concerted shift of our attention. We should not and cannot ignore the meanings to be found in cultural phenomena and their significance to people's identities and cultural membership, but we need to turn our attention to envisioning new cultural and political models for how we might live together in ways that meet people's material and emotional needs, equitably, justly, and in balance with the physical world.

I am not proposing that we create a new grand narrative or an ultimate solution. I am proposing that we develop potential models of communication processes that do not propose a particular kind of cultural content but rather identify the principles that will enable all people to interact, enjoy full rights of participation, and use communication technologies for the purpose of creating their own collective destinies. Without the identification of such principles, we cannot make judgments about what we should be advocating. As scholars of communication, we have not only the opportunity to provide this kind of intellectual leadership but also the responsibility.

Having made an argument that we need to turn our attention to creating new models, I now want to make an argument that the concept and experience of community should be at the center of our models. I realize that by raising the banner of community I may be dismissed by my Marxist colleagues as a naive holdover from the Chicago School and by my urban colleagues as a hopeless romantic for a bucolic paradise that never existed. Some of my feminist friends may worry that I am charting a course that will lead to women's return to the kitchen. I hope I am guilty of none of these. Instead, I believe I am proposing that we take the historic and contemporary American quest for community seriously.

The history of the concept of community in the social sciences is an uneven one. The Chicago School succeeded in the first few decades of the century in turning the attention of sociologists to community, trying to explain and chart a path for the social transformation caused by the migration and immigration they were witnessing, and culminating in an impressive collection of community studies in the 1920s. Functionalist social scientists knocked down their own "straw man" of a mass society by providing reassurance that, despite social dislocation, individuals were still embedded in networks of relationships that would provide social stability and keep the population governable. By the 1960s, sociologists had abandoned the concept of community because of its association with a conservative functionalism. Now we see a resurgence of interest in the concept of community among sociologists, because, in the words of Graham Day and Jonathan Murdoch (1993), "'community' is a concept that just will not lie down" (83).

This is not the case in cultural studies in communication. Some communication scholars have kept the interest in community alive (see Tichenor, Donohue, and Olien 1977; Christians, Schultze, and Sims 1978; and Schulman 1992), but the primary means by which community has been enjoined by cultural studies scholars in recent years has been through the notion of "interpretive communities" (see Nightingale 1986), a corollary to the cultural studies preoccupation with media content rather than with the range of structures and processes of social life. Interpretive communities refer to those members of audiences who share similar textual meanings by virtue of their social identities and location. Little discussion has taken place of the consequences of this shift in our thinking about the nature of communities because the concept of community itself seems to hold little interest for cultural studies scholars.

This lack of interest is a by-product of the way in which the concept of community was employed in the social sciences, which produced a received history of concern about community that makes any attempt to resurrect it suspect. This history is known as the "myth of the loss of community," exemplified by the progressives associated with the Chicago School, the myth itself immortalized by Robert Nisbet's book *The Quest for Community* (1953), and the source of the myth immortalized by Jean Quandt's book *From the Small Town to the Great Community* (1970). Current communitarian thinkers are criticized for the same unrealistic nostalgia for community. The philosopher Jean-Luc Nancy claims that the concept of community is suspicious because loss of community has always been a feature of the West, and therefore loss is constitutive of the concept of community itself (Bernasconi 1993, 4).

Is the contemporary American concern over community no more than a continuing nostalgia for something it never had, a golden age that never existed? Is the concept so fraught with theoretical pitfalls regarding the individual versus society, rural versus urban preferences, and the potentially conservative nature of a collective enterprise that community is not worth pursuing at all?

The answer lies in an alternative deconstruction of the concept that relies not on the received history of nostalgia but on the lived and contradictory experiences of people. If we attempt to reconstruct a new history of community in the United States—one that accounts for the experiences of women and all social groups, not simply middle-class, European American men—we will find that it is far more complex than the received history acknowledges. This new history would be a history of communities destroyed, created, and sacrificed for. It is a history of a struggle over place, identity, and political voice. It is a history that would help us account for the resonance of the term *community* for gays and lesbians, African Americans, Native Americans, and feminists and for the telling search for connectedness—for a "virtual community"—by white, middle-class professionals via the Internet (Schwartz 1995). Our accounting for the diversity of experiences and alternative conceptions of the concept of community should give us new ideas for models that break out of the tired dualisms that prevent us from moving ahead. Had Robert Bellah and his research group (1985), for example, looked beyond white, middle-class Americans, they might not have placed the primary tension of American society between private interest and public good. They argue, "These [middle] classes have traditionally provided the active public participation that makes free institutions work. In addition, the middle classes have been peculiarly central in American society" (iv). That they could so unabashedly justify their near exclusion of class and ethnic diversity is a telling indicator of their acceptance of the power structure of society and the reproduction of an ideological take on community that sheds little new light on a pressing social issue.

If nothing else, we cannot abandon the concept of community because at this moment in history the stakes are so very high. Racial and ethnic minority women and men and white women are being blamed for loss of both community and the virtues of care-giving, the rise of government spending and bureaucracy, the so-called balkanization of society, and a selfish clamoring for individual rights over collective responsibility. Cuts in government spending are placing economic and care-giving burdens on individuals, families, and locales in the name of community values at the same time that reversals in government policy on affirmative action and welfare requirements reduce their access to financial and political capital. Clearly, others are hard at work crafting a new social order. Scholars must propose new understandings of communities and articulate guidelines for social practices based on ethical principles of communication or prove ourselves once again irrelevant to the major issues of society.

Our efforts must take us beyond the current liberal-communitarian debate, as Elizabeth Frazer and Nicola Lacey (1993) so cogently argue. Liberalism, which begins from the standpoint of the autonomous individual, is unsatisfactory, particularly to feminists, because the individual subject must be conceived of as masculine by denying dependency or relational obligations (Haber 1991, 106). The private or personal cannot be an area of freedom for women because, as feminists proclaimed with the insight that had escaped everyone else, "The personal is political." The personal is where our gender identities are produced and reproduced (Frazer and Lacey 1993, 33) and where the structure of society is reproduced by the labor of subordinated economic and cultural classes. Those who would try to reconstruct a public sphere must recognize that a public sphere is built on the backs of those who are denied or have limited access to the only arena in which the very subject of their condition can be discussed and revealed. While communitarianism holds an attraction for feminists and others, current communitarian theory neglects a discussion of power, appealing to tradition and leaving institutions uncritiqued (Frazer and Lacey 1993). Although framed as a response to the individualism of liberal theory, it retains many of liberalism's features by failing to deconstruct the nature of the family, gendered identities, division of labor, and the economic. We have to construct alternatives that move beyond the debates of public and private.

Let me begin with a modest contribution to this undertaking by revealing some of the history of community in a U.S. context that I hope will contribute to laying to rest the received myth of the loss of community once and for all. Then let me suggest several elements from this history that will help us construct new definitions and models of communities that are not exclusively white, male, and middle class and that will help us construct new communities based on ethical principles of communication rather than on principles of individualism and competition.

A New History of Community

A new history of community in the United States would have to abandon a linear notion of change produced by small towns eclipsed by the migration to large cities. The history of the Native American experience of loss of community shows an important deviation from this explanation. Even though indigenous peoples had had centuries of successful communal life, the U.S. government refused to acknowledge their ordered and sophisticated social lives and implemented a policy that led to near genocide and eventual resettlement of remaining tribes onto reservations (see Bruchac 1993). In 1955, the American Indian Voluntary Relocation Program attempted to end reservations and treaty agreements by scattering Native Americans around the country (Willard 1994, 93).

Contrary to the perceptions of the invading European Americans, indigenous Americans saw humans as part of a natural world of communities, communities made up of extended families, unlike the European concept of a city of people who are strangers to one another and came together only in defiance of nature. Native communities lived in balance with the natural world:

> Among the native peoples of the Americas, therefore, community is not separate from nature, and the idea that the city is an "unnatural" place is a foreign concept. All cities feel nature, but the European city has most often tried to ignore it, fight against it, or miniaturize it into the manageable form of the city park or garden. The Native view is radically different in that the natural world is seen to include humans. It exists in terms of communities—of human people, animal people, plant people, and so on. Everything is alive, sentient, and ordered. (Bruchac 1993, 38)

The uprootedness from a physical connection with a particular part of the natural world and the destruction of social tradition have made the rebuilding of community on reservations a fragile undertaking, undermined by years of interference from the Bureau of Indian Affairs. Off the reservation, urban Indians have created their own communication systems and networks of people to, in William Willard's (1994) words, "prevent people from sliding off into the abyss of urban anomie" (96). The systematic destruction of indigenous communities and the efforts by Native Americans to retain and rebuild traditional relationships should add a significant new dimension to our understanding of American experiences and conceptions of community.

The history of community for African Americans must, too, account for the forced removal of Africans from their indigenous communities and the systematic policy in the United States of separating tribal members and families to prevent rebellion. The loss of a common language and culture did not prevent Africans from re-creating community as best they could, through the one social institution they were permitted—the church. According to Jack Daniel and Geneva Smitherman (1976), "The Traditional Black Church is both a sacred and secular community" that preserves black culture and communication processes (27). The church is both a symbol of and a mechanism for participation in the community. They argue that in the traditional African worldview, "[c]ommunities are modeled after the interdependent rhythms of the universe. Individual participation is necessary for individual survival. Balance in the community, as in the universe, consists of maintaining these interdependent relationships" (33).

This notion of community is embodied in the call-response communication pattern of the church, which places emphasis on commonality and the collective common good rather than on individuality. In secular culture, these same values still permit the individual to develop her or his own skilled signatures on communication practices, such as rapping, within the context of the community setting that calls for group cohesiveness.

Maintaining the black community has not been and is not easy, particularly with the dislocations caused by the migration of African Americans to the industrial north at the end of the last century that separated families and friends from the common culture of the rural south. American mass culture threatens to further erode the stories and histories of specific cultures and to replace racial and ethnic difference with a promise for equality based on consumption. By perpetuating such standards as beauty and femininity based on a presumption of whiteness, mass culture, as Jane Kuenz (1993) points out, "co-opts and transforms a history of communal and familial relationships it cannot otherwise accommodate" (424).

Michelle Wallace (1992) adds that the myth of a national black identity or black community needs to be demystified. Writing after the Anita Hill–Clarence Thomas hearings, she observed, "I share with [Anita] Hill and with all other black women the negative 'community' and negative 'identity' of being a silenced black female subject in a world in which we continue to be represented only as objects" (36). Hill "has begun to learn the one thing that unites us as a conceptual 'community,' which we might call the black feminist community." Membership in communities of race, gender, class, or sexuality cannot fully account for differences among black women. "What often has joined people together—forming perhaps the most powerful sense of community—has been the need to be heard" (37). Wallace is suggesting that community membership cannot occur on the basis of shared identity alone but also must include a shared meaning system about that identity. African American communities therefore must be seen as both remnants of a shared cultural tradition and the products of and response to a disempowering context of racism and sexism.

The role of women in creating community, particularly working-class and rural women, must be factored into our new history of community of the United States. The unpaid work of women, usually seen as an extension of their responsibilities for family and care-giving, in Mary Pardo's (1991) words, "creates community and the conditions necessary for life" (39).

Pardo's (1991) research on the role of Mexican American women in creating community documents their activist efforts, in the name of their children and families, to challenge and rebuild community institutions. They had a significant impact on improving the quality of life in their communities. The women expressed a sense of belonging to the community and to their families; conversely, they perceive their families and their communities as belonging to them. Their activities and their life stories support a strong notion of integration and membership in the larger community. The neighborhood constituted the immediate physical and social space for the family, and the women devised ways to influence its formation with limited resources (66).

Rural European American women perform a similar community-building role by extending their work for their families to the well-being of their towns, according to my own research, but without the racism and alienation from the economic system that makes other women resist oppressive institutional structures. In the community of Prospect (a pseudonym), a midwestern town of fewer than a thousand residents, women inherited most of the public spaces and institutions as men in the face of a changing national economy took up employment opportunities in neighboring cities. Through church, school, social organizations, and their own businesses, women provide the work—mostly unpaid—of holding together family networks and preserving a sense of community in the face of external pressures that threaten its economic and social viability (Rakow 1992).

The story of rural communities resisting their demise is another untold portion of the history of community in the United States. My research in another rural community, Crosby, North Dakota (not a pseudonym), revealed that, despite a strong sense of community among its residents, who feel as if they belong, who look after each other, and who "know what everybody knows," this community holds something in common with many contemporary communities across rural America. As I shared with its residents in a guest column in the weekly newspaper:

> But a cloud hangs over Crosby's future which everyone knows about. It's the threat to the community brought by a declining economic base and declining population. Young people leave because they do not have job opportunities in the area. Businesses close or fall into a spiritless downward cycle. The elementary school will soon experience the projected enrollment short-fall. The fate of surrounding small towns is a constant reminder that population decline can be fatal to a community. Though Crosby has endured in large part because it is the county seat and has the county's school system, can it survive in the long run? (Rakow 1995, 2)

Crosby, like some other rural communities, is trying to design a strategy to counter the forces that pull people away, but theirs is a difficult task, first, because they are up against such large and powerful national forces that long ago deprived small towns of their economic, political, and social autonomy, and second, because, like most European American communities, they do not have a process or a model for working together in such an activist fashion. Their dilemma is not unique. Loss of community is a real threat to many rural residents in the country because of a national communication, transportation, and economic system designed to favor urban areas at the expense of rural areas. The "myth of the loss of community" from our received history of community in the United States does not account for the real and impending losses that trouble rural communities in the present.

Not all residents of all communities find the sense of acceptance and shared meaning that characterizes some of the communities I have discussed. I already have pointed out some of the difficulties faced by African American women, for whom community and identity are more problematic than has been assumed. European American women, especially middle-class and urban women, have found that their communities can be stifling, restrictive, or, in the case of suburban women, perhaps nonexistent. For some of these women, alternative meanings about gender must be sought outside of their local communities to provide the kind of acceptance and sense of positive identity they seek. Linda Steiner (1983) argues that women's nineteenth-century newspapers and journals provided a new kind of community with other "like-minded" women in other parts of the country. In these publications, "women evolved intellectually and emotionally satisfying communal models for acting, thinking, judging, and feeling" (12).

Gays and lesbians often have had to look to new sources of community to find acceptance and a positive identity. As John Preston (1991) observes about gay men, they typically do not understand their identity until later in life, at which time they may feel they have to deny their gay identity or escape into the anonymity of urban life: "He had to hide his social and sexual proclivities, or else he had to give up communal life in pursuit of them" (xii). In the past few decades gays and lesbians have created their own communities in population centers, but the sense of a community lost is leading many back to the places where they were born, if not to live there, at least to come to terms with the loss (xiii).

Critical Characteristics of a New Social Model

This brief introduction to some of the diversity of experiences of community—communities built, destroyed, denied, reclaimed—should serve as a corrective to any simplistic accounting of a history of community in the United States. At the least, we can conclude that preserving or finding community is a strong desire for Americans of all kinds. But desire is not sufficient, and the outcome is not always satisfactory. Despite those successful attempts of creating or rebuilding community to which we can point, we remain a country of groups with disparate access to material resources, political power, and the sustenance of supportive social relationships.

A new social model with communities at its center would help provide a vision of how we might organize ourselves to produce the human, economic, and political relationships for a healthy and equitable society. Such a model should account for at least three factors that emerge from the beginnings sketched above of a new history of community in the United States: place, identity, and voice.

Social scientists who have downplayed the loss of place-bound communities by a migratory population point to the other forms of association—networks or "communities without propinquity" (Webber 1963)—as equally satisfying to the need for human connectedness, as do many who extol the virtues of a "virtual community" made possible by computer networking. Despite the assurances that any kind of human connection is equivalent to any other, the importance of a shared physical place for a primary community should not be ignored.

The lesson from indigenous cultures is that balance between the human community and the physical environment is critical for a universe in harmony. That European Americans have neglected such a balance is painfully obvious to those with an environmental conscience. As Native Americans observed about European American cities, these cities tried to defy nature. But Native American architecture corresponded to the natural world (Bruchac 1993, 37). As Black Elk said about the cities of the European Americans, "I could see that the wasichus [Lakota word for European American which means 'those who take all the fat for themselves'] did not care for each other the way my people did before the nation's hoop was broken. They would take everything from each other if they could, and so there were some who had more of everything than they could use, while crowds of people had nothing at all and maybe were starving. They had forgotten that the earth was their mother" (quoted in Bruchac 1993, 37). As this passage suggests, members of communities can and should take care of one another's physical and spiritual needs. Those who would suggest that social networks across distances are equivalent to those in a shared geographic locale neglect the need to integrate human activity with its natural environment, which can occur only when people share responsibility for the locale they inhabit, focusing their attention on their current environment.

Another reason for the importance of place to community is that we have to account for the amount of physical labor and attention human beings require, which primarily women provide for children, men, the sick, elderly, and disabled. Women have not been allowed to disengage from their bodies or their babies, which should make us all the more suspicious of an "information superhighway" populated by lone male cruisers escaping from the mundane world of the physical. Working-class women and women of color have drawn on the support system of other women in their local communities to share resources and care-giving, a sharing that is necessary for survival (Naples 1992). Patricia Hill Collins refers to the "community othermothers" of the black community, who, as part of the extended kinship networks, contribute to community development (described by Naples 1992, 443). In contrast, middle-class European American women have found their suburban care-giving a solitary and family-focused activity made more difficult by the distances across which their mothering must take place, a phenomenon Vija Navarro and I have called "remote mothering" (Rakow and Navarro 1993).

In addition to accounting for the community's relationship with the environment, then, any social theory of community needs to account for the physical care-giving required by children and adults and the physical support systems of neighbors and kin that individuals and families need, which require strong human relationships and commitment in a shared location. Without this context, we cannot envision a system of care-giving that does not exploit women and that spreads care-giving responsibilities across genders and generations.

But a shared location is not a sufficient prerequisite for community. It is certainly possible to live in a locale with others and not have a sense of community, as many mobile professionals and academics can attest. John McKnight (1992) describes how he discovered that people with developmental disabilities who were taken out of institutions and placed into communities were not in fact members of those communities. They could only be said to be living in the communities and receiving community services, but none of them had friends or knew their neighbors or belonged to any organization. McKnight concludes, "Indeed, the common life of North America is so segregated that the absence of experience with those who are excluded has led many citizens to imagine that labeled people are somehow inappropriate for community life" (57).

The experience of some people labeled as developmentally disabled parallels the difficulties faced by gays and lesbians and politically conscious women, illustrating that it is necessary to be accepted and valued by other members of a community on one's own terms. Again we can look to the principles of community valued by indigenous peoples—Native Americans and Africans—that value and acknowledge the interrelationships among all humans and all things, the balance required to sustain and support differences among individuals. In such communities as these, identity is not problematic. It is only when we have competing identities from which to choose and some identities are devalued or exploited by other members of the community that identities become problematic, as they are in a U.S. context.

Finally, our new social models of community must account for the need for voice—the ability to speak and to be heard, to be a fully participating member of a linguistic community within which the power to name is shared among all its members. Voice for each member within a community would take care of issues of identity and justice and distribution of power. Voice for each member within a community would produce healthy processes for the discussion and debate necessary for directing the community's destiny.

But communities also need a voice if their healthy existence is to be ensured in any larger social and economic order or collection of communities. The experience of Native Americans whose communities were destroyed and the experience of European American rural towns indicates that certain communities have been victimized by more powerful external forces. As members of communities need voice for equitable participation, a community needs the capacity for collective expression of its needs and interests while hearing similar expressions from other communities. Communities without the economic and linguistic resources for self-determination and without an equitable relationship with other communities are communities in danger of exploitation or extinction.

Communication technologies could be instrumental for achieving these ideals of intra- and inter-community voice, but not as they are currently designed, controlled, and used. They would have to be put to the use of communities for the purpose of sharing stories, experiences, and information among community members and between communities rather than to the use of corporate enterprises for the purpose of making money. We would need to stop asking, "What do the media do to people" and "What do people do with the media," and ask instead, "What could the media do for communities?"

Conclusions

My argument has been that we need to return to the concept of community in cultural studies if we are to address the central issues that face contemporary U.S. culture. An overreliance on the definitions and experiences of white men shaped the debate about community within and outside the academy during the twentieth century. The values and experiences of people of color, white women, and other groups struggling to change, preserve, or create communities of identity and geography can serve as a corrective to the terms of the debate. We need new models of community for a society torn apart by economic disparities, sexism, racism, homophobia, and nativism. We need to take seriously the various feelings of loss, anger, alienation, and lack of a transcendent meaning that have accompanied communities destroyed, left beyond, or undermined by more powerful economic and political forces. We need to uncover the transferable principles at work in successful communities and put to work by successful community activists and builders. The result could be a new social order, based on participation and built from the ground up.

Critics of this argument may well point to my own nostalgia for community that threatens to canonize different categories of community with the same uncritical acceptance that plagued American pragmatism. I trust that additional work on this new and needed history of community will correct any tendencies to mysticism and overgeneralization produced by these brief references to specific community experiences. We need to ask, in searching for helpful models of community, "Did it work? For whom? For whom didn't it work?"

Others will be concerned about what they might see as my attempt to prescribe or to advocate the prescription of a social order. But we already live within and struggle over and against prescriptions for the social order. As communication theorists, we can make a contribution that goes beyond understanding the meaning of the struggles to suggesting the principles that may be most useful for us to pursue collectively. That means coming to grips with our values as an academic enterprise. We cannot hide behind the safety of relativism, which is a corollary to journalistic and social scientific objectivity by virtue of its unwillingness to take responsibility for the political consequences of all positions, including, by default, support of the status quo.

My argument goes beyond the need to return to the concept of community. We need to return to our communities as cultural studies scholars. If we are to deal intellectually with issues of identity, difference, and community, we must look to our own segregation and difference from our nonacademic communities of place. I am not suggesting we should become community activists who start domestic violence shelters. I am suggesting we need to figure out how to integrate our intellectual work with the other kinds of work performed by other members of our communities. Our intellectual work is what we have to bring to the table; it is our contribution to the communal enterprise. Many have decried the separation of the academic from public debate. Certainly our communities (such as they are) have been the worse because of the absence of the historical and theoretical perspective that we could have provided. I propose that we not only reinvent the role of community in modern life but also reinvent our own role in modern life—through a return to community.

References

Bellah, R. N., R. Madsen, W. M. Sullivan, A. Swidler, and S. M. Tipton. 1985. *Habits of the Heart: Individualism and Commitment in American Life.* Berkeley: University of California Press.

Bernasconi, R. 1993. "On Deconstructing Nostalgia for Community within the West: The Debate between Nancy and Blanchot." *Research in Phenomenology* 23:3–21.

Bruchac, J. 1993. "The Families Gathered Together." *Parabola* 18 (4): 36–29.

Christians, C. G., Q. J. Schultze, and N. H. Sims. 1978. "Community, Epistemology, and Mass Media Ethics." *Journalism History* 5 (2): 38–41.

Daniel, J. L., and G. Smitherman. 1976. "How I Got Over: Communication Dynamics in the Black Community." *Quarterly Journal of Speech* 62:26–39.

Day, G., and J. Murdoch. 1993. "Locality and Community: Coming to Terms with Place." *Sociological Review* 41 (1): 82–111.

Frazer, E., and N. Lacey. 1993. *The Politics of Community: A Feminist Critique of the Liberal-Communitarian Debate.* Toronto: University of Toronto Press.

Haber, H. F. 1991. *Beyond Postmodern Politics: Lyotard, Rorty, Foucault.* New York: Routledge.

Kuenz, J. 1993. "'The Bluest Eye': Notes on History, Community, and Black Female Subjectivity." *African American Review* 27 (3): 421–32.

McKnight, J. L. 1992. "Redefining Community." *Social Policy* 23 (2): 56–62.

Naples, N. A. 1992. "Activist Mothering: Cross-Generational Continuity in the Community Work of Women from Low-Income Urban Neighborhoods." *Gender and Society* 6 (3): 441–63.

Nightingale, V. 1986. "Community as Audience—Audience as Community." *Australian Journal of Communication* 9 and 10:31–41.

Nisbet, R. 1953. *The Quest for Community.* New York: Oxford University Press.

Pardo, M. 1991. "Creating Community: Mexican American Women in Eastside Los Angeles." *Aztlan: A Journal of Chicano Studies* 20 (1 and 2): 39–72.

Preston, J., ed. 1991. *Hometowns: Gay Men Write about Where They Belong.* New York: Penguin Books.

Quandt, J. B. 1970. *From the Small Town to the Great Community: The Social Thought of Progressive Intellectuals.* New Brunswick, N.J.: Rutgers University Press.

Rakow, L. F. 1992. *Gender on the Line: Women, the Telephone, and Community Life.* Urbana: University of Illinois Press.

———. 1995. "Crosby Has Many Strengths but Needs a Common Vision." *Divide County Journal* 2 (August 2): 2.

Rakow, L. F., and V. Navarro. 1993. "Remote Mothering and the Parallel Shift." *Critical Studies in Mass Communication* 10:144–57.

Schulman, M. 1992. "Communications in the Community: Critical Scholarship in an Emerging Field." In *Democratic Communications in the Information Age,* edited by J. Wasko and V. Mosco, 28–41. Norwood, N.J.: Ablex.

Schwartz, E. 1995. "Looking for Community on the Internet." *National Civic Review* 84 (1): 37–41.

Steiner, L. 1983. "Finding Community in Nineteenth Century Suffrage Periodicals." *American Journalism* 1 (1): 1–15.

Tichenor, P. J., G. A. Donohue, and C. N. Olien. 1977. "Community Research and Evaluating Community Relations." *Public Relations Review* 3 (4): 96–109.

Wallace, M. 1992. "Whose Town? Questioning Community and Identity." *Aperture* 8 (Spring): 30–40.

Webber, M. M. 1963. "Order in Diversity: Community without Propinquity." In *Cities and Space: The Future Use of Urban Land,* edited by L. Wingo Jr., 23–56. Baltimore: Johns Hopkins Press.

Willard, W. 1994. "Indian Newspapers, or 'Say, Ain't You Some Kind of Indian?'" *Wicazo Sa Review* 10 (2): 91–97.

CLIFFORD G. CHRISTIANS

9 The Status of Moral Claims in American Cultural Studies

What is the status of moral claims in American cultural studies? From the Chicago School's commitment to Jane Addams's Hull-House through James Carey's work today, it is highly moralistic. Its notion of public life presumes a common discourse through value-laden language. What is the logic and rationale for moral knowledge from a cultural perspective? This essay pays tribute to narrative ethics over classical rationalism. But in terms of philosophy as a whole, to situate moral agents discursively is not as compelling as embracing an ethics of being. My argument puts the hand of death on rationalistic ethics, does a ritual dance with the contextual values of American cultural studies, and then contends for an ethics of being as an alternative to both.[1]

Ethics of Rationalism

In his *Meditations on First Philosophy* (1641), Descartes seeks an absolute proof that I exist. How can I distinguish the real from illusion? Is my nightmare or daily routine the reality? I fall asleep and dream of an igloo at high noon. I wake up, and it is a dark night in Champaign, Illinois. Presuming the most strenuous tests of skepticism, I must still perceive in either case. Whether dreaming appearances or negotiating the everyday world, my mind is necessary. My capacity to think is therefore indubitable, even if I doubt everything. *Cogito, Ergo Sum*—I think, therefore I am. The mind split off from the body. Disinterested pursuit of truth. Foundationalism where no power circulates. Humans as rational beings.

As the eighteenth century heated up around Cartesian rationality, Immanuel Kant (1724–1804) was schooled in Descartes, mathematics, and Newtonian science. In his early years as lecturer in Königsberg, he taught logic, physics, and mathematics. In 1755, his first major book, *Universal History of Nature and Theory of the Heavens,* explained the structure of the universe exclusively in terms of Newtonian cosmology. What is called the Kant-Laplace theory of the origin of the universe is based on it.

Then, in the *Critique of Practical Reason* (1788) and *Groundwork of the Metaphysic of Morals* (1785), Kant assimilated ethics to logic. He demanded that moral laws be universally applicable and free from inner contradiction. Society was presumed to have a fundamental moral structure embedded in human nature as basic as atoms in physics, with the moral law the analog of the unchanging laws of gravity. Through the mental calculus of willing my action to be universalized, imperatives emerge unconditioned by circumstances. I wish for everybody to keep their promises, and through this formal test, moral absolutes are identified precisely in the rational way syllogisms are divided into valid and invalid.

The modernist project is based on the belief that only through human reason can autonomous agents attain reliable knowledge to live well and die happy. In a context-free rationality, moral principles are derived from the essential structure of a disembodied reason. This is a correspondence view of truth, with an extremely narrow definition of what counts as morality. Instead of prizing care and reciprocity, for example, our moral understanding becomes prescriptivist, arid, and absolutist.

For ethical rationalists, the truth of all legitimate claims about moral obligation can be settled by formally examining their logical structure. Consistency requires that moral agents apply rules always and everywhere the same. Humans act against moral obligations only if they are willing to endure the illogic of self-contradiction. Modernity's confidence in the power of reason combines with the ancient emphasis on reason's universality to create ethical principles that are the same for all thinking subjects, every nation, all epochs, and every culture.

Narrative Ethics

Pragmatism and the symbolic interactionists turned the ethics of rationalism on its head. They contradicted the metaphysical foundations on which the Western canon was based. They worked from the inside out, from the backyard and the grass roots. Social constructions replaced formal law systems. Moral values were now situated in the cultural context rather than anchored by metaphysical abstractions. The moral life developed through community formation, not in essentialist sanctums of isolated individuals. Contextual values replaced ethical absolutes.

Cultural theory is decisively value-centered. Values and signification are the culturalist's stock in trade. If cultures are sets of symbols that organize life and provide it significance, then particular cultures are inherently normative. The distinctive quality of our knowledge is model-building, and in the process of constructing reality, our symbolic forms direct the ends of social practice and provide implicit standards for selecting courses of action. The only legitimate debate is over the character of valuation and our choice of the supremely valued, not whether values exist somewhere beyond facticity. Instead of an escapist value-neutrality, cultural studies promotes particular ideals (just allocation of resources, gender inclusiveness, nonpaternalism, for example).

In John Dewey's *Human Nature and Conduct* ([1922] 1948), our task in ethics is understanding those problem situations where we distinguish good conduct from bad. Conflict and a tangle of incompatible impulses prompt us to ask the question, "What is good?" These are the clues we need for a conception of values that is nonfoundational. Goodness and badness are not objective properties of things themselves (cf. Dewey 1929). But as Hume argued, values cannot be mere sentiment either. In our value judgments, we say something that we believe is true about the world and do not merely express subjective attitudes.

Thus Dewey's contextualism challenges both metaphysics and emotivism as possible homes for values. He is not seeking an ultimate normative standard but is investigating the social conditions under which we consider our assertions warranted. For Dewey, the only appropriate method is an interpretive, dialogic process rather than an appeal to pure reason or divine revelation.

In his *Contingency, Irony, and Solidarity* (1989), Richard Rorty situates moral theory within language. For making life worth living, he advocates the values of human fulfillment—creativity and freedom, community formation, shared rituals, inclusive discourse. He looks for those values that emerge when we clear the deck of normative ethics, enlightenment epistemology, theology, and metaphysics. Rorty seeks those autonomous conditions within which we contribute our own vocabulary to the ongoing human experiment. The narrative level constitutes our best shot for liberalism as a social myth to prosper and, at the same time, for authoritarianism in all forms to recede. In narrative, we rehearse our common doubts, affirm our mutual contingencies, and push away every kind of fundamentalism that purports to be the final answer. Through conversation, we legitimize questions that seek the common good.

For Rorty, literature rather than philosophy awakens us to the cruelty of particular social practices and to human solidarity. James Ettema and Theodore Glasser (1998) argue, "We can only enlarge and strengthen our sense of solidarity, one with another, as we listen to lots of different people tell their stories. These stories do not reveal some essential bond between us all but simply make us more reluctant to inflict suffering on one another. For this reason telling stories of those who suffer pain or injustice is especially important" (86–87). "The liberal novelist, poet, or journalist is good at that," says Rorty; "the liberal theorist is not" (87).[2]

Rorty abandons those moral problems that appeal for their salience to an abstract order beyond time and change. Instead of addressing issues irrelevant to democratic life, liberal culture, aware of its own contingency, concentrates on those questions that widen the arena of personal creativity and reduce the occasion for human conflict. For Rorty, liberals are ironists in that they are "never quite able to take themselves seriously"; they are "always aware that the terms in which they describe themselves are subject to change, always aware of the contingency and fragility of their final vocabularies, and thus of their selves" (73–74).

Ironists have radical and continuing doubts about their vocabulary; they have been impressed by the discourse of others, and these worries will not be resolved. They do not think their language is any closer to reality than others are. Ironists are not inclined to fight their way past appearances to the real. Believing in the arbitrariness of language to make whatever truth there is, they simply play the new off against the old, Rorty observes (73). He likens communication to biological evolution, new forms of life constantly killing off old forms—not to accomplish a higher purpose but blindly (16). Ironists who are analytical about this process do not ask of any given speaker or point of view, "How can you know that?" For Rorty, the important question is, "Why do you talk that way?" (29). They do not look for criteria that "put all our doubts to rest" (75). Liberal ironists have "no reason to think that Socratic inquiry into the essence of justice or science or rationality will take one much beyond the language games of one's time" (74). Ironists recognize they may have been socialized "into the wrong language game," but they "cannot give a criterion of wrongness" (74). "Nothing can serve as a criticism of a final vocabulary, . . . since there is nothing beyond vocabularies which serves as a criterion of choice between them. . . . So our doubts about our own characters or our own culture can be resolved or assuaged only by enlarging our acquaintance" (80). For Rorty's liberal society, there is "no purpose except freedom, no goals except a willingness to see how such encounters go and to abide by the outcome. It has no purpose except to make life easier for poets and revolutionaries while seeing to it that they make life harder for others only by words, and not deeds. It is a society whose hero is the strong poet and the revolutionary. . . . To see one's language, one's conscience, one's morality, and one's highest hopes as contingent products, as liberalization of what once were accidentally produced metaphors, is to adopt a self-identity which suits one for citizenship in such an ideally liberal state" (61; see also Rorty 1998, 1999).

It is a wholesale housecleaning of the worn-out mythologies of Western culture in favor of the processes that enable new contingencies to gain a hold in the marketplace of ideas. Solidarity does not arise from our common reason, but occurs in everyday happenstance. According to Rorty, truth is no longer "correspondence to reality" but "what comes to be believed in the course of free and open encounters" (68; see also Rorty 1999).[3]

Dewey and Rorty illustrate narrative ethics. Clearly, for the communications enterprise, the shift from principle to story, from formal logic to community formation, is an attractive option. Stories are symbolic frameworks that organize human experience. Narration gives order to social life by inducing others to participate with us in its meaning. Through stories, we constitute ways of living in common. Humans are narrative beings aware of discursive coherence (whether or not a story hangs together) and of narrative fidelity (whether or not a story rings true) (Fisher 1987; see also Fisher 1984, 1985, 1991). Rorty pleads for wisdom rather than epistemic certainty, for an ethics closer to the ground where the moral life takes place.

Narratives are linguistic forms through which we think, argue, persuade, display convictions, and establish our identity. They contain in a nutshell the meaning of our theories and beliefs. As Renato Rosaldo (1989) points out, "Not only men and women of affairs but also ordinary people tell themselves stories about who they are, what they care about, and how they hope to realize their aspirations" (129–30). "I have learned from Zimbabwe and Zambia," writes Michael Traber (1991), "that storytelling is fundamental to human life and at the very heart of communication, both interpersonal and technically mediated. Descartes' dictum, 'Cogito, ergo sum,' would, in Africa, have to be changed to 'I am a story teller and I sing and dance, therefore I am'" (chap. 4, 1).

"Narrative prose fiction like real world discourse is," Adam Newton (1995) argues, "subject to an 'ethics.' One of the discursive worlds it inhabits is an ethical one, manifesting certain characteristics which resemble features of everyday communicative experience" (25). For Theodore Glasser (1991), storytelling "cuts through abstractions and other obscurities," enables us "to think creatively and imaginatively" about "the endless details of . . . a disorderly world," and in the process transforms "essentially private experience into a shared and therefore public reality" (235–36; cf. Mander 1987). The stories of Nelson Mandela's twenty-six years in prison, Paul Revere's ride, the Selma march, the demolition of the Berlin Wall, Kosovo's history, and the "velvet revolution" in Czechoslovakia were fodder for political revolution. Ethnic narratives are particularly meaningful for the displaced—Palestinians, Armenians, Kurds, and Misquito Indians, for example. In contrast, word and image bites of mayors cutting ribbons and heads of state waving from airplane stairs are pseudostories that do not engender common commitments.[4] Public indifference to the frivolous character of such discourse indicates in itself that great storytellers—as opposed to mere image-makers—probe deeply into our belief systems and shape the social landscape.

Narratives mediate our common understanding of good and evil, the tragic and deliverance. Stories stitch together, in George Gerbner's (1988) words, "the seamless web of culture that shapes who we are, how we live, whom we love or hate or kill . . . and how long we shall survive" (6). Everyone has general views on the meaning of life and death, of happiness and of reward. People may be wrong about their deepest beliefs or may not articulate them imaginatively. But, as Newton (1995) points out, "finding oneself 'addressed' by ethical demands, in effect, establishes one's place in regard to others as well as to one's own life; it locates, in a word, one's 'address'" (299). Communities are constituted by a set of values that specify their members' roles and aspirations. "A community is at bottom," Walter R. Fisher (1991) notes, "an ethical construction" (22).[5]

Hermeneutics has taught us that language is the matrix of the social order. Rorty's great conversation, Hauerwas's social ethics, Gadamer's intersubjectivity, Pierce's semiology, and literary journalism's news as narrative are compatible with important trends toward symbolic theory in communications and interpretive studies in the social sciences (see Denzin 1997). Taking ethics out of the ether and situating values in context are paradigmatic revolts of historic proportions. Narrative ethics to date has structured itself in contrast to ethical rationalism and therefore stakes out its territory in radically different, foundational terms (see Ellos 1994; and Kagan 1998, 296–98). But after decentering rationality, it yields arbitrary definitions of goodness. After providing a thick reading of how societies work in a natural setting, narrative ethics is mute in its own terms on which valuing to value. Whatever is identified experimentally cannot in itself produce normative guidelines. If phenomena situated in firsthand space and present time are presumed to contain everything of consequence, the search for values outside immediacy and particularity is irrational.

Ethics of Being

Cornel West's *American Evasion of Philosophy* (1989) opens the door to another path—an ethics of being. He argues that Rorty's neopragmatism kicks the philosophic props from under liberal democratic societies but requires no fundamental change in our cultural and political practices (206). What then are the ethical and social consequences of Rorty's neopragmatism? In West's terms, it has virtually no impact on the macro level. Rorty promotes the basic practices of liberal bourgeois capitalism, but, according to West, he makes his project "seem innocuous by discouraging philosophical defenses of such societies" (206).

West celebrates Rorty's antirealism and joins the Emersonian swerve away from philosophy centered on epistemology. But West believes a truncated version of American cultural studies ought to give way to scholarly accounts that go beyond a straight-line tradition from Emerson to Dewey to Rorty; a thicker genealogy of pragmatism can account for oppositional movements outside a narrow historicist rendering (210, 230). Pragmatism's common denominator is a "future-oriented instrumentalism" that "deploys thought as a weapon to enable more effective action" (5). However, this tradition does not simply represent a deliberating populace in contrast to "Cartesian and Kantian models of epistemology" (210). It includes as its heritage confrontational "analyses of class, race, and gender and oppositional movements for creative democracy and social freedom"—particularly among pragmatists with a religious orientation (206; see also 206–19).

Like William James, Reinhold Niebuhr, and to some extent W. E. B. Du Bois, West holds a religious conception of pragmatism. For him, the Christian epic, stripped of decrepit dogmas, is a "rich source of existential empowerment and political engagement" (233; see also West 1991 and 1999, 45–55). Mark Wood (2000) argues that "West's Christocentric orientation vigorously animates his belief that class, race, and gender oppression will not 'have the last word on how far democracy can go' and existentially sustains his tireless efforts to foster the development of more just, democratic, and equitable conditions of existence" (8).

Prophetic pragmatism West calls it, giving prominence to degraded otherness and subaltern marginality—to the poor peoples of color, women, and workers. Prophetic pragmatism for West is a deeply American response to the end of the Age of Europe, racism and oppression at home, and the decolonization of the third world (237; see also West 1993).

The narrative ethics of American cultural studies has generally reflected a humanistic worldview. Locating the habitat of values in the social context obviously articulates to the humanistic project as a whole. In fact, Walter Lippmann argued for humanism in his *Preface to Morals* (1929) as the only basis for a public ethics in a pluralistic and increasingly secular society.

But Cornel West highlights another tradition in American cultural studies: Christian theism. He includes Reinhold Niebuhr, for example, in his genealogy of pragmatism, along with the traditional canon. West locates his own prophetic version of pragmatism within this theistic strain, bringing it up from the footnotes to the intellectual center.

Religious pragmatism is my concern as well, though with a different intent. One way to take the measure of contextual values is through that layer of American cultural studies that has never come to peace with narrative ethics. In addition to Reinhold Niebuhr and Cornel West, Peter Berger (1990, 1997), Stanley Hauerwas (1981, 1989, 1997), and H. Richard Niebuhr (1963) should be noted and—back to Chicago—Paul Tillich (1952, 1959, 1969), Paul Ricoeur's sacred symbols (1995; cf. Kemp and Rasmussen 1989), David Tracy's (1994; cf. 1998) appeal to quality conversations, and Langdon Gilkey's (1993) ultimacy in his theology of culture. Together they point to a morality of being at odds with both a rationalistic ethics and one of narrative.

Paul Tillich's philosophical theology revolves around symbol and culture. For Tillich (1959), religious symbols disclose the "dimension of depth" in culture; "they open up a level of reality which otherwise is not opened at all, which is hidden" (59; cf. Church 1999, 45–56). In *What Is Religion?* (1969), he argues, "In the cultural [process], the religious is substantial; in the religious act the cultural is formal" (60; see also Deile 1971). Ultimacy and depth are synonymous. Religion is our ultimate concern, and ultimate concern is directed to what Tillich calls "the ground of being," "being itself," and "God." But as Jay Van Hook (1979) points out, God is not an "existent entity having certain properties which can be conceptually grasped and propositionally stated" (93). As hermeneutics has made obvious, symbolic constructions enable us to live in several domains simultaneously—in everyday worlds of meaning; in Tillich's depth dimension also—that is, purpose, our worldviews, love, and justice; and in terms of our ultimate concern with being itself, with transcending finitude.

In a celebrated dispute with William Urban (1940) over Tillich's totally symbolic system, Tillich (1952) claimed one literal statement that does not point beyond itself—God or the ground of being (334). Tillich (1959) concluded that all knowledge and experience cannot be of a symbolic character (61–62). Symbolic language has meaning for him only in contrast with the nonsymbolic. Make the concept "symbol" all-embracing, and it becomes contentless. Analogously, if all the universe expanded simultaneously and in exact proportions, how could we know of such expansion? The symbolic realm as well must be limited by something unsymbolic. Beginning with some nonnegotiable ultimate claim therefore establishes the possibility of interpreting all other activity symbolically. In the process, Tillich points to a God who is ground of being. As a result, all mental functioning remains finite. Any promise of fulfillment through rational self-realization within the human cosmos is thereby denied as a kind of epistemological nirvana that will never arrive. Human beings have neither the power to formulate adequate "orderings" fully nor the will to achieve them. Rather than exhortations to just start believing, Tillich is not afraid to ask, "How could I?" (see Church 1999, 13–31).

Cornel West (1989) calls Reinhold Niebuhr *the* Emersonian figure in midcentury America and the most respected social critic of his time: "With one foot in Protestantism and another in . . . pragmatism, Niebuhr . . . sustained a generation of Americans on the left, center, and right." His "ebullient style and sparkling personality" were similar to William James's. "And, as with Dewey, his social activism touched on nearly every issue of importance to middle-class reformist Americans" (150). Niebuhr's realism sought to link a Christian tragic perspective on evil "with a tempered Emersonian stress on human creative powers" (163). Niebuhr simultaneously had an imaginative grasp of life's possibilities and an accurate picture of its realities. As Niebuhr (1972) declared in his most famous aphorism, "Man's capacity for justice makes democracy possible; but man's inclination to injustice makes democracy necessary" (xiii). He recognized the moral ambiguities of the political order while not abandoning human aspirations. Hans Morgenthau (1962) considered him America's "only creative political philosopher since Calhoun" (109). For West, Niebuhr rivals Tillich as the most ambitious and influential theologian throughout twentieth century America (159).

Niebuhr ([1941] 1964) was preoccupied with validating a Christian understanding of human nature, which paradoxically claims "a higher stature for man" while "taking a more serious view of his evil than other anthropology" (18). This is the conceptual core of his major books, *Moral Man and Immoral Society* (1960), *Man's Nature and His Communities* (1965), *An Interpretation of Christian Ethics* ([1935] 1979), *Beyond Tragedy: Essays on the Christian Interpretation of History* (1937), and his magnum opus, the two-volume *Nature and Destiny of Man* (1941, 1943). In discussing Niebuhr and Christian realism, Robin W. Lovin (1995) notes, "Unlike divine command metaethics, for example, Christian Realism does not argue that moral imperatives are meaningful only insofar as they can be understood as commands of God. . . . Moral systems fail when their norms become unrelated to human nature or, more usually, when they are formulated in relation to only a part of it" (16).

Tillich's ground of being within symbolism and Niebuhr's human being within pragmatism illustrate an ongoing struggle in American cultural studies among intellectuals not content with contextual values and the narrative ethics derived from it. The less luminous in the religious sector—Berger, Tracy, Gilkey, and Hauerwas—have no intention either of resurrecting a rationalistic ethics of the metaphysical.

Their discontent is a narrative ethics of the empty center. An equitable process is protected, values are clarified, but no appeals are possible except a quest for discovery and revision. A cultural studies of collective values settles for the short-term goals of better education and a socially responsible press as prerequisites for generating truth. Democratic institutions are viewed as a cooperative experiment, lurching along without an axle. But its gaping hole in the middle leaves the integrity of the entire structure in doubt. Richard Neuhaus (1984) labels it the problem of the naked public square.

For Rorty (1988), the vacant center is a virtue. No agreed-upon cosmology is required to hold a free society together. He opts for a self that is historically contingent all the way through. Egalitarian democracy, he insists, should stay on the surface and create a set of operations for democratic life distinct from matters of ultimate importance. But what if the context within which values are supposed to percolate is fractured and tribalistic? Values clarification without social cohesion is meaningless. If we look north and south, the Canadian philosopher Charles Taylor and Antonio Pasquali of Venezuela quarrel with U.S. cultural studies exactly along these lines. Pasquali's (1997) "morals of intersubjectivity" is at odds with Mead's descriptive I and Other. Taylor's (1989) insistence that all humans have "uncommonly deep and universal" moral concerns has a Niebuhrian inflection (3–8; see also Taylor 1995).

Tillich's ground of being and Niebuhr's human being point to an ontological ethics. Instead of appealing to rational abstractions or to the social order, the root of this paradigm is animate nature. The rationale for human action is reverence for life on earth, respect for the organic realm in which human civilization is situated. The Enlightenment defined nature as spiritless materiality. But a reductionism to matter and motion cannot account for at least one determinate goal—life itself, evident in its own reproduction. In the ethics of being, nature has a moral claim on us for its own sake and in its own right.

Our duty to preserve natural life is similar to parents' responsibility for their children. The progenitors' duty to children is an obligation outside subjectivity that is timeless and nonnegotiable. For Emmanuel Levinas, nurturing life has a taken-for-granted character. As James Olthuis (1997) puts it, "[T]he face of the other commands me not to kill. . . . The face is the epiphany of the nakedness of the other, a visitation, a coming, a saying which comes in the passivity of the face, not threatening but obligating. It is looking into the face of the other that reveals the call to a responsibility that is before any beginning, decision or initiative on my part" (139; cf. Levinas 1979, 1981). When new life or the beckoning face of the needy other appears, in Levinasian terms, I see human life as a whole. Human existence cannot be renounced without destroying my own. Our mutually sacred life across cultural, racial, and historical boundaries situates the moral order in our creatureliness. In Olthuis's terms, "Being ethical is a primordial movement in the beckoning force of life itself" (141). Given the oneness of the human species, universal solidarity is the basic principle of ethics. Reverence for life on earth bonds us universally into an organic whole (Christians and Traber 1997, 6–8). Our obligation to sustain one another defines our human existence. Since human beings, in Kwasi Wiredu's (1996) words, "have a basic natural sympathy for their kind," we can endeavor to live by the principle of "sympathetic impartiality" (41).

One ethical principle inscribed within this ontological model is human dignity. This principle is widely known as the Universal Declaration of Human Rights, established in 1948 by the United Nations General Assembly: "Recognition of the inherent dignity of all members of the human family is the foundation of freedom, justice, and peace in the world" (Preamble). Every child, woman, and man has sacred status without exception. Inspired in large part by the atrocities of World War II, the declaration expresses the moral aspirations of participating nations across the globe. On the basis of our unassailable dignity as human beings, we begin to articulate an ethics of social justice.

The primal sacredness of life establishes a level playing floor for cross-cultural collaboration in ethics. Representatives of various societies articulate this protonorm in different terms and illustrate it locally, but each brings to the table a fundamental respect for the others gathered there. If moral claims are assumed to be presuppositionless, the possibility of doing ethics at all is jeopardized. Without a starting point, moral reasoning falls into infinite regression, and ethical imperatives are always indeterminate.

Prophetic Witness

Ontological ethics enables us to witness prophetically to authentic being. There are few oases left today where the moral imagination can prosper undisturbed. The best we can manage is ongoing struggle. Pockets of resistance are possible, though often marginalized. Ontological ethics provides a legitimate basis for making emancipatory appeals on behalf of the primal sacredness of life.

In Cornel West's terms, prophets speak with a thirst for justice. Surely they react fiercely; they carry a burden on their souls and are stunned at blatant greed and our plundering the wretched of the earth (West 1989, 233–35; see also West 1988; cf. Wood 2000, 41–62). But their purpose is not flagellation for its own sake; they call the wayward home (Heschel [1962] 1969–71). And how can they do so without elitism and hot-tempered moralism? Except for a defensible conception of the good, rooted in universal human solidarity, even prophetic witness is arbitrary and thereby oppressive.

Narrative ethics, Thomas McCarthy (1990) argues, "deprives us of resources for examining and criticizing 'basic cultural practices or basic institutional structures'" (648). Without an external perspective, Matthew Festenstein (1997) observes, we are "ultimately committed to parochial standards and practices . . . exalting the status quo" (185). This is the longstanding charge of pragmatic acquiescence originating contra Dewey and unresolved by narrative ethics specifically or cultural studies generally.[6]

From the perspective of ontological ethics, the narrative paradigm is fundamentally flawed on the issue of normativity. Cultures need general principles beyond their own indigenous context to be self-critical. As Samuel Fleischacker (1992) notes, "Only an 'outside' lets us know that we are limited, and defined by these limitations: only an 'outside' shapes us and recalls us to our 'internal principles'" (223). Without norms that are more than contingent, dehumanization cannot be condemned except on the grounds of personal preference or emotional makeup.

While narrative ethics legitimately opposes foundationalism, it illegitimately contradicts all versions of universal norms. Festenstein (1997) concludes that Rorty, for example, "underestimates the motivation to employ general and philosophical argument on the part of even the liberal political thinkers whom he admires, including Dewey" (128). While Rorty properly insists that liberals are defined by their opposition to cruelty,[7] his appeal does not meet Julia Kristeva's (1991) objection offered in another context: "The Nazis did not lose their humanity because of the 'abstraction' that may have existed in their notion of 'man.' On the contrary, it is because they had lost the lofty, abstract, fully symbolic notion of humanity, and replaced it with a local, national or ideological membership, that savageness materialized in them and could be practiced against those who did not share such membership" (13).

The challenge is an interactive universalism that is not modernist, formal, or static (cf. Benhabib 1992, 1995). The ethics of being entails universal humanness and meets this test. Obviously not every community ought to be celebrated. Through a commitment to human solidarity, we resist those communal values that are exclusivistic and divisive. Short of a moral order rooted anthropologically, we will do only quandary ethics of a minimalist sort.

Cultural studies that draw too straight a line through American pragmatism from Dewey to Rorty are themselves subject to Cornel West's critique. They tend to make moral claims in terms of narrative's social context and therefore hold definitions of goodness in arbitrary terms. Understanding the normative domain through being is a compelling alternative.

Notes

1. An abbreviated, nontheological version of this typology appeared in Christians (1998).

2. For an application of Rorty's irony in understanding the press as a social institution, see Ettema and Glasser (1998, chap. 4). They demonstrate that investigative reporters use irony as a rhetorical device to work within the boundaries of objectivity while developing "a morally charged vocabulary for condemnation of the villains to whom we have foolishly entrusted our public affairs" (12).

3. For elaboration of this section on Rorty's moral philosophy, see Fackler (1992).

4. The examples in this paragraph are elaborated in Traber (1991). Traber distinguishes foundational stories, parables, and pseudostories and sets narrative within the context of ritual (cf. White 1980).

5. Fisher elaborates on this thesis in terms of Dewey, Buber, Hauerwas, and Gadamer and includes an extensive bibliography.

6. Edward W. Purcell (1973) argues that Dewey and other scientific rationalists were accused in the 1930s of providing no normative foundation for defending democratic institutions against the threat of totalitarianism.

7. As Rorty (1989) puts it, "I borrow my definition of 'liberal' from Judith Shklar, who says that liberals are the people who think that cruelty is the worst thing we can do. . . . Liberal ironists are people who include among [their] ungroundable desires their own hope that suffering will be diminished, that the humiliation of human beings by other human beings may cease. [However], for liberal ironists, there is no answer to the question 'Why not be cruel?'—no noncircular theoretical backup for the belief that cruelty is horrible" (xv). Festenstein (1997) concludes, "The injunction to avoid or minimize cruelty is a placeholder for the ironist's ethical beliefs rather than an account of them. For what counts as cruelty or humiliation is left open" (131).

References

Benhabib, S. 1992. *Situating the Self: Gender, Community, and Postmodernism in Contemporary Ethics.* Cambridge: Polity.

———. 1995. "Cultural Complexity, Moral Interdependence, and the Global Dialogical Community." In *Women, Culture, and Development: A Study of Human Capabilities,* edited by M. Nussbaum and J. Glover, 235–55. Oxford: Clarendon.

Berger, P. 1990. *The Sacred Canopy: Elements of a Sociological Theory of Religion.* New York: Doubleday.

———, ed. 1997. *The Limits of Social Cohesion: Resurgent Religion and World Politics.* Boulder, Colo.: Westview.

Christians, C. 1998. "Critical Issues in Communication Ethics." In *Communication: Views from the Helm for the Twenty-First Century,* edited by J. Trent, 270–75. Boston: Allyn and Bacon.

Christians, C., and M. Traber. 1997. *Communication Ethics and Universal Values.* Thousand Oaks, Calif.: Sage.

Church, F. F., ed. 1999. *The Essential Tillich.* Chicago: University of Chicago Press.

Deile, C. C. 1971. "Paul Tillich's Philosophy of Communication." Ph.D. diss., University of Illinois.

Denzin, N. 1997. *Interpretive Ethnography: Ethnographic Practices for the Twenty-First Century.* Thousand Oaks, Calif.: Sage.

Dewey, J. [1922] 1948. *Human Nature and Conduct.* New York: Henry Holt.

———. 1929. *The Quest for Certainty.* New York: Minton, Bolch.

Ellos, W. 1994. *Narrative Ethics.* London: Blackwell.

Ettema, J. S., and T. L. Glasser. 1998. *Custodians of Conscience: Investigative Journalism and Public Virtue.* New York: Columbia University Press.

Fackler, M. 1992. "Debates in Contemporary Theory: Richard Rorty versus Charles Taylor." In *Conference Proceedings of the Second National Communication Ethics Conference,* 26–34. Annandale, Va.: Speech Communication Association.

Festenstein, M. 1997. *Pragmatism and Political Theory from Dewey to Rorty.* Chicago: University of Chicago Press.

Fisher, W. R. 1984. "Narration as a Human Communication Paradigm: The Case of Public Moral Argument." *Communication Monographs* 51 (March): 1–22.

———. 1985. "The Narrative Paradigm: In the Beginning." *Journal of Communication* 35 (4): 74–89.

———. 1987. *Human Communication as Narration: Toward a Philosophy of Reason, Value, and Action.* Columbia: University of South Carolina Press.

———. 1991. "Narrativity and Community." In *Proceedings of the Conference on Narrativity and Community,* edited by M. Casey. 1–34. Malibu, Calif.: Conference on Christianity and Community.

Fleischacker, S. 1992. *Integrity and Moral Relativism.* Leiden, Netherlands: E. J. Brill.

Gerbner, G. 1988. "Telling Stories: The State, Problems, and Tasks of the Art." Paper presented at Institute of Communication Research Fortieth Anniversary, University of Illinois at Urbana-Champaign, March 19.

Gilkey, Langdon. 1993. *Nature, Reality, and the Sacred: The Nexus of Science and Religion.* Minneapolis, Minn.: Augsburg Fortress.

Glasser, T. L. 1991. "Communication and the Cultivation of Citizenship." *Communication* 12 (4): 235–48.

Hauerwas, S. 1981. *A Community of Character.* Notre Dame, Ind.: University of Notre Dame Press.

———. 1997. *In Good Company: The Church as Polis.* Notre Dame, Ind.: University of Notre Dame Press.

Hauerwas, S., and L. G. Jones. 1989. *Why Narrative? Readings in Narrative Theology.* Grand Rapids, Mich.: Eerdmans.

Heschel, A. J. [1962] 1969–71. *The Prophets.* 2 vols. New York: Harper and Row Torchbooks.

Kagan, S. 1998. *Normative Ethics.* Boulder, Colo.: Westview.

Kemp, T. P., and D. Rasmussen, eds. 1989. *The Narrative Path: The Later Works of Paul Ricoeur.* Cambridge, Mass.: MIT Press.

Kristeva, J. 1991. *Strangers to Ourselves.* Translated by L. S. Roudiez. Hemel Hempstead, U.K.: Harvester-Wheatsheaf.

Levinas, E. 1979. *Totality and Infinity.* The Hague, Netherlands: Martinus Nijhoff.

———. 1981. *Otherwise Than Being or Essence.* The Hague, Netherlands: Martinus Nijhoff.

Lippmann, W. 1929. *A Preface to Morals.* New York: Macmillan.

Lovin, R. W. 1995. *Reinhold Niebuhr and Christian Realism.* Cambridge: Cambridge University Press.

Mander, M. S. 1987. "Narrative Dimensions of the News: Omniscience, Prophecy, and Morality." *Communication* 10 (1): 51–70.

McCarthy, T. 1990. "Ironist Theory as a Vocation." *Critical Inquiry* 16:644–55.

Morgenthau, H. J. 1962. "The Influence of Reinhold Niebuhr in American Political Life and Thought." In *Reinhold Niebuhr: A Prophetic Voice in Our Time,* edited by H. R. Landon, 97–116. Greenwich, Conn.: Seabury.

Neuhaus, R. J. 1984. *The Naked Public Square.* Grand Rapids, Mich.: Eerdmans.

Newton, A. Z. 1995. *Narrative Ethics.* Cambridge, Mass.: Harvard University Press.

Niebuhr, H. R. 1963. *The Responsible Self.* New York: Harper and Row.

Niebuhr, R. [1935] 1979. *An Interpretation of Christian Ethics.* New York: Seabury.

———. 1937. *Beyond Tragedy: Essays on the Christian Interpretation of History.* New York: Charles Scribner's Sons.

———. [1941, 1943] 1964. *The Nature and Destiny of Man.* New York: Charles Scribner's Sons.

———. 1960. *Moral Man and Immoral Society.* New York: Charles Scribner's Sons.

———. 1965. *Man's Nature and His Communities: Essays on the Dynamics and Enigmas of Man's Personal and Social Existence.* New York: Charles Scribner's Sons.

———. 1972. *The Children of Light and the Children of Darkness.* New York: Charles Scribner's Sons.

Olthuis, J. H. 1997. "Face-to-Face: Ethical Asymmetry or the Symmetry of Mutuality?" In *Knowing Other-Wise: Philosophy at the Threshold of Spirituality,* edited by J. H. Olthuis, 134–64. New York: Fordham University Press.

Pasquali, A. 1997. "The Moral Dimension of Communicating." In *Communication Ethics and Universal Values,* edited by C. Christians and M. Traber, 3–23. Thousand Oaks, Calif.: Sage.

Purcell, E. A. 1973. *The Crisis of Democratic Theory: Scientific Naturalism and the Problem of Value.* Lexington: University Press of Kentucky.

Ricoeur, P. 1995. *Figuring the Sacred: Religion, Narrative, and Imagination.* Translated by D. Pellauer. Minneapolis, Minn.: Augsburg Fortress.

Rorty, R. 1988. "The Priority of Democracy to Philosophy." In *The Virginia Statute for Religious Freedom,* edited by M. D. Peterson and R. C. Vaughn, 257–82. Cambridge: Cambridge University Press.

———. 1989. *Contingency, Irony, and Solidarity.* Cambridge: Cambridge University Press.

———. 1998. *Truth and Progress: Philosophical Papers.* Vol. 3. Cambridge: Cambridge University Press.

———. 1999. *Philosophy and Social Hope.* New York: Penguin Books.

Rosaldo, R. 1989. *Culture and Truth: The Remaking of Social Analysis.* Boston: Beacon.

Seigfried, C. H. 1996. *Pragmatism and Feminism: Reweaving the Social Fabric.* Chicago: University of Chicago Press.

Taylor, C. 1989. *Sources of the Self: The Making of the Modern Identity.* Cambridge, Mass.: Harvard University Press.

———. 1995. *Philosophical Arguments.* Cambridge, Mass.: Harvard University Press.

Tillich, P. 1952. "Reply to Interpretation and Criticism." In *The Theology of Paul Tillich,* edited by C. W. Kegley and R. Bretall, 334. New York: Macmillan.

———. 1959. *Theology of Culture.* Edited by Robert C. Kimball. New York: Oxford University Press.

———. 1969. *What Is Religion?* Translated by J. L. Adams. New York: Harper and Row.

Traber, M. 1991. "Narrativity and Community: A Cultural Studies Approach." In *Proceedings of the Conference on Narrativity and Community,* edited by M. Casey, ch. 4, 1–24. Malibu, Calif.: Conference on Christianity and Community.

Tracy, D. 1994. *Plurality and Ambiguity: Hermeneutics, Religion, Hope.* Chicago: University of Chicago Press.

———. 1998. *The Analogic Imagination.* New York: Crossroad.

Urban, W. M. 1940. "A Critique of Professor Tillich's Theory of the Religious Symbol." *Journal of Liberal Religion* 2 (Summer): 34–36.

Van Hook, J. M. 1979. "The Problem of Communication in Paul Tillich's Philosophical Theology." *Communication* 4 (1): 87–102.

West, C. 1988. *Prophetic Fragments.* Grand Rapids, Mich.: Eerdmans.

———. 1989. *The American Evasion of Philosophy: A Genealogy of Pragmatism.* Madison: University of Wisconsin Press.

———. 1991. *The Ethical Dimensions of Marxist Thought.* New York: Monthly Review Press.

———. 1993. *Prophetic Reflections: Notes on Race and Power in America.* Monroe, Maine.: Common Courage.

——— 1999. "Interview: Philosophical Faith in Action." *Harvard Review of Philosophy* 7 (Spring): 45–55.

White, H. 1980. "The Value of Narrativity in the Representation of Reality." *Critical Inquiry* 7 (1): 5–27.

Wiredu, K. 1996. *Cultural Universals and Particulars: An African Perspective.* Bloomington: Indiana University Press.

Wood, M. D. 2000. *Cornel West and the Politics of Prophetic Pragmatism.* Urbana: University of Illinois Press.

CAROLYN MARVIN

10 *Media Rituals: Follow the Bodies*

This essay looks at media as part of an ordered system of bodily gestures, or rituals, that hold enduring groups together.[1] *Enduring groups* are those for which members may be persuaded to lay down their lives. They include, but are not limited to, nation-states, ethnicities, and sectarian faiths. In contemporary mass media, nation-states are the most visible enduring groups. By *mass media,* I mean the complex of national print and electronic outlets that share a similar agenda of stories on a periodic schedule. *Ritual* is a more complex term. By *ritual* in the largest sense, I mean memory-inducing behavior that has the effect of preserving whatever things or ideas are indispensable to the group. On the presumption that all important things in society are ritualized, this definition deliberately encompasses a large range of events.

Operationally, I follow Roy Rappaport's (1979) definition of ritual as the performance of more or less invariant sequences of formal acts and utterances not encoded by performers (175). To explore mass media as a ritual genre, I examine the first part of this definition. Bodily performance is so fundamental to ritual that theorists conventionally assume that only events in which all necessary components (meaning performers, congregants, and objects) are immediately copresent may count as ritual.[2] Since the body cannot be physically alienated from ritual time or space in this strong definition, mass media presentations appear to be strictly disqualified from being classified as rituals. I argue that mass media presentations are a type of ritual genre because they do satisfy the bodily performance requisites of ritual practice, even if they seem at first glance to be the antithesis of whatever ritual means.[3]

Bodily performance in ritual is a kind of bodily re-presentation. It quasi-magically re-presents every body that has previously incarnated whatever ritual archetypes offer a model for contemporary reenactments. Whatever power such re-creations have derives partly from these antecedent performances. Even a wedding that consciously departs from previous ritual forms depends on the accumulated memory weight of previous reenactments of the archetype to make the departure meaningful. Just as ritual archetypes confer conviction and transforming power on subsequent reincarnations, every reincarnation confirms the archetypal status of the model to which it hearkens.

While notions of performance and drama have always been central to cultural studies, they are modeled on the playful distance from life that typifies art or fiction. Bodily performance in ritual and dramatic performance in this discursive, textual sense function differently. In cultural studies, performances are treated as distant from what is dead-serious in the way that texts may be said to be distant from embodied life. Just as symbols are not what they stand for, performances are treated as constructed and not to be taken at face value. They are suspect, in a word. Because of its focus on discourse and language as the key to the social, cultural studies has not been much interested in ritual, though discourses of the body have received plenty of attention, most famously from Michel Foucault (1972).

In the most basic sense, the chief task of societies is to organize and dispose of bodies. Mary Douglas (1982) argues that our notions about the body are always notions of social order. Foucault is more radical, arguing that power in society is registered directly on the physical body. Jean Comaroff (1992) claims that the constitution of social relations is a visceral matter. This is why, as the fundamental mode of group communication, the body is the medium and focus of ritual. Through bodies, rituals address who belongs to the group and how to keep it together through cycles of birth and death. Roy Rappaport (1979) makes the most useful statement about ritual: it is the basic social act (174). The reason, explains Mircea Eliade (1959), is that it repeats the act of creation. In human experience, creation begins with the body. Ritual works on bodies, is performed by bodies, and models them in significant ways.

Conceiving of ritual form as bodily re-presentation instead of discursive representation is a departure from the usual cultural studies approach. It proposes consequences in the world for sociability based on the universal human experience of having a body. Discursive textual culture floats free, as symbols do, from social action. The discursive sign is insubstantial. In ritual, by contrast, the body is an indexical sign of performers' relation to the liturgical and social order they incarnate and to which they submit (Rappaport 1979). The ritually performing body is not insubstantial; it is what it communicates. The body is a real and constitutive element of social action. Its impact qua body must be taken into account. By *body*, I mean the heat-seeking skin packages we all inhabit. *Heat-seeking* refers to our desire for connection and warmth, our innate social capacity. Our skins are "social skins," culturally permeable boundaries. As cultural studies theorists recognize, the body is also a model through which social actors imagine themselves and the world. It can be argued that this model also travels more successfully than text across human experience.[4]

Though it is no surprise that academicians find a congenial model for culture in text, the reach of that conceptualization across less textually focused cultures remains limited.[5] Even in highly textualized cultures like our own, the body is never absent or unimportant. The unending struggle for dominance between bodies and texts is one of the constitutive dramas of advanced industrial societies (Marvin 1994). A theoretical and empirical focus on the body offers a remedy, finally, for a sometimes too blunt-edged social constructivism in cultural studies by exploring the tension between what is given in human experience, as the body is, and how culture emerges from social wrestling with that given.

What does any of this have to do with media ritual, which many theorists consider to be an oxymoron or at least an impoverished and corrupt version of more authentic, body-based ritual experiences. The term *media ritual* includes face-to-face rituals presented through media and patterns of presentation and audience engagement peculiar to media, especially news coverage of community triumphs, dangers, and disasters. Logically, the distinction between so-called mediated and so-called face-to-face rituals is an unstable one. Since every ritual refers to already established (previously encoded, in Rappaport's terms) structures of sociability, every ritual recalls persons, processes, and events that are not immediately present. These include ancestors whose ritual deeds may be remembered, reliance on a traditional liturgical order of events, and invocations of prior moments and places of significance. In point of fact, every ritual is mediated.

Still, the most obvious difference between mass media rituals and other mediated ritual forms is the way in which bodies are incorporated in them. In traditional rituals, performers and congregants occupy each other's immediate presence for the ceremonial duration. In media rituals, performers are physically separated from viewing and reading congregants, and congregants are separated from one another. If all rituals are mediated presentations, differences in bodily presence are issues not of ritual authenticity but of ritual power. The most powerful ritual magic, or transformations, are worked directly on the bodies of supplicants in the physical copresence of congregants, who may include other performers or simply witnesses. The most important rituals do the most dramatic things to supplicants' bodies. The ritual of war, for example, dramatically transforms the bodies of group members. (Since war is the most powerful group-forging ritual in contemporary nation-states, I refer to it frequently.)

Media displays of blood sacrifice images and text that re-presents sacrifice in words are clearly not the referred-to sacrificial event but re-presentations of it. The transforming power of re-presentation differs from that of face-to-face events; the power of re-presentation is generally but not always less.[6] The crucial ritualizing function of media is to re-model blood sacrifice on which group cohesion depends. In concrete terms, media retell important stories of group sacrifice. This happens every time a newscast references these experiences even in passing and whenever books, films, plays, songs, paintings, parades, exhibits, and other mediated forms take these stories for their subjects. It also takes place when mass media re-present body-to-body commemorative rituals for wider circulation.

Enduring groups rely on media, but not just mass media, to learn about foundational blood sacrifice. Media preoccupation with violence may be seen both as a re-presentation of defining blood sacrifice and as a ritual rehearsal for it. "Television dotes on death, the violent kind," writes Max Frankel (1995, 28), expressing a widely shared belief, and David Halberstam (1991) observes that American media are "interested in foreign news only when it happens point-blank to Americans, preferably violently" (A21). This is not all media do. They re-present a great variety of events, objects, persons, and symbols that concern the group to whom they address themselves and of which they are a part. But in times of social emergency, group members go to media. The greatest emergencies are those in which group members' lives are at stake, when bloodletting is imminent on behalf of the group. At such times, media are ritually essential.

The rest of this discussion sketches out some essential propositions for understanding the relation between bodies and rituals and builds a case for classifying media presentations along a continuum of ritual practices that engage enduring groups.

1. *Ritual mimics and transforms bodies.* As biological bodies reproduce the species bloodline, ritual reproduces the social species, the group. Ritual systems for perpetuating enduring groups are homologous with natural systems that perpetuate species. Biological bodies are transformed in the process of producing new bodies. Puberty, sexual intercourse, pregnancy, and childbirth visibly transform bodies. Bodies are also imitated in biological reproduction and nurturance. Each generation produces the next by mimicking bodies that know how to do this already. New biological bodies turn out to be reassuringly familiar. There is comfort in seeing the physical features of parents in children.[7] Biological replication thus displays species and social continuity. Across the generations, we value the same gestures, the same posture, the same laugh. Baby Ruth has Aunt Helen's nose, Dad's jawline. A body with discernible similarities to other bodies can be connected to a social kinship system and invested with responsibility for creating future generations. For species to have a future, present bodies must be transformed. Present bodies are transformed by imitating past bodies.

From the beginning, physical bodies are fashioned into group-sustaining social bodies. This is done by imitating rituals that have transformed others. Just as every child is a biological homologue of its parent, every ritual event is a homologue of an imagined ritual archetype. Every ritually transformed citizen body is a homologue of the social body. Rituals cease to be useful when their archetypal models no longer convincingly sustain themselves in the present to the group. As biological sociability re-creates species, ritual sociability re-creates groups. New social bodies are intelligible because we see the old ones in them. A ritual quest by the American nation-state to depose Saddam Hussein is worthy because the president designates it as the child of the ritual quest to depose Hitler. As in sexual reproduction of biological bloodlines, ritual reproduction creates long-term stability in social structures by absorbing and exploiting short-term changes.

2. *Blood is the most important ritual substance; rituals about blood are the most important for enduring groups.* First blood for males is a symbol of fighting readiness. First blood also establishes female fertility in menstruation. It accompanies birth. Its appearance at death signals the breakdown of body borders. Its importance for biological bodies makes it central to sacrificial and regenerative rituals of the group. The blood sacrifice of bodies on a scale and in a manner to impress its members is the sustaining ritual of enduring groups. Bodies sacrificially transformed by blood in war are ritually returned to the homeland and "planted" in ritual burial as the socially regenerative seed of future generations. Each

new bloodletting points back to creation-sacrifice, the bloodletting that originates society. Here, too, rituals imitate biology. As each biological birth mimics an ancestral event filled with blood and peril, each group rebirth mimics a generative bloodletting. Group life is ritually sustained by draping new disorders and bloodlettings that imperil the group in the familiar garments of an originating myth about how the group is formed and how to keep it together. Just as birth and death are fundamental to biological bodies, rituals that rivet group attention concern birth and death in the social body. Events full of real or potential death—impeachments, moon landings, hurricanes, wars, and murder trials—get more attention from media than the national budget does. Equating the social body to the natural one by attending to its death and resurrection is what concerns the group in its primitive guise as an entity that constructs the social out of the body.

3. *Gesture is the essential communicative mechanism of ritual.* Society consists of relationships among bodies. Bodies relate to other bodies in two modes. They touch (transform) one another out of affection or hostility. They conform to (imitate) one another in socially coded ways to a greater or lesser degree. These two ritual modes of contact and modeling correspond to Sir James Frazer's categories of magical action. In contagious magic, agency or substance flows communicatively from the ritual object to those who receive it. Substance flows into substance, violating and breaching form. The transforming principles are contiguity, contact, and connection. Contagious magic transforms by touching, by infecting, by suffusing. It crosses boundaries and exchanges substance. The power of sympathetic magic resides in mimesis. It communicates form through re-creation. Supplicants do not receive the ritual object or symbol so much as they perform it by speaking its gestures and putting on its forms. The power of sympathetic magic is acquired through modeling and imitation. Contagious and sympathetic magic has meaning only in reference to the experience of having a body. Both are elements in the most magical of enduring-group rituals, blood sacrifice. To shed another body's blood or to have one's own blood shed, as in war, is to alter bodily and social boundaries and thereby perform contagious magic. To multiply mimetically the contagious magic of killing and dying—to broadcast a war, for example—is magically to re-present the originating body to body event (with weaker transformative effect, to be sure, but without news re-presentation there would be no effect beyond the immediate performers) by sympathetically repeating it.

4. *The transforming power of ritual depends on its proximate relation to the sacrificed body.* Ritual events vary in how much they struc-

ture the life of the group. These variations depend on their capacity for sympathetic magic, which is the degree to which they copy ritual events, and their capacity for contagious magic, or transforming power. The chief transforming power that rituals have is to stop time, to cut out and frame from the flow of existence an event to which group history is ever after referenced. Generally speaking, battlefield death is more transformative for those who see it close up than press reports about it are for media audiences. Yet if the press does not capture it (or in a different kind of culture, if storytellers do not pass it along), blood sacrifice cannot become creation-sacrifice and execute its group-unifying function. Media choose and organize coverage of events according to a blood sacrifice myth that maintains the group. Fredric Jameson (1981) has written, "History is what hurts" (102). Body language is necessary to describe it. The biggest history is about the biggest hurt, which is sacrifice. Media witness and model sacrifice. Though media have no power to perform real sacrifice, they scratch the itch in small ways and at regular intervals. They provide maintenance and memory until a big sacrifice comes again. Then they become the channel through which knowledge of sacrifice moves to the nation. Ritual recalls events that in re-modeling become something other than strictly real. They are re-presented, which is to say, mediated, with elements added and subtracted in the service of group myth. Mediation does not ensure ritual success, though in groups that are too large for all members to know one another personally—which includes virtually all nation-states—it is necessary. Media mythically tidy up and polish events that contain ritually usable elements, as all ritual form does. Even failed rituals instruct congregants in what proper rituals should be. Successful rituals give the group a new or renewed sense of itself, and they do it for an extended period. World War II was a more successful ritual than the Gulf War because its unifying effects stayed with group members longer.

5. *Media track the bodily engagement of congregants and participants in ritual events.* The most effective ritual magic is exercised directly on bodies. Though media rituals do not act directly on bodies, they restore the illusion of bodily presence for ritual re-presentation. Media show bodies performing ritual acts and often observe the bodily reactions of congregants. The more media focus on the body, the more important the ritual is likely to be. Media track bodies anticipating ritual outcomes, responding to them, making new connections to one another, and offering testimony about ritual success or failure.

Media restore bodies to ritual by re-presenting them in images and words and commenting on the bodily efforts of congregants and performers. The more ritually engaged the bodies of congregants and performers and the more media report on this engagement, the more important the ritual to the group. "Read my lips!" declared the presidential candidate George Bush in a 1988 campaign promise not to raise taxes. The electorate punished him in 1992 for breaking his body oath. "I did not have sexual relations with that woman," President Bill Clinton told the American people and punctuated the statement by jabbing the air with his finger. This gesture, more than any other act or statement, came to most represent the president's having broken faith with the American people and precipitated an impeachment trial.

Media rituals convey whether many or a few bodies are ritually participating and watching. Successful rituals engage many congregants. According to the *New York Times,* "More people watched the two-hour long address [by Minister Louis Farrakhan at the Million Man March] on CNN than any other speech this year, including Mr. Clinton's State of the Union Message and the Pope's address to the United Nations" (Holmes 1995, A1). "Millions of people in millions of places seemed to spend 10 spellbinding minutes yesterday doing exactly the same thing," the *New York Times* wrote about the O. J. Simpson verdict (Kleinfeld 1995, A1). "Never before in any election have I seen crowds like these," declared a Quebecer waiting to vote on the future of the province (quoted in Farnsworth 1991, A12). Since genuine ritual magic requires the transformation of bodies, bodily engagement must be apparent. In words and pictures, media charted flag-waving, singing, and painted Quebecois faces, contagiously and sympathetically connecting the bodies of the faithful to their flags: "In downtown Montreal, a crowd estimated at 150,000 waved the Maple Leaf flag of Canada and the fleurs-de-lis flag of Quebec and sang the national anthem, hoping to convince the French-speaking people of Quebec to vote No in their independence referendum on Monday" (Farnsworth 1995, 1).

When the pope visited Sacred Heart Cathedral in Newark in 1995, the media recorded the ritual: "The sounds of the organ and thunderous applause filled the cathedral, echoing off the stones laid in place in 1898 by workmen long dead, as the Pope appeared. Rejuvenated by the joyful greeting, he stretched out his arms, taking 10 minutes to walk up the aisle past moist-eyed priests and nuns, many of whom stood on their pews like excited schoolchildren and reached out to kiss his ring" (Stout 1995, B1).

When Israeli Prime Minister Yitzhak Rabin was assassinated, metaphors of bodily suffering were plentiful. A CNN reporter described Israel as "paralyzed with grief" (Rogers 1995). An Israeli citizen told the *New York Times* correspondent that "his pain was as searing as an ulcer" (Jehl 1995, A1).

There is ritual consternation when bodies are unavailable. When Valujet Flight 592 plunged to earth in 1996, rituals for repairing the social trauma caused by the deaths of group members were missing their most important element, as Rick Bragg (1996) reported for the *New York Times:* "Rescue workers found no survivors. They found no bodies. When Valujet Flight 592 dropped out of the sky and into the Florida Everglades on Saturday afternoon, it was as if 109 people aboard the DC-9 were just erased. . . . 'How can you have a funeral?' said Ms. Hinley, who answered questions about her future daughter-in-law graciously and patiently, until the notion of the burial and how it would be arranged brought her to tears" (A1). How can you have a ritual without a body? By imaginatively restoring it as media do. But as congregants, we know the difference, and it is not the same.

Effective rituals build uncertainty about the fate of the group in advance of a ritual outcome and express this uncertainty in bodily terms. In a good ritual, there is doubt (it may be real or manufactured) about how the ritual will come out. There is testimony to this fact. Awaiting the O. J. Simpson verdict, a friend of mine wrote by e-mail, "I keep staring at the clock. I cannot believe the jury came up with a verdict so quickly. The anticipation is KILLING me."

As the Quebec independence referendum approached, this newspaper headline conveyed ritual suspense in bodily terms: "Canada Holds Its Breath as Quebec Votes." The more uncertain the outcome, the greater the ritual magic that must be summoned. The greater the magic required, the more bodily transformation will play a part; the greater the benefit to the social body if the ritual succeeds, the greater the peril if it fails. When a ritual outcome is prescribed in advance, as in a wedding ceremony, uncertainty shifts to the suspense of bringing off the certain outcome. Will Aunt Edna faint? Will the groom make it to the church on time? Will the bride trip going down the aisle?

In effective rituals, well-defined outcomes are rendered in bodily terms. For several days, television repeated the moment in the O. J. Simpson trial that determined whether the group would sacrifice him. When the verdict was read, the press reported that sobs sounded, audiences gasped, jaws dropped, people cheered and spoke. "I felt the verdict in my sinuses," Jeffrey Toobin (1995) wrote for the *New Yorker.* He also registered the time-stopping clarity of the outcome. "I thought how rarely life is like this—a single moment when everything changes. I urged myself to seize it, capture it, write something profound in my notebook" (48). This is the ritualizing impulse. Televisual and print media did seize it, repeatedly re-presenting the transformation of the defendant's face in the moment that uncertainty became acquittal. Media also endlessly re-presented the postures and facial expressions of congregants in different racial groups reacting to the verdict.

Successful rituals multiply connections among bodies. These are social connections. They include every body-to-body interaction precipitated by ritual events. New rituals of solidarity are generated among congregants. Michael Matza (1995) reported that as voting returns came in on Quebec's future, "separatists gathered for what they hoped would be a great victory party. They banged on drums. They stomped their feet. They cheered and whistled wildly. In front of a giant video screen on which the returns were projected, they swooned with ecstasy with each new village recorded for oui and recoiled at every non" (A6).

The pope's visit to Newark was depicted in the *New York Times:* "The faithful broke into reverent cheers shortly before 6 p.m. as two huge television monitors showed the Pontiff's vehicle circling the block. Murmurs and ripples of excited chatter filled the French Gothic church" (Stout 1995, B1).

Reuters World Service described the reaction to Prime Minister Rabin's assassination: "Hundreds of Israelis waiting outside a Tel Aviv hospital broke into screams and tears when a spokesman announced Prime Minister Yitzhak Rabin's death from an assassin's gun. . . . Others simply clutched their heads in disbelief. Grown men wept openly. . . . Teenagers lit candles, placed them on the sidewalk and sat in circles around the small lights flickering across from the hospital where Rabin, the only Israeli leader to be assassinated, was taken spattered with blood" (Gur-arieh 1995).

A successful ritual brings the group to a new sense of itself as a corporate body.[8] When rituals are successful, congregants say so. After the kidnapping and murder of eight-year-old Polly Klaas in California, a neighbor explained that Polly "means everything to this town, because she made it really small again. She solidified what we have" (quoted in Gross 1994, A12).

When a talented New Jersey high school senior died in a car accident, her friends put aside (thereby, it should be pointed out, sympathetically sacrificing) their own work to complete her science contest project, which won a posthumous prize. A school official recalled the rituals of bodily connection and group unity her blood sacrifice had created: "Day after day the pain was so intense. . . . Everybody was hugging, touching. We kept pulling together rather than separating apart. I really feel we have a connection through this that will keep us together for the rest of our lives" (quoted in Stewart 1995, 29).

But here is a description of an old photograph, an early twentieth-century mediation of a ritual event that gets closer to the process by which blood sacrifice unifies groups and by which groups gesturally forge and renew themselves: "A large group of men and women were standing near a tree. Hanging from that tree was a bloodied corpse. Smiling men, women and children stood at the base of that tree, pointing up at the dead black man as if directing the camera's eye toward the corpse. These white people beamed. There were great smiles on their faces, as if they took great pride that this bloody black corpse hung from that tree. They had done it, you see. They had killed the man. And they were glad" (Gaiter 1994, 21).

The most important task of ritual is fostering group cohesion. When it does this successfully, it is moral by the lights of the group performing it. The criterion for successful ritual performance is not whether it accords with an elusive universal morality but whether it generates a corporate group sense. As there is testimony about ritual success, there is testimony about ritual failure. "After Quebec votes to stay, it is as split as ever," read a headline following the referendum on independence for Quebec. This is an unsuccessful ritual. The group remains divided and perhaps has become more so. "Jury Clears Simpson in Double Murder; Spellbound Nation Divides on Verdict," reported the *New York Times*. "We knew we were a divided society," the columnist Anthony Lewis (1995) wrote. "But not before had the depth of the division been so instantly dramatized." He concluded with a powerful metaphor of group disunity: "It was as if we lived in different countries" (A31).

Conclusion

Society organizes bodies. Rituals organize society. Rituals recall, mimic, and transform bodies to reproduce the social bloodline. Their transformative power depends on how much they alter participant bodies at key moments of group birth and death. Ritual seeks embodiment because whatever is vital, including groups, must be embodied. While the most obvious attribute of mediated rituals is that the bodies of congregants and participants are separated from one another, media are ritually driven to offer the illusion of bodily presence restored. Since this presence cannot actually be restored, the transformative power of ritual re-presentation in media is weaker than the transformative power of body-to-body rituals. Still, media use ritual formats to sculpt current events for re-presentation, instruct congregants to ritual procedures, and recall rituals past. By this means, they help sustain enduring groups whose members are physically separated from one another at important ritual moments. By re-presenting bodies at critical moments of group transformation, they play a critical role in keeping nation-states cohesive.

Notes

1. The arguments in this essay are based on the author's book with David W. Ingle, *Blood Sacrifice and the Nation: Totem Rituals and the American Flag* (1999). See also Marvin and Ingle (1996).

2. This territory has been trod by others but somewhat differently. Ronald L. Grimes (1987) argues for "the primacy of the human body" in ritual studies but limits this primacy to the body's "capacity to enact social roles and body forth cultural meanings" (423).

3. On media ritual, see Rothenbuhler (1998); Dayan and Katz (1992); Bell (1997); Farrell (1989); Coleman (1994); Elliott (1982); Schudson (1994); Ettema (1990); Deegan (1989); and Real (1975).

4. See van Gennep (1960); Mauss (1973); T. Turner (1980); V. Turner (1967); Bourdieu (1977, 1990); Douglas (1982); and Bell (1992). See also Goody (1977).

5. A key argument in this area remains Clifford and Marcus (1986).

6. Sometimes it may be more powerful. See Marvin and Ingle (1999).

7. Not all progeny are accepted. Some biological reproduction creates consternation and fear. Some ritual reproduction works the same way.

8. For a discussion of systematic factors in ritual success, see Marvin and Ingle (1996).

References

Bell, C. 1992. *Ritual Theory, Ritual Practice.* New York: Oxford University Press.

———. 1997. *Ritual.* New York: Oxford University Press.

Bourdieu, P. 1977. *Outline of a Theory of Practice.* Translated by R. Nice. Cambridge: Cambridge University Press.

———. 1990. *The Logic of Practice.* Translated by R. Nice. Stanford, Calif.: Stanford University Press.

Bragg, R. 1996. "Search Called Off for Survivors of Crash in Everglades." *New York Times,* May 13, A1.

Clifford J., and G. E. Marcus, eds. 1986. *Writing Culture: The Poetics and the Politics of Ethnography.* Berkeley: University of California Press.

Coleman, S. 1994. *Redefining Solidarity: Media Technology, Ritual, and Protestant Fundamentalism.* Ovieda, Spain: International Sociological Association.

Comaroff, J. 1992. "Bodily Reform as Historical Practice." In *Ethnography and the Historical Imagination,* edited by J. Comaroff and J. Comaroff, 69–91. Boulder, Colo.: Westview.

Dayan, D., and E. Katz. 1992. *Media Events.* Cambridge, Mass.: Harvard University Press.

Deegan, M. J. 1989. *American Ritual Dramas: Social Rules and Cultural Meanings.* Westport, Conn.: Greenwood.

Douglas, M. 1982. *Natural Symbols.* New York: Pantheon.
Eliade, M. 1959. *Cosmos and History: The Myth of the Eternal Return.* New York: Harper and Row.
Elliott, P. 1982. "Media Performances as Political Rituals." *Communication* 7 (1): 115–30.
Ettema, J. 1990. "Press Rites and Race Relations: A Study of Mass-Mediated Ritual." *Critical Studies in Mass Communication* 7 (4): 309–31.
Farnsworth, C. H. 1991. "Canada Holds Its Breath as Quebec Votes. *New York Times,* October 31, A12.
———. 1995. "150,000 Rally to Ask Quebec Not to Secede." *New York Times,* October 28, 1.
Farrell, T. B. 1989. "Media Rhetoric as Social Drama: The Winter Olympics of 1984." *Critical Studies in Mass Communication* 6 (2): 158–82.
Foucault, M. 1972. *Discipline and Punish: The Birth of the Prison.* Translated by A. M. Sheridan. New York: Pantheon.
Frankel, M. 1995. "News of a Lifetime." *New York Times Magazine,* June 11, 28.
Gaiter, L. 1994. "American Mantra: Blame the Black Man." *New York Times,* November 12, 21.
Goody, J. 1977. "Against Ritual: Loosely Structured Thoughts on a Loosely Defined Topic." In *Secular Ritual,* edited by S. F. Moore and B. G. Myerhoff, 25–35. Amsterdam: Van Gorcum.
Grimes, R. L. 1987. "Ritual Studies." In *The Encyclopedia of Religion,* vol. 12, edited by M. Eliade, 423. New York: Macmillan.
Gross, J. 1994. "California Town Mourns Abducted Girl." *New York Times,* December 6, A12.
Gur-arieh, D. 1995. "Israelis Weep, Scream at Rabin's Death." *Reuters World Service,* November 5.
Halberstam, D. 1991. "Where's Page 2 in TV News?" *New York Times,* February 21, A21.
Holmes, S. A. 1995. "After March, Lawmakers Seek Commission on Race Relations." *New York Times,* October 18, A1.
Jameson, F. 1981. *The Political Unconscious.* Ithaca, N.Y.: Cornell University Press.
Jehl, D. 1995. "A Moment of Disbelief and Uncertainty." *New York Times,* November 6, A1.
Kleinfeld, N. R. 1995. "The Day (10 Minutes of It) the Nation Stood Still." *New York Times,* October 4, A1.
Lewis, A. 1995. "An American Dilemma." *New York Times,* October 6, A31.
Marvin, C. 1994. "The Body of the Text: Literacy's Corporeal Constant." *Quarterly Journal of Speech* 80 (2): 129–49.
Marvin, C., and D. W. Ingle. 1996. "Blood Sacrifice and the Nation." *Journal of the American Academy of Religion* 64 (4): 35–48.
———. 1999. *Blood Sacrifice and the Nation: Totem Rituals and the American Flag.* Cambridge: Cambridge University Press.
Matza, M. 1995. "Quebec Rejects Proposal to Secede." *Philadelphia Inquirer,* October 31, A6.
Mauss, M. 1973. "Techniques of the Body." Translated by B. Brewster. *Economy and Society* 2:70–88.

Rappaport, R. 1979. *Ecology, Meaning, and Religion.* Berkeley, Calif.: North Atlantic Books.
Real, M. 1975. "Super Bowl: Mythic Spectacle." *Journal of Communication* 25 (1): 31–43.
Rogers, W. 1995. "Rabin Assassination." *CNN News,* November 4, Transcript #614-1.
Rothenbuhler, E. 1998. *Ritual Communication: From Everyday Conversation to Mediated Ceremony.* New York: Sage.
Schudson, M. 1994. "Culture and the Integration of National Societies." *International Social Science Journal* 46 (1): 63–81.
Stewart, B. 1995. "After Tragic Death, Students Fulfill Their Friend's Dream." *New York Times,* January 14, 29.
Stout, D. 1995. "On Newark's Highest Hill, Faith and Joy Overflow." *New York Times,* October 5, B1.
Toobin, J. 1995. "A Horrible Human Event." *New Yorker,* October 23, 48.
Turner, T. 1980. "The Social Skin." In *Not Work Alone,* edited by J. Cherfas and R. Lewin, 112–40. Beverly Hills, Calif.: Sage.
Turner, V. 1967. *Forest of Symbols: Aspects of Ndembu Ritual.* Ithaca, N.Y.: Cornell University Press.
van Gennep, A. 1960. *The Rites of Passage.* Translated by M. B. Vizedom and G. L. Caffee. Chicago: University of Chicago Press.

JAMES W. CAREY

11 The Sense of an Ending: On Nations, Communications, and Culture

In the fall of 1965, the British literary critic Frank Kermode delivered the Mary Flexner lectures at Bryn Mawr College, later published as an influential little book, *The Sense of an Ending* (1966), from which I take my title. Fictions that imagine "the end" and relate it to "the beginning" are pervasive and persisting features of the human imagination, enduring expressions of one of the ways we try to make sense of our lives. Kermode noted that while the apocalyptic and prophetic genre is general, there are particularly intense historic moments of this imaginative form when people come to believe that *no* earlier way of satisfying the need to know the shape of life will suffice: everything must come to an end to have a new beginning.

While we no longer believe the literal end is imminent, the shadow of the Apocalypse is cast across all our sophisticated imaginings. As Kermode says, "[W]e may speak of it as immanent" (6). If we were always serious and literal in speaking of "the crisis" or the "end of an era," we would be living in ceaseless transition (7), as Harold Rosenberg (1959) and Raymond Williams (1961) told us we were. There are, however, certain fundamental chronological markers—Kermode calls them saecula—that, while quite arbitrary, are made to "bear the weight of our anxieties and hopes." The sense of an ending may be a permanent feature of our imagination, but certain markers of the end are projected onto history that create a "perpetual calendar of human anxiety" (11). The end of a century is one such marker.

Today the most popular title in our literature takes the form "The End"—The End of Art, Architecture, Conversation, Democracy, History, Sovereignty, Racism, Belief, Religion, Kinship, Equality, Ideology, Science, Marxism, the Family, the Modern, the Bourgeois Class—take your pick. This is the "structure of feeling," to use Raymond Williams's felicitous phrase, of our time, mingling apocalyptic and redemptive endings. Nothing signals this structure better than the notion of the postmodern, combining as it does images of ultimate fulfillment with recipes of disaster: the postmodern moment is either denouement, where everything of value is running to red ruin, or another Eighth Day, the day after creation, of a new beginning.

In an essay in the late 1960s, I examined images of communications and technology as millennial impulses resurfacing in response to the disorders of the decade and early anticipations of the year 2000 (Carey and Quirk 1970). But if we live with the sense of an ending, what is it precisely that is ending, and what is beginning? That is the context in which I discuss space, time, culture, and nations at the end of the twentieth century, a discussion that takes the form of a prolonged meditation on Harold Innis's epigrammatic sense of an ending, namely, that Western history began in time and is ending in space.

On October 24, 1998, the 350th anniversary of the Treaty of Westphalia was observed, though without much notice in the United States beyond the *Chicago Tribune*, which, alone among American newspapers, devoted a portion of a front-page article to it (Longworth 1998). Yet the treaty is of some importance both to an understanding of the history of nations and to the history of communications. As conventionally understood, the treaty brought to an end the Thirty Years' War and recognized the sovereignty of the German states. More important, it marked the end of the Holy Roman Empire as the defining presence of Western history and civilization. The treaty also established the principle, though only the principle, of religious tolerance and the separation of church and state, with its utopian hope for a universal citizenship. Finally, it marked the beginning of the modern European state system, the polar star and model of the international system to this day.

The anniversary reminds us of just how modern the system of nations really is. Prior to the treaty, people belonged to—better, were organized by and took their identities from—empires, civilizations, principalities, and religions but not to nations.[1] There are very few nations that predate the modern era: France assuredly, England perhaps (but not Great Britain), and maybe Japan (Pfaff 1993). Nations were, by and large, formed within modern history and are the major expression of that history, just as nationalism is the dominant form of ideological bonding in the modern era. We are misled on this by the way nations write their histories for, not surprising, most trace their beginnings to the mists of time, to myths and legends of origin that posit the preternatural existence of the nation. Despite that, the nations we know are products of the eighteenth, nineteenth, and, above all, the twentieth century: products, that is, of modern thought and modern technology.

Nations, like all political and social organizations, have definite physical limits; that is, they live within geography or space. Similarly, they have definite temporal limits; that is, they live within history or time. This is so obvious that it usually goes without saying, but its implications are hardly explored. Duration and extent define the borders of social organization. But where are the origins and limits of these borders? What purposes do they serve? How do spatial and temporal borders act as technological containers shaping the lives of peoples consigned to different locations along them? How does technology, among other things, figure into the establishment and maintenance of these frontiers? How are spatial and temporal boundaries reciprocally related?

The epigram that Western history began with time and ended in space means, as a first approximation, that religion was the dominant form of social organization at the point of origin of the "imaginary community" of Western civilization, what we generally call, with all its limitations, Western Christendom. This was a civilization with vague and imprecise geographic boundaries stretching from portions of Britain to a line that runs down the borders of what are today Finland and Russia and somewhere in the middle splits Belarus, Ukraine, and Romania. At that point Western Christendom ran into other religious traditions that provided relatively impermeable barriers—Eastern Orthodox and Islamic. The space of Western civilization was occupied unevenly, however, with rivals, religious and political, everywhere within its borders. The weakness of the church in maintaining spatial sovereignty was compensated for by a monopoly over language—a portable sacred language, Latin, and stable, orally transmitted vernaculars—which controlled the coordinates of memory and posterity—past and future—the basic temporal framework within which identity and loyalty were constructed and enacted. The control or monopoly of the church was exercised in time by the construction of history or narrative.

The Treaty of Westphalia signaled the beginning of the end of a civilization based on religion and time as the basis of social organization and its replacement by the nation, politics, and space. Religion did not disappear, of course, but moved in three alternate directions. Religion was assimilated by the nation in the form of national religions—One Nation under God—thereby giving up its claim to universality and sovereignty to serve, in return for state protection, as a legitimation of politics. Or, religion became submerged in the geological structure of national societies, a religion again of the catechumens, lying about in monuments and language, waiting for a moment of reassertion. Or, alternatively, it took the form of what Robert Bellah (1967) has called "civil religion": multireligious nations were sacralized by merging the vocabulary and myths of the dominant religious traditions within its borders.

Nations differed from religions as a form of social organization in their emphasis on *spatial* borders. Nations sealed their frontiers and regulated their relations to surrounding space through defined apertures. The border (or frontier) became the basic political institution, for the border defined the center and allowed for the imposition of internal order and form. As Malcolm Anderson (1996) says, the "linear and exclusive state frontier, in the sense currently understood, scarcely existed before the French Revolution" (1). Since then, the frontier has defined, in a legal sense, a sovereign authority. The identity of individuals and their claims to nationality and the exercise of rights of citizenship were delimited by the frontier. The modern state is, in Gianfranco Poggi's (1978) words, the "sole exclusive fount of all powers and prerogatives of rule" (92), and such power could be realized only if the state brooked no rivals to that sovereignty—from religion or anything else—and if it made its frontiers impermeable to unwarranted external influences. As a matter of prudence, the state may grant privileges and immunities to religions or other institutions and groups, but it will tolerate no nation within the nation, that is, no contestant for sovereignty. That is what makes the nation space-binding.

However, a price is exacted for such spatial control. Nation-states experience perpetual problems of temporal instability and psychological displacement. The terms *anomie* and *alienation* were invented to describe this chronic problem. As Thomas Jefferson recognized and turned to a virtue, every generation of the nation is sovereign relative to the past and future; nations live for the moment, though I am of course exaggerating, sacrificing control over the past and future, tolerating perpetual revolution in time for control over borders and space. We have had, for example, many French republics within fairly constant geographic boundaries. There are, however, some people who have lived in three or four different nations in this century while never having moved from the house in which they were born.

Harold Innis (1951) initiated the argument that nations are creatures of, or made possible by, the printing press, by a light, portable means of communication that was easily movable, thereby effecting control at a distance. Print was also subject—compared with, say, the oral tradition—to deterioration in time. Language may be more portable in the hand, but it is more durable in the head. Since Innis's pioneering work on the relation of print to the nation, Marshall McLuhan (1965) and many others, principally Elizabeth Eisenstein (1983) and Robert Darnton (1989) in the United States, have produced a remarkable body of research that has extended, corrected, and filled in the wide gaps in what we know about the printing press in relation to, among other things, the politics of nations.

The most influential work on nations and nationalism in recent times has been Benedict Anderson's (1983) analysis of print capitalism as the agent creating "the imaginary community of the nation." In Anderson's analysis, nations are defined as a people who in the main never meet, who never know one another in any ordinary sense, but who nonetheless identify with one another, assume they possess outlooks in common, and live lives that flow, by and large, in steady harmony and uncoordinated coordination. As Anderson puts it, "An American will never meet, or even know the names of more than a handful of his 240,000,000-odd [now 280,000,000] fellow Americans. He has no idea of what they are up to at any one time. But he has complete confidence in their steady, anonymous, simultaneous activity" (31). This is the psychology of the nation as a sociological organism that moves calendrically through homogenous time: a solid community, invisible and anonymous, united by a shared reality existing under the date of a newspaper or the dailiness of television broadcasts. That psychology is the product of or, better, made possible by certain mass ceremonies, significantly performed, in the main, in silent privacy, "in the lair of the skull" or in the relative isolation of the private domicile. Anderson continues:

> Yet each communicant is well aware that the ceremony he performs is being replicated simultaneously by thousands (or millions) of others of whose existence he is confident, yet of whose identity he has not the slightest notion. Furthermore, this ceremony is incessantly repeated at daily or half-daily intervals throughout the calendar. What more vivid figure for the secular, historically clocked, imagined community can be envisioned? At the same time, the newspaper reader, observing exact replicas of his own paper being consumed by his subway, barbershop or

residential neighbors, is continually reassured that the imagined world [the world imagined in the newspapers] is visibly rooted in everyday life . . . creating the remarkable confidence of *community in anonymity* which is the hallmark of modern nations. (39–40, emphasis added)

Printing, Anderson suggests, defined the nation as a uniform reading space. This implies, as a corollary, privileging the vernacular in print, radically simplifying orthography and literate form, controlling the circulation of foreign languages, creating a uniform educational system, centralizing administration in the vernacular, and downgrading sacred languages from a lingua franca to a particular antique dialect.

The consequences of printing were intrinsically contradictory. The printing press, as Elizabeth Eisenstein (1983) has pointed out, both eliminated and preserved languages, effaced old borders and erected new ones, and spread secularism along with a narrowly focused piety. Printing drove down barriers within states as it erased dialects and regional languages and blunted cultural difference. But it also created or significantly hardened barriers between nations as it constructed new borders by insisting that linguistic frontiers be mapped onto national ones, defining in effect the category of the "foreign." For example, *La France Profonde* slowly consolidated and imposed a degree of uniformity on Normandy, Brittany, Occitania, the Basque country, Provence, Berry, Lorraine, Alsace, and Savoy. The same movement sharpened, made linear and exclusive, the frontiers with Spain, Italy, and Germany. For Benedict Anderson, as with Innis, it was the newspaper—light, transportable, easily distributed over a wide space as a uniform commodity—that created the "imaginary community of the nation." The state used printing to assist in defining and sealing frontiers, allowing cross-border communication only through defined apertures, which it struggled, not always with success, to control.

Once unified, European nations developed the power to leap: to transcend national boundaries and to implant New France, New England, and New Spain in the New World. While this power to leap was the product of advances in the arts of shipbuilding and navigation that allowed the transport of a nation and its furniture through the cultureless void of the ocean, that power was facilitated, and its limitations determined, by the printing press. The ships of exploration were expressions of state power and ambition, but they contained a culture within their hulls. The printing press expedited the transport of a culture, not merely a state, and maintained tenuous ties of correspondence over vast distances. While this movement is rightly seen as the beginnings of colonialism—the creation of wider markets and greater venues for profits—it was also a moment in the history of nations, for it obeyed the most ruthlessly compulsive axiom in the moral geometry of nations: wherever there was a vacant space, that is, a space not occupied by something recognizably a nation-state (for example, a tribe, kingdom, religion, principality, empire, or civilization), it was only right to implant a nation in full dress—religious, political, and economic.

North America is an expression of the power of the nation-state system of Europe to leap its boundaries onto a new continent. The motives were mixed—mercantile, religious, political—and, therefore, the movement in space overdetermined. Nonetheless, whether tying together markets, congregations, or political administrations, the spatial bias of modern, print-based communications was both cause and effect of the impulses of nationalism and the formation of nations. That Europe *overleapt* its bounds in the seventeenth and eighteenth centuries—that communication was so slow that peoples so widely separated could not be kept to the same "clock of awareness," in William Gilmore's (1989) happy phrase, and, as a result, creole nationalism (though it was *creole*) grew in the imperial hinterland—does not reverse the general point of the motives both embodied and realized in the technology.

The nature and power of the modern nation-state were starkly revealed in North America, for here the state was stripped of its ancient and medieval background.[2] Alexis de Tocqueville ([1835] 1961) studied European developments in North America because in that setting the state was accessible in its essence, unencumbered by feudal and traditional baggage that might otherwise conceal it. He was the first to grasp the new structures of authority that emerged with the modern and putatively democratic nation-state. Like other nineteenth-century social theorists, he began with a contrast between the traditionally dispersed authority of the ancien regime and the centralized authority of the modern democratic state that had emerged in France following 1789, which he could see forming in the United States when he visited in the 1820s. For Tocqueville, the modern European state, for which France was the model, represented a major historical change in the structure of society and, more especially, in the structure of authority (Holton 1996, 37). Tocqueville recognized the totalism of the modern territorial state. The state claimed complete sovereignty over society and swept aside the more dispersed and partial sovereignties of religion, feudalism, and aristocratic rule. The modern state claimed total control over the entire geography of the nation. National law was used to override the ascriptive status rights of competing social formations and underwrote the claim of a monopoly of sovereignty within a given territory. The assertion of these claims required the dismantling of the dispersed, pluralistic, self-governing, and fiscally autonomous powers of such bodies as estates, guilds, and churches. Not surprising, such medieval restraints on state power were not present in the United States, except as vanishing moments of colonial rule, which increased the tendency toward centralism and totalism.[3]

Tocqueville recognized compensating mechanisms, freshly innovated (a vast national geography, separation of powers within the state), that limited or contained state power in the United States, though he had doubts about their long-term efficacy. Principal among such countervailing forces was the autonomy of voluntary organizations within civil society. However, he also recognized that the real distinction of the nation-state was its claim to be a rational system of governance that justified the power of the centralized state over any older, traditional authority that might mount a challenge to state prerogatives. A nation may tolerate, even support, subordinate social formations—religious, ethnic, regional, racial—within its borders, but it will brook no authority, human or transcendental, as a competitor to its rule.

Tocqueville had well-known fears, expressed through the notion of the "tyranny of the majority," concerning the autonomy and freedom of individuals living under the totalizing, centralized modern state. He commented that the democratic state "covers the surface of society with a network of small complicated rules, minute and uniform . . . [that] does not destroy but compresses, enervates, extinguishes and stupefies a people, till each nation is reduced to . . . a flock of timid and industrious animals of which the government is the shepherd" (Tocqueville [1835] 1961, 2:381). This views democracy not as a system of unambiguous freedom but, as Robert Holton (1996) points out, in "major respects, as an unprecedented form of penetrating power" (38). Trends toward suffocating centralized control were by no means inevitable. The state could be arbitrary and despotic or moderate and republican in its impact on society, depending on the extent to which voluntary groups, for example, were capable of placing limits on state power. To complete the system of warnings, he added that the major stumbling block to republican democracy is the tendency toward privatism among individuals. He thought the modern state promoted—indeed, had a vested interest in—the absorption of the individual into private concerns inhibiting participation in public life, creating what we would call today a consumer's rather than a participant's involvement in politics. The political actions of the state were thereby judged by citizens in terms of the private, personal advantages that might accrue rather than in terms of a wider public interest. Privatism also discouraged the formation of political associations that might exert a countervailing effect on the centralized state.

The potential tyranny of the nation-state stems from the simple fact that in the modern world everyone belongs to a nation; that is the one nonpsychological fact of human identity in our time. However much peoples may think of themselves as members of minorities, subnations, ethnic groups, or religions; however much they may think of themselves as speakers of such transnational languages as French, Russian, German, English, or Spanish; however much they may think of themselves as self-invented individuals—citizens of the world or particles of the cosmos—no one can cross a frontier without an identity card: a passport must assign one to a nation, however marginally. One needs an identity card, as well, to vote in an election, hold a job, or participate in or, more often, avoid the draft. National identity is not a matter of taste and preference. The most deprived and vulnerable status in the modern world is to be stateless, ever more so the less wealth one has, which is why the Peruvian economist Hernando de Soto (1980) calls nations "the skin of the poor" and why the strength of nationalism varies inversely with social class.

Because nations are, in part, the product of communications media, they live in not only geographical space but also media space, in not only Greenwich time and historical time but also media time. The printing press, through the periodical, established a definite temporal horizon within given spatial frontiers. The newspaper established the day as the basic unit of keeping time within the spatial organization of the nation, though in such large countries as the United States it acted to link the city to the nation.

National geography exists in not only physical space but also media space. The boundaries nations maintain are simultaneously geographic and symbolic. Geographic boundaries are the most common and clearest: the customs and immigration points at which one passes into and out of the physical space of the nation. At such boundaries, identities are confirmed and implanted: citizen, migrant, guest worker, alien, green card holder, and, on rarer occasions, enemy. In political terms and from the standpoint of the nation, these are points of passage between sacred and profane space—space where one is "known" and protected or unknown and unprotected.

Nations are also symbolic spaces—spaces of meanings, values, and identities. Geographic and symbolic space come together in the immigration office on the national frontier. But symbolic space, while bounded, is inherently vaguer than geographical space, for it refers to the points at which people, even if they stay put, pass out from under the sacred canopy of the nation—the system of meanings, values, and identities that legitimate membership. Nation-states, as Carolyn Marvin and David Ingle

(1999) have argued, organize and deploy bodies, which is perhaps the key to Max Weber's definition of the state as the legitimate monopolist of violence. Nation-states therefore require means of identifying bodies, of stigmatizing them, so that they might be otherwise allocated to or segregated from the tasks required by nations. Nations are sociological organisms, but unlike crowds, gatherings, classes, and status groups, they are boundary-maintaining ones. "Passport control" is a place where these boundaries are maintained, where people are marked or are asked to mark themselves, asked to put on the involuntary stigmata of citizens, apostates, heretics, outsiders, interlopers, foreigners, subversives, traitors, or, in the favorite term of one country, un-American. But media also exercise a form of passport control—as will be illustrated later—for within their confines are places and occasions where entire groups are marginalized, defined as minorities, though not as nations, symbolically segregated from the core values and impulses of the nation. Symbolic space and media space are highly contestable because they are inherently vague and indeterminate, constituting invisible and shifting boundaries that are as likely to be stumbled across as much as deliberately breached.

Each communication medium imposes its own distinctive spatial order and confirms it within a steady stream of ongoing reality—the existence of an external world that is in order within a shared social space of awareness—and a particular organization of time: the month, the week, the day, the hour, the minute, the pico second. As one radio slogan has it, "You give us twenty-two minutes and we'll give you the World."

The remarkable confidence in the "community of anonymity" of which Benedict Anderson speaks refers to the ordinary, daily habits through which the world is confirmed in communication. He notes Hegel's line that newspapers serve modern individuals as a substitute for morning prayers, implying that the line dividing the modern from the premodern was drawn when people began their day attending to their state and nation rather than to their God. At the level of culture rather than social organization, media time gradually displaced both liturgical time and natural time and provided the temporal architecture of daily life. In turn, the rhythms of the media were in significant part the rhythms of the state (and the capitalist economy) because cycles of the news were tied to those institutions. When newspapers broke through into the Sabbath, when attending to the Sunday paper became as common as attending religious services, a new qualitatively different rhythm was imposed on the week.

The symbolic space and time of the nation are continuously contested and reshaped in the very media that implant and express them. In other words, the symbolic space of the nation is primarily represented in the media and accounts for the often ferocious struggles among groups over the portrayal of identities, conduct, and values in news and entertainment. At any given historical moment, the medium may differ, for at various times in the past newspapers, magazines, or film have served as the dominant form or medium in which the nation talked to itself. Over the last fifty years, television has constituted, in David Thorburn's (1988) term, the moral or consensus narrative: the site of a daily and largely invisible struggle, one that goes on behind the screen and the front page and in the silent "lair of the skull" over the values and identities that form the symbolic space of the nation and its most general terms of inclusion and exclusion.

The printing press and, above all, the newspaper may have been able to create a uniform reading space and the imaginary community of a nation for European states, but these are, comparatively speaking, geographically small nations. The largest of the Western European nations, France, would find plenty of room inside California and Oregon. To create a nation the size of a continent with an emphasis on "united" rather than on "states," a nation that even at its founding was incomparably large—500 by 1,000 miles—required something more than a printing press, good roads, fast horses, and an efficient post office. The united states were just that—states but hardly united—until a faster more powerful infrastructure could be found to shape their intercourse. It required the railroad and the telegraph in combination to turn a loose collection of political sovereignties into an integrated nation, one in which a national identity and a national community predominated. The building of that infrastructure began early in the Republic's history, but its major episodes occurred between 1840 and 1890. Until then, the states were largely united in common defense and by a common tariff against the reassertion of colonial rule. When the states survived the major episode of disunion, the Civil War, and, more important, when Britain, which supported the separatist efforts of the Confederacy, signaled the end of its designs on North America by granting Canada quasi-independence in 1867, the shape of a continental nation was decided, except for the aggressive tidying-up of relations with the old Spanish Empire.

To understand the process by which nations were formed in North America, let us turn to one arena of long-term intellectual dispute: the role of the "frontier" in U.S. and Canadian history. Despite the similar settlement histories of Canada and the United States, American historians of the West, with a few notable exceptions, follow Frederick Jackson Turner's (1920) emphasis on the frontier as a thin, moving line separating savagery from civilization, thereby underscoring the frontier's role as the site of authentically democratic impulses and institutions and disconnecting the frontier from the urban centers of the East Coast. Even when American frontier historians focused on cities, they rarely emphasized the relationship between the country and the city but treated them instead as independent entities. Canadian historians, led by Harold Innis, have more or less rejected the Turnerian frontier notion and in its place have focused on the emergence of cities of outstanding size that dominated both the surrounding countryside and other cities and their countrysides. Entire metropole-hinterland areas were understood as organized by the metropolis, through control of communication, trade, and finance. Together they form one economic and social unit, focused on the metropole, that regulates trade with the world. Beneath the central metropolis are smaller cities, playing similar but less extensive roles. The relationship of cities is like a chain of feudal vassalage in which one city may stand as tributary to a bigger center and yet be the metropolis of a sizable region of its own.[4] To put it more formally, the relationship between the metropolis and the hinterland was homologously reproduced in the relations of smaller cities and hinterlands. Particular metropole-hinterland relations, organized around the production of staples and other commodities, constituted the source of distinctive regional and national cultures in Canada and the United States.

In North America, this emphasis on the interdependent relations of the rural and the urban, the frontier and the city, the metropole and hinterland highlighted relations among regions knit together by a long-distance, spatially biased system of communication focused on New York. This underscored the process by which the United States developed through an imperial competition among cities—Boston, New York, Philadelphia, Baltimore. For example, Chicago could be understood only by taking literally its complaining self-description as "The Second City." It grew as an outpost of New York and was decisively shaped by interurban competition that created the corridor of communication and transportation joining it to New York. Chicago was the western outpost of a metropolitan economy centered on New York, which in turn mediated relations with European trading capitals. On the streets of Chicago, products of different ecosystems, different though interdependent economies and interdependent ways of life, came together and exchanged places. In the United States, an artificial corridor had to be built, for there were no natural ones like the St. Lawrence River. It was built by rail and canal, lock and dam, national highway and country road. It was a corridor of fairly cheap transport that appeared like a fault line across the diverse cultural and economic zones of the American West. The railroad, canal, and telegraph broke radically with geography, for they made possible the straightest possible line, a geometrical route through areas with high market demand and low operating costs. These technologies—unlike the foot, boat, horse and carriage—operated pretty much independent of climate and therefore evened out the seasons that controlled the rise and fall of economic cycles. They straightened time by controlling time zones and substituted the regularity of mechanical time for seasonal time, merging night and day, winter and summer, wet times and dry times. When one entered a railroad car or the telegraph system, one entered an environment separated from the outside world and with its own sense of time and space. Wherever the railroad and telegraph extended, frontier became hinterland. And, as people prospered in the hinterland, they became more dependent on distant, remote, unknown institutions: grain elevators, commodity brokers, railroads, vaudeville circuits, traveling minstrels, and wire services.

Turner chose to see the frontier as a rural place, the very isolation of which created its special role as a cradle of a distinctively American democracy. It is not that this view was totally wrong, but it obscured much that had to be rescued. Against Turner's romantic view, it was necessary to demonstrate what now seems merely obvious: the country would not be there without the city in which to sell its crops and products; the city would not be there without a countryside to feed it. These relations had gone invisible and were scorched over by ideological work. This invisibility served to isolate human life from the physical and cultural ecosystems that sustained it, a process intensified, as we shall see, a century later by the Internet and World Wide Web.

By 1800, New York was the crucial geographic node in the American communication system, and it needed an interior city that it could control as its gateway to the staples beyond: hardwoods from Michigan and Wisconsin, ore from the Mississippi basin, crops from the prairies. If Chicago was to be a tributary of New York, then Chicago would act as a great catch basin, drawing 700,000 square miles of western territory into its feeder system and concentrating it at its mouth. This demanded the transformation of a natural landscape into a spatial economy. Western cities came into existence when eastern capital created remote colonies in landscapes that contained few people. "Front-tiers" were thereby linked to "back-tiers" and to an international system of cities. Chicago and New York were nodal points of a trunk communications system, and the principal problem of communication was to link them closer together in space and coordinate their activities in time. Chicago, in turn, attempted to draw hinterland cities into the same relation and to stave off competition from other hinterland cities, such as St. Louis and Milwaukee. The frontier may have been the outer edge of a wave, but it was more than a wave of civilization and migration. The frontier also marked the extension of market relations into the ways humans used land and one another. The penetrative power of the price system sometimes paralleled, sometimes preceded, and sometimes followed the penetrative power of the state; both, not the extension of democracy, were major forces in national expansion, though to emphasize them does not demean the importance of the democratic impulse. In a thinly settled country, effective markets—markets effective enough to compete with the denser markets of Europe—required the extension of physical markets beyond rimmed and identifiable places. It required creating everywhere and nowhere markets, markets bound together not by face-to-face trading relations but by the spatial bias of modern media (Chandler 1977).

The metropole-hinterland relations in the U.S. system of cities were reproduced in the relations between the United States and Canada. Although Canada was never an American colony, its relation to the United States was homologous to Chicago's relation to New York: Canada and Chicago were shaped by staple commodities, and their relations to the manufacturing world and the international system of cities and countries were mediated by trade relations governed largely, though never exclusively, by the United States and New York and their monopolistic control over trade routes and, to a lesser extent, communication and culture.

These relations, engraved into the physical, symbolic, and media ecologies of North America, lasted through the age of television. Such geographic trunks and tributaries, for example, formed the infrastructure for long-distance telephony, which, in turn, carried network radio and television. Such routes were fundamentally modified only after the deregulation of jet travel and the launching of satellites for broadcasting and point-to-point communication.

Frederick Jackson Turner celebrated 1890 as marking the closing of the frontier, but it was also the enclosing and definition of national space. Such space was enclosed in two senses. First, the nation was enclosed, reaching its manifest destiny as a prelude to a leap beyond its own borders in imperial expansion. The expansion of the railroad and telegraph had connected the major cities into a national system of transportation and communication, and in the later years of the nineteenth century, the vacant spaces were backed and filled, hooking "island communities" into a national society (Wiebe 1967). This process everywhere met local resistance, but the "system was the solution," and communities everywhere were either integrated into it or circumvented and left to die. The second closing resulted when national networks of communication invaded the space of local institutions. That is, local institutions of politics, commerce, and culture were reconfigured as end points or nodes in national structures. Local political organizations became outposts of national parties; local businesses became elements in chains; local newspapers, lectures, performances, concerts, and educational institutions became stops on, in a manner of speaking, a national circuit. They lost their autonomy and, increasingly, their local identity.

As the spatial frontier was closing, time was opened as a "new frontier." Time was, first of all, standardized into a national grid so that everyone was on the same clock of awareness. The telegraph organized and controlled time zones so that organizations and activity could be coordinated nationally. But new "times" were also opened as commercial and other forms of activity broke into the Sabbath and then upward, through the electric light, into the nighttime. As I suggested earlier, the invasion of time began with the Sunday newspaper's occupation of the Sabbath. Eventually, nationally produced communications would occupy and monopolize every space and every time: every office, home, street, city, and institution; all time, sacred and secular, seasonal and annual, daytime and nighttime. One would never be out of earshot or eyeshot of national media. This imperialism of images spread the representation of the national into all geographic times and spaces and into all cultural times and spaces as well. The system represented an imperative that every social time and space should be filled by commerce and communications. The national system, the system of the modern, was, in the case of the United States, formed in the 1890s, and subsequent developments in communications—motion pictures, radio, television—were, from this perspective, protracted and relentless mopping-up operations—perfections in what Innis would call the particular spatial bias of American media.

These changes also produced a crisis of representation; they raised the disorienting specter of an unknowable society lacking the terms or vocabulary necessary to ingest these changes into consciousness. The maturing of the wire services, the growth of national magazines, the development of national retail organizations and catalog sales, rural free delivery, national advertising and marketing, and national political parties all had the effect of eclipsing the local, of terminating the existence of self-contained island communities. Urbanization, industrialization, the maturing of industrial capitalism (with increasingly international connections), the closing of the frontier, and the eclipse of agriculture as a predominant way of life and with it the country town as a cultural force were events that closed the nineteenth century and marked the true foundation of a national communication system.

At that closing, three distinct ecologies were knitted into one continuous social organization. The first was a purely physical ecology, as the landscape was technologically inscribed via communication and transportation and social groups formed settlement patterns, whether in the city or the country, by radiating over the networks. This was at one level a purely physical struggle, as groups battled to find and maintain an ecological niche—literally a biospatial home. But there was also a symbolic ecology, for the struggle for space was inevitably transmuted into a series of symbolic fronts. People engaged in biospatial struggle had to name and identify one another, opponents and partners had to be characterized, symbolic space and group values had to be rendered intelligible. The pastoral language of the country and the city and the terms and epithets derived from it—local and cosmopolitan, red neck and city slicker—were the residues of such struggle, as were the identities, sacred and profane, that ethnic groups bestowed on one another. There was a media ecology that overlaid both the physical and symbolic struggles. Newspapers, magazines, and eventually radio and television stations rendered these underlying physical and symbolic struggles intelligible by narrativizing them and, not so incidentally, displacing and devaluing the "local knowledge" by which the struggles were originally understood.

The city, at one level a purely physical world, also contained an imaginative world of social relations. Media were overlaid on these baser ecologies, producing yet another imaginative world, one articulated to and integrated with the national community. The communities of the city were in every case transmuted or diasporic communities. Some were formed out of the physical diaspora of migration—nationally and internationally; others were formed by such imaginative diasporas as the new professionals who lived in the national worlds of medicine, law, journalism, and the other professions; still others inhabited even more ephemeral but equally imaginative worlds: the art world, the fashion world, and so forth. These diasporic groups were twisted and knotted into one another in urban life; they were given form by the symbolic interactions of the city and the ecology of media that reported on and defined these groups to one another, fostered and intensified antagonisms among them, and sometimes even sought forms of mutual accommodation.

The modern era of communications begins for the United States during the decade of the 1890s. Greater precision is unnecessary, for that decade can serve as the approximate moment when space and time were enclosed, when it became possible to think of the nation as everywhere running on the same clock of awareness and existing within a homogeneous national space. The telegraph and the railroad from the 1830s forward gradually laid the infrastructure for a national society that linked every town and time into a regular and periodic national system of communications, a system with a beat as steady as a heart and a space as enclosed as a body. Of course, long after 1890, many people continued isolated existences, many communities held on even though bypassed or only superficially penetrated by modern technology, and the struggle of local life against the national system continued throughout the twentieth century. Nonetheless, by 1890 everyone, in principle, was keeping to the same clock and was accessible to the same media on a regular basis. However intermittently, everyone became part of the great audience, the imaginary community of the nation, capable of a singular focus of attention at a determined time. No longer could people live, except by heroic efforts, in isolated island communities, exclusively attuned to local rhythms and customs, dimly aware of a nation beyond local borders except as news irregularly arrived or national emergencies precipitated a heightened consciousness of the nation.

The perfection or completion of this national system took place over many decades and required the invention of other, more flexible and "lighter" means of spatial conquest—film, radio, and television. Because technologies of communication and transportation come in matched pairs, national relations were mediated progressively by telegraph and train, film and automobile, television and aircraft. Despite differences in these technologies, they formed a complex ecology governed by a common end: the construction and integration of a national society in which distant centers of political, economic, and cultural authority could form direct relations with individuals circumventing the interference of local, immediate, and proximate institutions. Such technologies therefore ought not be artificially bracketed and hived off into distinct histories. Instead, their meaning and import must be understood within a complex ecology governed by a common project.

If, at the outset of the process, the daily novel of the newspaper, the dominant form of popular printing, created a uniform reading space and the imaginary community of a nation, television turned entire countries into congregations devoted to worship of the idea of the nation. Television cemented and rendered visible what was less apprehensible in the age of the printing press: a particular structural relation between the state, technology, and the economy in which *the authority of the state, the economy, and the national culture* was nailed metaphorically to every tree via a television signal, dominating all the partial and particular cultures and authorities contained within national borders. The master narrative was the story of the nation, which assumed the sacred vocabulary, compulsory ritual, and inescapable obligations of membership once accorded the church. As Carleton Hayes (1960) observed, the nation adopted patriotic rituals that resembled religious ones, elevating the state, as giver of private as well as public morality, into a simulacrum of the deity.

Television completed and perfected the national system, finishing what the printing press, wire services, and national magazine had begun. Television became a wall-to-wall, everyday medium. It blanketed social space and social time in their entirety; no time or space was left uncovered. With television, every home in the nation and, with only slight exaggeration, every individual within the home could be linked to every other home and individual through a common medium, which is to say, through a centralized source of supply, a truth that held, irrespective of whether television was organized as a state monopoly or a commercial oligopoly. The first cable systems, the last mile of the national system of communication and, as it turned out, the first mile of the new global system, linked those places inaccessible to over-the-air signals and fulfilled the social imaginary of the nineteenth century—the eclipse of time and space: one nation under a common system of communication ("one nation under television" as J. Fred MacDonald [1994] usefully called it), sitting down to be counted together, at the "same" time and for the same purposes. In country after country, whether driven by commercial or political imperatives, the names of television companies expressed the desire and the result: the American Broadcasting Corporation, the British Broadcasting Corporation, systems that could endow individuals with an identity, members of the great audience who were also part of a great national community.

The American South provides one compacted example of the nation-forming process that will be useful later in this essay. Historically the South was isolated from the rest of the nation by every measure of transportation and communication available: number and circulation of newspapers and magazines, miles of highway and railroad track, per capita penetration of telephones and motion picture theaters, and so forth. While this can be partly explained by disparities in per capita income, such regional variations have been true throughout the history of the country and do not fully account for the relative absence of communication between the South and the rest of the nation or the low levels of intraregional communication in the South.

More important, the South was bypassed as the United States developed on an east-west axis, with the major roads, highways, railways, telegraph and telephone lines—the basic infrastructure of communication—running on routes from New York to San Francisco and from Baltimore/Washington to Los Angeles. The historic South remained at best a spur on the major trunk lines. Because the South developed in relative isolation from the rest of the country, it evolved and maintained a distinct culture, expressed in many different ways but particularly through race and religion.

Following the Civil War, regional disparities in communication were reduced but were not eliminated until the network television system penetrated the South. At this point, the flow of communication ran largely in one direction—from northern production centers into the South, with fairly low levels of return or feedback. Television made the South part of the national congregation. It radically increased the knowledge southerners had of the rest of the country without a corresponding increase in northerners' knowledge of the South, with an important exception. Although southern television stations tried to restrict the flow of images of race and race relations coming into the region from New York and Los Angeles, they ultimately failed. Black actors started to appear on television programs viewed in the South, and news flowed into the region contradicting the images of race and the norms of race relations long cherished by the South. Since race was one of the keystones in the arch of Southern culture, this led, eventually, to a civil rights movement focused on the South that became a staple of television news, entertainment, documentary, and docudrama. In short, the introduction of television into the South put the region on the same clock of awareness and enclosed it within the more homogenous space of the nation. Television robbed the South of control over its culture, its peculiar practices; television centralized the authority of national politics and culture over the region and made the South more northern. It did much more, however, to which I turn later in this essay.

Our understanding of television and the nation-state has been greatly advanced by Daniel Dayan and Elihu Katz's (1992) analysis of media events. Whereas Benedict Anderson concentrated on the historical formation of nation-states at the dawn of modernity via the printing press, vernacular languages, and a shared imagination of historical time, the media events that have engaged Dayan and Katz come from a later stage in the history of the nation-state or in the life of new states, born after World War II, such as Israel, or reborn, such as postcommunist Poland, in the age of television. Television permitted a level of national integration in both large and small states that was difficult to achieve, except on a reduced scale, in the age of the printing press. The "high holidays of the media," as Katz (1980) termed televised media events, had their more ephemeral and transitory counterparts in the "extras" of newspapers, the moments when the natural priorities of the telegraph were suspended to achieve a relatively simultaneous focus of attention among widely dispersed readers, or in extraordinary public gatherings where news was read or repeated to the entire community. In the age of television, media events burst localized confines and took on a national and even international character because of the migratory habits of television signals and the emphasis they gave to the relations of peoples rather than merely states.

Media events, then, are episodes in the history of the nation-state and, in the age of television, the relations between states, nations, and peoples. They are among the most important forms in which the imaginary community of the nation is created and sustained. While television created distinctive conceptions of space and time, media events were eruptions within this spatio-temporal framework, altering both media and natural routines. Media events declare holidays, a time out, from the everyday character of both media time and natural time, the time of communication and the time of history. They also upset spatial frameworks, declaring "space-outs," substituting sacred for profane space and periodically redrawing the geography of the nation, dragging the expatriate and foreigner into the national space as coparticipants in the ritual.

Media events reconfigure attention by disrupting the predictable regularity of the real, the habitual flow of routines of reading and viewing. They are deviations from the norms of the media and the ongoing certainty of history and of the nation itself. As Michael Ignatieff (1998) puts it, "In a culture overwhelmed by massive amounts of promiscuous representation, there must be some practice by which the real . . . is given a place of special attention, a demarcation that insists that it be *seen*" (30). While it is often said that modern culture is impoverished in sacred ritual, Dayan and Katz have detailed sacred occasions in modern, secular culture for which television has devised its own rhetoric and ritual, enfolding viewers in a sense of the pious importance of these moments: the hushed voice of the commentators, loving attention to uniform and vestments of power, meticulous attention to stage and set, and, above all, the tacit inference that what is being represented is a rite of national significance.

Dayan and Katz treat media events as collective social rites, an anthropology of celebration that draws on central sacral codes of the social order in which the elementary process underlying the dramatic forms is the rite de passage. Media events integrate a diverse set of expectations into a narrative genre. The media event is an exceptional public performance where the nation through the medium of television partakes in a ceremony celebrating its core, sacred values or memories of its collective history. But whatever the outward resemblance of media events to religious rituals and however much these events utilize symbols and narrative forms drawn from the warehouse of religions, they remain celebrations of national memory and national deities. They are dramaturgical displays of the nation to itself and occur in a "fictional register," something made, not found. The rituals, contrived and fictitious, speak to the desires of the audience in a subjunctive key: rites that display what a society most essentially is, what the nation should be, or what the nation desires to be—its scared ideals as compared with its mundane, vulgar realities. Those practical realities are not ignored on television. Indeed, the strength of everyday television is the degree to which it forms a consensus narrative (Thorburn 1988) concerning the contours of everyday life. Consensus does not refer here to a common body of belief or agreement about collective needs and values. Just the opposite: a consensus narrative is agonistic in the precise sense that it represents the conflicts and struggles within a nation over what to believe, what to need, what to value.

Media events are partly distinguished from other news and entertainment on television by the peculiar role of the audience; the audience's participation is central to the narrative of the rite. Such fundamental social rituals require public witness from those who represent the primordial power of the nation before it is organized by institutions, regulated by rules, and delegated to legitimate authority. The rite of transition invokes the primordial power of the populace as the basis of the democratic order and suggests that the transitional rites and powers have been properly delegated by citizens to the legitimate officers of the nation.

This emphasis highlights the key aspect of media events as analyzed by Katz and Dayan: media events are moments of reconciliation and reunification, a reintegration of the nation in its commitment to shared values and goals. "The message is one of reconciliation, in which participants and audiences are invited to unite in the overcoming of conflict," they declare (8). "Almost all of these events have heroic figures around whose initiatives the reintegration of society is proposed. Even when these programs address conflict—as they do—they celebrate not conflict but reconciliation" (12).

In all of these matters, they follow Victor Turner (1969) in considering social dramas a progressive sequence that moves from conflict to reconciliation. Conflict is a stage that is surmounted in the drama or ritual. The dominant motif, in short, is not social division or reflexivity and enhanced public discussion. Furthermore, the congruence of accounts provided by government, media, and social institutions and the ingestion of the population in the central dramatic spectacle mean that rites are not especially polysemic or multivocal. The thesis that media events are an expression of society's central values, combined with the notion that central social institutions must necessarily agree to the production of the ceremonies, means that all media events are characterized as largely integrative.

Such rites involve moments of *communitas,* for they display the collective society as a undivided group outside of the privatized roles and differentiated statuses of individuals. They speak in the neo-Durkheimian spirit that holds that mechanical solidarity—a sense of membership, similarity, equality, familiarity—is at the foundation of the organic solidarity of differentiated, to say nothing of postmodern, politics (Durkheim 1961). Here they point to Durkheim's special role for rituals, not just as social integration but in the creative construction of the social categories underlying the social order.

The weakness in the analysis of Dayan and Katz lies in their exclusive focus on media events as instances of integration and reconciliation and the lack of attention paid to ceremonies that end in consolidating divisions, excluding groups, and polarizing opposition. Media events do more than integrate society, celebrate consensus, and overcome conflict. There are also distinctive rites that break through ordinary media time and space as moments of disintegration, moments that highlight unresolved and unresolvable conflict and threaten the basis of social consensus and the capacity of the society to adapt. Contests, conquests, and coronations, the categorical structure Dayan and Katz employ, do not exhaust the classification of media events. Occasions of degradation, shame, and excommunication are also fundamental to the genre. These are ceremonies that reinscribe cultural geography into explicit rites of passage during which bodies are stigmatized, reputations destroyed, and citizens expelled into the guild of the guilty.

While episodes of integration and national reconciliation are fundamental and of critical importance, they should not obscure that media events, like the religious rituals on which they are based, also consolidate divisions in society, polarize opposition, and exclude groups from the sacred center of social and symbolic space. Rites of excommunication on television are of particular interest, for the readmission of the stigmatized to official society must then be conducted in the same medium that was the site of the expulsion (Carey 1998).

Degradation ceremonies and the larger family of events of which they are a part do not meet a model of the celebration of consensus. They touch on core, sacred values but are episodes in the production of dissensus, episodes in the re-creation, indeed redefinition, of lines of social demarcation and exclusion. Instead of uniting the audience and the polity either in expectation or fact, they divide it ever more deeply. Their central element is not merely conflict but also bitter discord and struggle. The event produces neither catharsis nor relief but ever widening and expanding ripples of civil disquiet. Media events include drama without rest or resolution, drama without catharsis or consensus, drama that divides people more sharply and intensifies the perception of social difference, drama involving confrontation that spills outside its ritual frame to contaminate and reconfigure social relations at large. Media events are often exercises in social cruelty that teeter on the edge of legitimacy and bear dangers beyond purely ritual ones. They threaten civil society because they suture the audience into systematic cruelties and institutionalize civil discord.

While Dayan and Katz do not cite the work of Robert Bellah, their analysis shadows his conception of the role of civil religion in modern, complex, differentiated, multireligious societies. Bellah (1970) suggested that formal declarations of the separation of church and state and the insistence on the modern state's secular character had not denied the political realm a religious dimension. Alongside clearly differentiated churches, a well-institutionalized civil religion existed. Although matters of strictly religious belief, worship, and association were considered to be private affairs, a common religious orientation was shared by the great majority of members of modern societies. Bellah argued that "civil religion, at its best, is a genuine apprehension of universal and transcendent religious reality as seen or, one could almost say, as revealed through the experience of . . . people. Like all religions, it has suffered various deformations and demonic distortions. At its best it has neither been so general that is has lacked incisive relevance . . . nor so particular that it has placed society above universal human values" (179–80). These values play a crucial role in the development of institutions and provide a religious dimension for the whole fabric of life, including the political sphere. The public religious dimension is expressed in a set of beliefs, symbols, and rituals manifest on formal occasions of state: inaugurations, funerals, declarations of war, the return of war dead—in other words, on the occasion of media events. Civil religion is also present in the specific languages of ceremonial politics; in the American case, the language of Exodus, a New Jerusalem, a Chosen People, a Covenant creating a City on a Hill, Blood Sacrifice, Rebirth, Witness, and Civic Virtue.

Media events, then, at least as they exist in the United States, express a social contract of moral obligation essentially in Protestant theological terms for the simple reason that the founders of the nation were Protestant. Robert Bellah and Phillip Hammond (1980) suggest that when the founders expressed noncontractual ideas, they employed familiar terms from Protestantism, especially the Puritan tradition, centered on "a notion of covenant, while at the same time denying ecclesiastical claims to exclusiveness" (203). This view seeped into and informed the American code. The civil religion was neither sectarian nor Christian, though it had much in common with Christianity. While originally formulated out of the central terms of the Protestant pulpit, over time it was steadily broadened and distanced from its Protestant origins. By the time of the Civil War, a war directed by Protestant elites and fought, in significant measure, by a Catholic army, the language of Protestantism had to be extended to envelop broader Christian traditions. In the twentieth century, the code words were enlarged to include the Judeo-Christian heritage, and, in recent years with the influx of Muslim immigrants, civil religion has been increasingly identified as "Abrahamic." But civil religion is not merely inclusive. Such religions set definite narrative terms for telling the story of the nation, and, like media events, such religions establish boundary conditions; they exclude as well as incorporate, stigmatize as well as honor, excommunicate people from discourse as well as interpellating them into it.

Civil religion and media events share one other thing in common: both notions arrived on the intellectual scene at the moment the phenomena they described were disappearing. Little of the civil religion remained intact, despite its historic importance, amidst the clamor of the Vietnam War and the civil rights movement. While both of these movements of protest were originally expressed in the language of civil religion (think of Martin Luther King Jr.'s famous "I Have a Dream" speech at the Washington monument or the Port Huron statement of Students for a Democratic Society), by the late 1960s that language was thoroughly displaced; a vocabulary of political power and violence displaced the more reassuring biblical images of a sacred quest for individual rights. To many of its critics, the notion of civil religion suggested a cargo cult or ghost dance: an attempt to avoid or deflect real social conflict by invoking a mythic past at the moment the religion and the civic culture the myth supported were "gone with the wind." More important, the idea of civil religion provoked the scorn of clergy, for it seemed a clear competitor to church religion and an attempt to erode it. In other words, the nation-state could dominate religion as long as the relation was not explicitly noted, theorized, and privileged. If that was done, the attempts to reform the churches in the image of civil religion (for example, turning denominations into branches of the Democratic or Republican parties) would meet determined resistance in the name of the separation of church and state.

A further blow to civil religion came from the growing strength of the conservative movement following the Vietnam War, a movement containing contradictory elements of libertarian and religious conservatism. On the one hand, the libertarian wing of hard-core conservatism argued that civil religion was unnecessary. The social bond of modern nations was properly a purely rational one, provided exclusively within an economic framework of costs, prices, and utilities. Conservatives argued that economic exchange alone could provide sufficient social solidarity for modern life and that it was merely atavistic to believe that exchange, uncontrolled by the culture of civil religion, promoted anarchy, unbridled power, and a Hobbesian war of all against all. Economic exchange, the argument went, provided an awareness of interdependence, of the link between self-interest and the collective good, and nothing more than this purely secular framework was necessary or appropriate to modern society. On the other hand, the religious wing of conservatism sought to destroy the tepid morality of civil religion and to substitute a narrowed, rejuvenated, and fundamentalist Christianity.

Two strengths of Bellah's analysis of civil religion, unappreciated by many of his critics, were, first, his emphasis on the plural and negotiated status of the sacred and, second, the recognition that the link between self-interest and collective good, while not necessarily religious, must be understood as transcending human choice if it is to achieve legitimacy and be more than merely coercive. Prior to the triumph of the market, this link between self-interest and collective good had been embedded in a metaphysical apparatus taken to be in the nature of things and therefore could serve as the source through which people interpreted their fate, understood good and evil in their lives, and made sense of the rituals conferring collective identity: something lived rather than contemplated, natural rather than invented, given rather than constructed, embraced rather than tolerated. Religion and nation, separably or together, have been such identities for they are the source of a shared and general culture rather than a partial and limiting one.

Media events have suffered a fate similar to that of civil religion and for parallel reasons. Most obvious, the structural conditions of media events—the ability to assemble the nation as a congregation—were undermined by the rise of cable and satellite television. The great audience assembled by oligopolistic commercial networks or public service television organizations has been fragmented into segments small enough that it becomes impossible to imagine the conditions under which it might be reconstituted, except for the most dire of national emergencies. In short, the ritual character of media events and civil religion has evaporated into multichannel, postnetwork television systems.

The cause of the shift in the television system was in part purely technological: the ability to construct through cable, computer, and satellite an economically feasible, indeed profitable, multichannel system. However, an equal cause, though the language of cause and effect hardly makes sense here, was the same conservatism that undermined civil religion. When the notion emerged that "choice" should be the sacred term of communication, though the term was taken to be rational rather than sacred, justifications of communications policy based on culture, or a shared ritual experience, or collective good became incoherent. Not only was there no longer an economic need for a common television system, but there was no longer a cultural or political need either. Politics, culture, and religion could be turned into consumer goods subject, at least superficially, to individual choice rather than common appropriation. That is approximately where we are as the twenty-first century opens.

The national system of communication that embodied, symbolized, and ritualized a common national narrative and civil religion held until sometime in the 1970s, when a decisive unraveling began with the launching of satellites for direct-pay television, the inauguration of Home Box Office, and the subsequent transformation of small cable systems, which were merely adjuncts of network television, into independent competitors of the networks. Finally, and perhaps most important, the great private and public monopolies in telecommunications were broken up, deliberately in most cases, and the entire sector of communications deregulated. The changes that took the national communication system apart beginning about 1975 had many precursors, and the process set in motion would continue for decades.

The consequences of these changes on both the national and international stage were contained by geopolitical factors for more than a decade in much the same way that the introduction and consequences of television were delayed and contained by World War II. With the end of the cold war, the restraints imposed by world politics were shattered, and the new configuration of cable, satellite, and computer technologies, reinforced by changes in public policy, opened up novel conceptions of time and space, individual identity, and social action; they opened up social, political, and economic possibilities that transcended the boundaries and restraints of national communication, national identity, and national religion.

In the wake of these technological changes, every modern nation has witnessed a dazzling array of new communication services, the proliferation of computers and cell phones as consumer goods, the breakdown of the structure of national broadcasting, disarray in political parties and processes, alterations in patterns of settlement, the emergence of new dominating firms, a new plutocracy unknown two decades ago, and the bursting of borders and boundaries of all kinds, political as well as personal. At the international level, there has been a breakdown in governmental authority and the breakup of states; the intensification of tribal, ethnic, and religious conflict; the migration, forced and voluntary, of large numbers of people; and the proliferation of weapons of aggression, the spread of terrorism, and a new wave of massacres and ethnic cleansing.

However dangerous and frightening, there is something alarmingly familiar about these phenomena. Postmodern technologies and flows of communication have produced phenomena parallel to those that accompanied the creation of the modern system of communication in the late nineteenth century: the eruption of new social movements that attempt to reconstruct politics, economics, and social life; a new world of space and time brought about by new communications technology; a new migration that unsettles established social fronts of the city, nation, and globe; and the international expansion of capitalism that keeps the whole pot boiling.

If the disturbances of the world were confined to the "objective" sphere of the economy and politics, they might be seamlessly assimilated. However, these objective conditions are subjectively experienced as the displacement of identity, or, in more fashionable terminology, the decentering of the subject. This is experienced as a category crisis or cultural meltdown in which established conceptual schemes no longer make adequate sense of the self or the world and result in frenzied attempts to build new conceptual schemes to account for changed circumstances. Taken together, deconstruction and postmodernism attempt to delegitimate old patterns of understanding and create new categorical structures as replacements.

Throughout national cultures, we are confronted by category crises, failures of definitional distinction, and transgressive leaps. Borderlines between cultural categories become increasingly permeable, and crossings between fundamental distinctions—between objective and subjective, black and white, male and female, the normal and the abnormal, rich and poor—are both common and problematic. To generalize, everything has been placed in doubt, is under erasure. We can no longer take the established categories of culture for granted, whether they are seen as constructed or biological. This represents a displacement of fixed and given subjectivities and sets in motion a restless search for new identities that can act as the countersigns of new practices. In turn, the category crisis sets in motion the search for new metanarratives with which to tell the story of our lives.

Of this much we can be sure: the consequences of these technological changes in communications will be contradictory. Contradiction is the essence, not just an accidental by-product, of the process. As I argued earlier, the printing press broke down some barriers or borders but simultaneously created others. Printing opened the borders separating learned languages from the vernacular and therefore widened the possibilities of communication across existing barriers of class. It also lowered the barriers separating many forms of communication: philosophy and the crafts, for example. But printing simultaneously created new borders; it hardened the barriers between the sciences and humanities and between various vernacular languages, sharpening the distinction between, say, French and German, and it also led to the elimination of Latin as a lingua franca of transnational scholarship, isolating national scholarly and religious traditions. Printing illustrates the maxim that improvements in communication make communication more difficult, for the technology, while effacing some ancient borders, led to the creation of new and equally problematic ones.

It is a cliché of the cyberspace literature that a new and borderless world is under construction because of the computer and satellite. This is partly true but misleading. There is no doubt that nations, for example, are losing control of their borders, whether understood as geographic or symbolic. Nations are more easily penetrated not only by transnational flows of communications but also by flows of people. Even such island nations as Britain and Japan, always the most resistant to these flows, have lost control of their borders. Nations find themselves under two kinds of pressures, one from above and one from below. Globalization puts pressures on the external borders of nations, and sovereignty over affairs gravitates upwards to transnational collectives: trading blocs, nongovernmental organizations, and corporations. Similarly, nations are being collected into new and institutionalized regional coalitions, such as the European Union, an expanded North Atlantic Treaty Organization, the North American Free Trade Area, and a still primitive but growing Asian sphere. Such supranational organizations as the World Trade Organization, the International Monetary Fund, and the World Bank exercise dominion over matters that were once solely at the discretion of nations.

Nations are also under pressure from below, the most conspicuous of which are separatist movements that bedevil every country. Equally important are barriers and borders based on race, class, ethnicity, and gender that have emerged as fault lines of intensified intranational conflict.

If some borders are going down, one can be sure that other borders are going up, though the latter are much less visible and difficult to detect than the former. Cultural fragmentation and postmodern homogenization constitute contradictory, dialectically related trends of a single global reality (Appadurai 1996). Examples abound. Quebec desires not only an exit from Canada but also membership in the nations of North America. Catalan wants greater autonomy from Spain but greater presence within Europe and a strengthening of the Council of the Regions. Elites in every advanced nation desire more independence and isolation from the restraints of locality, while, as Zygmunt Bauman (1998) points out, "the rest of the population finds itself cut off from and forced to pay the heavy psychological, cultural and political price of ensuring the isolation and freedom of elites" (21). Nations, caught in the contradiction between homogenizing and fragmenting forces and unable to resolve it, are torn as sovereignty simultaneously evolves upward to the transnational and devolves downward into regional, class, ethnic, and racial segments. Many take pleasure in the rending of nations because they see the nation-state and nationalism as malevolent forces. But even if that judgment is warranted (and I believe it must be highly qualified), the dislocation of sovereignty produces new ambiguities, dangers, and conflicts and, most menacingly, throws into doubt received understandings of democracy and civil liberties.

We exist, then, in a "verge" in the meaning Daniel Boorstin (1978) gave that word: a moment between two different forms of social life in which technology, among other things, has dislodged all human relations, and nothing stable has replaced them. The world seems to be imploding and exploding at the same time, experienced imaginatively as simultaneously coming together and falling apart (Barber 1996). In the mid-1970s, we entered a new phase in the history of the compression of space and time. As telecommunications has burst the constraining boundaries of the nation-state, social structures that have defined the modern world and established its direction have been thrown into disarray, and national cultures have been forced into cognitive and affective meltdown. Two briefly developed examples—moral space and computer time—can serve to represent the ambiguities and contradictions of these developments.

In 1996, the BBC television broadcast a moving documentary, *The Crying Room,* filmed when three reporters smuggled cameras into China to record the treatment of children in rural orphanages. It was a morally disturbing, indeed heartbreaking, program, as one watched children filling gymnasium-sized rooms, sitting tied to potty chairs for the entire day, and rhythmically rocking back and forth in the autistic sway. While it must have affected the rate of adoption of Chinese children, though that was not its announced purpose, the documentary contained a larger lesson, which I paraphrase from Michael Ignatieff (1998).

At about the time of the Vietnam War, television began to mediate, through its graphic images of suffering and death, the moral relations among strangers. This is one of the clearer and positive manifestations of Marshall McLuhan's notion of the global village created by advanced electronics. Strangers are understood here as those outside the imaginary community of the nation. It was a contradiction to say that one's compatriots were strangers. The moral space of the nation had been contained within television from the outset, and the civil rights struggle in the United State was a powerful example of the inclusion of hitherto isolated towns and villages into this moral space. In the 1960s, that moral space was widened to include the daily appearance of war, famine, disease, and pestilence from around the globe, bringing the suffering of strangers into the living room. Television helped forge a direct relation between people that cut across national boundaries to become a new kind of electronic globalism, more so in news than in entertainment, linking the conscience of almost everybody with almost everybody else. Television thus contributed to a more universal moral citizenship, breaking down barriers of geography, race, religion, and nation that divided the moral landscape into those for whom we were responsible and those beyond our ken. While Western humanism always contained this element of moral universalism—what is liberalism without it?—it was always enclosed by national borders that surrounded the arena of natural sympathies. The nation was the primary container of moral space and moral sympathy.

Television, at the end of its network era, created a new kind of moral universalism built on a new experience of wrongdoing: the crime against humanity. With it came a new politics of nongovernmental organizations—Amnesty International, Medicin sans Frontières, and Oxfam are but a few examples—that refused to make a distinction between good corpses and bad ones, famines that are our concern and famines that are not, diseases that are ours and diseases that are theirs. As Michael Ignatieff (1998) observes, these are organizations that assess nations and ideologies by the victims they leave behind.

Global television takes as its domain the world. This is clearest in the commercial sector with its self-serving slogans: "The world is our audience" (Time-Warner), "We see the world as one civilization" (Archer Daniels Midland Company). But commerce is hardly the only source of national transcendence. The moral space of the nation is increasingly penetrated as well. Cultural and psychological barriers that divide suffering into classes with whom we identify because they are "like" us and those whom we are privileged to ignore because they are "unlike" us can no longer be easily maintained, which is why the Balkans present a moral as well as a political problem for all the parties.

If moral space is being redrawn, so too is psychological time, and here the computer is the site of struggle. Computer time is kept in coordinates fundamentally different from the older systems of clock time because its underlying code is expressed in micro, nano, and pico seconds. Recently proposals have come forth for rebuilding the coordinates of time to bring them in line with computer logic.

The British were the navigation timekeepers and Greenwich, England, ground zero for temporal reckoning in the modern period, the age of territorial navigation. The Swiss emerged as the pure timekeepers, those who kept time independent of space, and, perhaps not surprising, the first proposal to establish a new standard of computer time has come from Switzerland, a time country rather than a space country.

The Swiss Watch Company, Swatch, has created a standard appropriate to the Internet and World Wide Web. Dubbed Swatch Internet Time, the new system divides the day into beats rather than minutes or seconds. One beat equals 1.0 minute and 26.4 seconds, and each day consists of 1,000 beats. The meridian for Swatch time runs through the company's headquarters in Switzerland. Thus, the new day begins at midnight central European time: @000 (identifying time with the common email address symbol). Midday central European time is @500. On America's East Coast, a new day begins at midnight EST or @250, and the day on the West Coast begins at @375. On the other side of the earth, a new day begins in Tokyo at @667, and midday local time is equivalent to @167. Those variations disguise the fact that Swatch time is uniform time calculated independent of space: every Swatch watch would read the same time wherever a person is in the world and wherever the sun is in its orbit.

Cyberspace or Internet time is a coordinate without seasons and has neither night nor day. Internet time is absolute for everybody. It is advertised as time without politics because it is global rather than national. One of the first adopters was CNN, which now offers on its home page an Internet time version of its latest updated banner and a converter from local time to Internet time. Netscape tells time in Swatch time. In January 1999, Swatch began selling watches that display both local time and Internet time.

While Swatch Internet Time might seem fanciful, no more than a gimmick, the product of the publicity department of the Swatch Watch Company, it is wise to remember that standard time, the dominant time frame we live in today, was a product of the railroads. In the United States, it was New York Central Time before it was railroad time. Railroad time existed for thirty-five years before it was officially adopted by the U.S. government as the standard system for measuring and regulating time during World War I.

Despite the evidence of fundamental social change, I must return in closing to the lessons of Frank Kermode in "the sense of an ending." We may be at the beginning of the third millennium, but we are hardly at the end of history. We have not as yet taken up residence in the postmodern, nor have earlier ways of making sense of life come to an end. Chiliasm is a "natural" mood of writing and reading in this time, but the actual fin de siècle is much more mundane. Despite cultural fragmentation and postmodernist homogenization—both of which are real tendencies in the empirical world—we are not yet at the end of the nation-state or the modern; the world is both less fragmented and less homogenous than it seems.

Of course, the nature of the nation-state is being changed because of the declining capacity of governments to control much of the traffic in persons, goods, and information that flows across borders. Other social formations, usually weaker and less cohesive imagined communities, may be now better able to transcend the confines of the state, and myths of regional, continental, and hemispheric unity will therefore grow in tandem with an unstable mix of racial, ethnic, religious, and gender-based myths of particularity.

But even if the penetrative power of the price system is now, as it was in the early modern period, virtually unrestrained across national and institutional boundaries and even if much commerce is hypermobile and corporations, investors, and institutions move information and capital over vast distances at blinding speeds by fax and modem, the world system still relies on legal, financial, and other services that are part of a geographically situated infrastructure and cluster in cities within nations. The continued importance of national currencies alone, as the European Union has discovered, is enough to restrain the vision of a globalized and borderless world. The global, in fact, is not out there; it is embedded in national regimes, even though such regimes now stand in differing relations to one another. Corporations, even global ones, come and go, disappearing when their power to command a market evaporates or when they fail to control costs or keep pace with technological change. Nations, however, do not fail in the same way corporations fail. Except in special and especially important circumstances, they are not "merged" into other nations or subdivided into constituent parts. While nations may be happy or unhappy with their economic performance, they have no well-defined bottom line.

Nations go bankrupt only in a metaphorical sense; their creation and destruction are attributable to something more than economic factors. Despite all the forces seeking to transcend the nation, today nations remain the sturdiest of collectivities and nationalism the most rampant ideology. The evidence for this lies in the relationship between the centers and margins of social formations. The most powerful centers are national ones, and the critical margins are, simultaneously, external borders, the ambiguous geographic points at which nations meet, and internal borders, where lines are drawn between those who belong to the nation and those who do not. Both are points at which national identity threatens to evaporate.

As long as national borders, internal or external, define the critical margins in the minds of most people and nations retain the monopoly on legitimate coercion and violence, national consciousness will continue to be deeper and more powerful than global consciousness or consciousness based on race, class, gender, and the like, and nations will remain for some time more solid and enduring realities than either sub- or transnational formations. And the nation will remain, to anticipate yet another argument, a cultural rather than an ideological prototype, its character the outcome of history and culture, including the history and culture of its economy, rather than of ideology.

The principal power among men and women, like it or not, is still nationalism. As early as the late middle ages the nation began to displace religion as the strongest bond of community among large numbers of people, as Benedict Anderson has emphasized. Carolyn Marvin and David W. Ingle's (1999) remarkable work has shown how nations continue to possess a religious character and are formed, maintained, and repaired through ritual, particularly rituals of blood sacrifice and atonement. Nations are not merely textual communities, Anderson's useful insights notwithstanding; they are embodied in their citizens or subjects and the sacrifices they are periodically called upon to make, in body and imagination, to the gods of the nation.

All this makes national cultures even more psychologically recalcitrant than individuals; generation after generation, instead of year after year, they display the same traits. However much these traits may be reshaped, adapted, and newly proportioned, they are, relatively speaking, intransigent. A central character in many cultures, the trickster, can stand as an archetype of the cultural process, for the trickster represents the persistent, recurrent, and contradictory impulses of a people. Thernadier in *Les Miserables,* to chose an accessible representative of the trickster, continually reappears, always an optical illusion that takes us a moment to recognize. While the guise is always different, the character—ambitions, motivations, moods, and desires—are always the same and serve to both mock and highlight the more serious and pretentiously resolute character types in the culture. Despite the fact that tricksters embody antisocial attitudes, despite the fact they are often on the side of the irrational and evil, audiences are asked to identify with them. The trickster provides an example of the way the broad, rich, community-forming meanings of culture are embedded and opposed to the narrower identities of race, gender, and class.

Still, there is evidence, as I have emphasized throughout, that we are returning to what Samuel Huntington (1996) has called a "pre-Westphalian condition," in which culture breaks loose from its national moorings and is realigned in transnational and subnational linkages. Huntington's primary example of this change is religion. As he puts it, "the separation of church and state, an idiosyncratic product of western rationalization, is coming to an end and religion is increasingly likely to intrude in international" and domestic politics as well (54). The age of ecumenism, cultural as well as religious, may have passed at both the local and international levels. A period in which moral values and cultural outlooks were taken to be private matters and tolerance a shared value may be giving way to antagonism and difference as cultures universalize their particularity in transnational movements and particularize their universality in more rigidly bounded local communities and formations.

The nation is no longer the focus, explicit and implicit, of the social imaginary. Peoples and countries with similar cultures are coming together. Peoples and countries with different cultures are coming apart. Alignments defined by ideology and superpower relations are giving way to alignments defined by culture and civilization. Political boundaries increasingly are redrawn to coincide with cultural ones. Cultural communities are replacing cold war blocs, and the fault lines between civilizations are becoming the central lines of conflict in global politics. Because the roots of culture remain religious (as the old saw has it, always inquire of an atheist whether he or she is a Protestant, Catholic, Jewish, or Muslim atheist), a shift to political blocs based on culture and civilization means that religion displaces nation as a primary axis of human identity and a force in politics at all levels. That is Huntington's argument, barely paraphrased, and it captures a real tendency and its potentially destructive consequences at the opening of the twenty-first century. But even if that is true, transnational religious particularities remain expressions of or enclosed by national cultures. The Islamic, Jewish, and Christian diaspora has rendered Mecca, Jerusalem, and Rome, if anything, more important as controlling sites of memory, but it has not rendered national capitals irrelevant.

In an essay thirty years ago (Carey 1967), I suggested that one way to understand the global processes then emerging was to recognize that human diversity was disappearing, at least in a spatial sense. Communications, technology, and economic modernization were reducing the variations in conduct, culture, and human institutions throughout the world. The contrasts that remained were, to use Clifford Geertz's phrase (2000), paler and softer than those detailed in the anthropological texts. All of us were increasingly living one uniform way of life under very similar economic and political circumstances.

However, I also suggested that the end of diversity and social conflict was not yet at hand for two reasons. First, as spatial diversity decreased, temporal diversity increased. As differences among people in space declined, differences among people in generational terms increased. The axis of diversity, in other words, had shifted from the space to time, from differences between societies to differences between generations within societies. The sharpest evidence of this was the development of new age-segregated patterns of living and, more important, the generational styles of popular culture that bore discontinuous outlooks and sensibilities. Again, generations are embedded in a contradiction: generational differences increase, but age hierarchies become blurred. Adults in their different ways become more like children, and children, in their different ways, become more like adults, for which contrasting images of grade school murders and twelve-year-old mothers stand alongside geriatric baseball games and pregnant grandmothers as tropes.

But spatial differences, rather than simply decline into some softer and paler version, true as that is, also become relocated from there to here. The age of large undifferentiated total societies facing off against one another, as Geertz (2000) suggests, is gone. The old comparisons of East versus West, primitive versus modern, developed versus underdeveloped, anthropologist versus native do not work anymore. There is no longer an East here and a West there, a primitive in Malaysia and a modern in New York. The natives are everywhere, and so are we. If someone is predicting the weather from the entrails of a pig, chances are that person is living next door. If there is widow burning going on, it is likely to occur outside of town rather than halfway around the world. The most publicized case of cannibalism encountered in recent years did not occur in some dark continent elsewhere but in relatively enlightened Milwaukee. The communication and transportation system is now running in reverse, cultures are imploding, taking up residence next to one another on the television set and in the housing subdivision. You can sample many of the tribes of world by taking a one-hour stroll through the neighborhoods of most large cities or grazing through cable television channels.

If I can shift the metaphor to an aesthetic one deployed by Geertz, we can no longer understand the world as a still life through the standing back of perspectival painting. Rather, every society is a collage of conflicting and randomly assorted elements in which the artist is absorbed into the art. We live now amidst enormous cultural and social diversity, part of it the persisting traces of older ways of life and part of it generated on such new axes of differentiation as sexuality. There seems to be no end to the delicacy and invidiousness with which we can describe, impute, and elaborate human difference. We can no longer count the number of tribes—old and new—that array themselves before us.

These differences are both less stark and more pronounced than ever before. The "narcissism of small differences" (Ignatieff 1998) governs the social world, rendering it both more uniform and more conflictual. Difference may be paler and softer, but the struggles over the differences that remain are more intense. Even if conflict over religion and ethnicity persist, other, historically more trivial differences take on an unprecedented intensity and animus.

This is a displacement in which, to again borrow a formulation of Clifford Geertz (2000), a world of integral societies in distant communication disappears into a collage of side-by-side and jumbled societies of clashing sensibilities and unavoidable conflicts (85–87). The redistribution of culture in space makes variant structures of subjectivity and alternative models of the life world more readily available for imitation and adoption. We are exposed, in short, to an increasing, rather than diminishing, number of ways in which people think their thoughts, live their lives, and arrange their institutions.

In making the argument for the decline of spatial diversity, I assumed that the modernization process worked more uniformly than in fact it does. What seems to be closer to the facts would go something like this. For much of the nineteenth century and the twentieth, the technological, scientific, cultural, and political forces emanating from the advanced nations had the effect of spreading a thin layer of similarity onto a global grid so it appeared that cultural difference was being effaced. Subsequently, however, the spread of the modern system of communication ran into a deeper, more fundamental resistance, a resistance easily dismissed as cultural lag but actually a process of indigenization, whereby technologically imported culture was nativized in the very act of being absorbed. Arjun Appadurai (1996) has argued that as fast "as forces from various metropolises are brought into new societies, they tend to become indigenized in one or another way; this is true of music and housing styles as much as it is of science and terrorism, spectacles and constitutions" (32).

He is suggesting that as the pace of modernization increases, indigenization replaces modernization as the primary axis of social change. Eventually, the rate of modernization declines, and local cultures, infused now with power borrowed from the very modernizing forces that were resisted, go through a revival. Further modernization then alters the balance of power between nations, bolstering the self-confidence of previously dominated societies and strengthening their commitment to native or indigenous culture.

This is true even in such a country as the United States. I earlier argued that television broke the barriers that separated the South from the rest of country and brought isolated southern communities into a national civic congregation. Let me close by using that case as an exemplar. In the American South, television was both powerfully resisted and transforming at the same time. The South could not go backwards or remain the same. Even those who resisted change developed vested interests in the aspects of the new ways of life opened up by an enveloping national society. In a sense, people could not go home again, but they did not want to leave home either. The old structures of community were no longer satisfying even for those who did not want to leave home. The simultaneous resistance and adaptation resulted in a new southern culture—more modern, liberated, aggressive—and, at the same time, a "southernization" of the entire country. Small-town southern religion had to adapt to a national culture, and its ministers wanted a national stage on which to operate. As a result, the evangelical and ecstatic versions of Christianity spread nationally and gave southerners a new vested interest in the nation and in national class and status distinctions. The South was freed from isolation to work a larger effect in both shaping the future and reconstructing understandings of the past.

It comes as no surprise that a separatist movement, still small, has broken out in the American South. The Southern Party, which immediately suggests an inverted, American version of Italy's Northern League, has as short-term goals merely the election of state and local candidates with the aim of sending enough party members to Congress to work toward a more distant horizon: a separate southern nation. The web site of the party asserts that "the shotgun wedding forced upon the South at Appomattox has reached a dead end, and it is time for a political divorce for the good of all parties concerned." Its propaganda even invokes sacred personages: "Lincoln once said that a house divided would not stand. Lincoln was wrong. A house divided will stand. It's called a duplex." The criteria for forming a southern nation are particular and religious: "We believe the United States in general and the South in particular are defined by their historically European and Christian ethnic, linguistic and cultural core . . . This cultural majority represents the true fusion of blood and soil that defines what the Southern nation is" (quoted in "Secession Party" 1999, A8). Interestingly, the newly conceived southern nation has imperial designs, incorporating from the outset the old border states of Missouri, Kentucky, West Virginia, and Maryland in an attempt to surround the District of Columbia by the "old South."

The message of the Southern Party is this: if the United States prefers to stay a multiethnic, civil religion nation linked to the wider world through the North American Free Trade Agreement, then the South will join the community of European Christian nations—another Catalan. This effort will fail, of course, but that is not the point, for in failing it will, with only modest electoral success, change the United States.

While the American South has been modernized, the American nation has been southernized. This distinctive American phenomenon can serve as both model and metaphor for the world at large. Contrary to my earlier belief, the spread of technology has a differential impact during the modernization process, advancing modernization at one point and promoting or at least leading to resistance at others. In the first phase, increased contact between nations promotes modernization. In the second phase, such contact promotes demodernization, first, by strengthening the political and economic power of hitherto dominated nations and subnations and, second, by generating, through anomie and alienation, a return to established culture forms, though of a more ecstatic and passionate version than that embraced by modernizing elites themselves. At this point, a reconstructed and emotionally appealing version of an age-old established culture is better able to interpret, grasp, and deal with the novel needs of people wrenched painfully out of tradition, whether that tradition is ancient or, like the American South, a product of an earlier phase of the modernizing process itself.

In recent years, the precipitous increase in the flows of information, goods, and services between civilizations and the innumerable human encounters that result, whether they are personal or only electronic, leave their mark on literally everyone. The resulting flood of discrepant messages clamoring for attention has led to a reemphasis on the local cultural heritage, affirming its superiority to anything and everything outsiders have to offer. A growing popular response to uncomfortable encounters with outsiders, whether direct or mediated, is withdrawal into the cave of a familiar, primarily religious past and an emphatic reaffirmation of local habits and customs. This always has been the first, most elemental, and popular reaction to novelties that threaten established verities and routines of life. But it is not the only one. The "old" culture of locale and tradition does more than merely resist the new; it transforms it. The process runs not only in fast-forward but in reverse as well. As the new culture of advanced electronics has penetrated the hitherto relatively isolated villages of the world and the few remaining "island" communities of advanced countries, an ever-denser web of exchanges occurs among civilizations, and local self-sufficiency becomes impractical and undesirable. Those who engage in such communication haphazardly expose themselves to strange ideas and attitudes. They are inevitably affected and develop powerful vested interests in the continuance of such exchanges. These new patterns coexist awkwardly with the need of displaced and uprooted persons for a secure moral community, even though such traditional communities no longer provide a satisfactory way of life for the majority of human beings.

As cultures, old and new, transform one another, we all are transvested or, as I put it earlier, nativized and globalized at once. Such is life and the cultural process engendered by television in the new world that is "after television."

Notes

1. There are terminological problems in the discussion of nations. European usage makes a distinction between nations and states. *Nations* refer to peoples, whereas *states* are formal political organizations. Thus, political identities have not always corresponded to the frontiers of modern sovereign states. There are nations without states (the Scots and until recently the Palestinians); nations that are part of two or more states (the Basques); states that are nations, though they do not include all of the nation (Ireland); states that are nations (the French or Germans by their own reckoning); and states that are multinational (the United States). Such groups as Gypsies and Jews have no geographically defined frontiers yet have retained, until recent times, strong boundary-maintaining mechanisms. Distinctive human groups without states have come to be known as minorities, and they have conflicted with the objective of creating a homogeneous national identity bounded by the frontiers of states. Americans use the word *nation* to refer to most or all the above cases and use *state,* only rarely, to refer to national or subnational governments. *Nation-state* gets around the terminological vagueness but has limitations itself. There is a similar confusion over the word *frontier.* In American usage *frontier* refers to the thin and shifting line separating "barbarism" from "civilization," whereas *borders* are the boundaries between nations (states). In Europe, *border, frontier,* and *boundary*—though they can have slightly different meanings—can all mark the space separating states. I largely follow the American usage in this essay.

2. The visibility of the American state derives from the fact that nothing stands behind it. There is no independently existing people who are given expression by the state. If the American state ceased to exist, there would be nothing left to which to give expression. One would have to invent a new state and give it a new name to define a new people.

3. Portions of this paragraph and those immediately following are indebted to and paraphrased from Holton (1996).

4. The discussion that follows is indebted to the exceptional historical work of William Cronan (1991).

References

Anderson, B. 1983. *Imagined Communities.* London: Verso.

Anderson, M. 1996. *Frontiers: Territory and State Formation in the Modern World.* Cambridge: Polity.

Appadurai, A. 1996. *Modernity at Large.* Minneapolis: University of Minnesota Press.

Barber, B. 1996. *Jihad vs. MacWorld.* New York: Ballantine Books.

Bauman, Z. 1998. *Globalization: The Human Consequences.* New York: Columbia University Press.

Bellah, R. 1967. "Civil Religion in America." *Daedalus* 96 (Winter): 1–21.

———. 1970. *Beyond Belief.* Berkeley: University of California Press.

Bellah, R., and P. Hammond. 1980. *Varieties of Civil Religion in America.* San Francisco: Harper and Row.

Boorstin, D. J. 1978. *The Republic of Technology.* New York: Harper and Row.

Carey, J. W. 1967. "Harold Adams Innis and Marshall McLuhan." *Antioch Review* 27 (Spring): 5–37.

———. 1998. "Political Ritual on Television: Episodes in the History of Shame and Degradation." In *Media, Ritual, and Identity,* edited by T. Liebes and J. Curran, 42–70. London: Routledge.

Carey, J. W., and J. J. Quirk. 1970. "The Mythos of the Electronic Revolution." *American Scholar* 39 (Spring): 219–41; 39 (Summer): 395–424.

Chandler, A. D. 1977. *The Visible Hand: The Managerial Revolution in American Business.* Cambridge, Mass.: Belknap Press.

Cronan, W. 1991. *Nature's Metropolis.* New York: W. W. Norton.

Darnton, R., and D. Roche, eds. 1989. *Revolution in Print.* Berkeley: University of California Press.

Dayan, D., and E. Katz. 1992. *Media Events: The Live Broadcasting of History.* Cambridge, Mass.: Harvard University Press.

Durkheim, E. 1961. "On Mechanical and Organic Solidarity." In *Theories of Society,* vol. 1, edited by T. Parsons, T. Shils, K. Naegele, and S. Pitts, 208–13. New York: Free Press.

Eisenstein, E. 1983. *The Printing Revolution in Early Modern Europe.* Cambridge: Cambridge University Press.

Geertz, C. 2000. *Available Light: Anthropological Reflections on Philosophical Topics.* Princeton, N.J.: Princeton University Press.

Gilmore, W. J. 1989. *Reading Becomes a Necessity of Life.* Knoxville: University of Tennessee Press.

Hayes, C. J. H. 1960. *Nationalism: A Religion.* New York: Macmillan.

Holton, R. J. 1996. "Classical Social Theory." In *The Blackwell Companion to Social Theory,* edited by B. S. Turner, 25–52. Oxford: Blackwell.

Huntington, S. P. 1996. *The Clash of Civilizations and the Remaking of World Order.* New York: Simon and Schuster.

Ignatieff, M. 1998. *The Warrior's Honor.* New York: Henry Holt.

Innis, H. 1951. *The Bias of Communication.* Toronto: University of Toronto Press.

Katz, E. 1980. "Media Events: The Sense of Occasion." *Studies in Visual Communications* 6 (3): 84–89.

Kermode, F. 1966. *The Sense of an Ending.* New York: Oxford University Press.

Longworth, R. C. 1998. "Nationhood under Siege." *Chicago Tribune,* October 25, A1.

MacDonald, J. F. 1994. *One Nation under Television.* Chicago: Nelson-Hall.

Marvin, C., and D. W. Ingle. 1999. *Blood Sacrifice and the Nation: Totem Rituals and the American Flag.* Cambridge: Cambridge University Press.

McLuhan, M. 1965. *The Gutenberg Galaxy.* Toronto: University of Toronto Press.

Pfaff, W. 1993. *The Wrath of Nations.* New York: Simon and Schuster.

Poggi, G. 1978. *The Development of the Modern State.* London: Hutchinson.
Rosenberg, H. 1959. *The Tradition of the New.* New York: Horizon.
"Secession Party Says It's Not Just Whistling Dixie." 1999. *Providence Journal,* June 20, A8.
Soto, H. de. 1980. *The Other Path.* New York: Harper and Row.
Thorburn, D. 1988. "Television as an Aesthetic Medium." In *Media, Myth, and Narratives: Television and the Press,* edited by J. W. Carey, 48–66. Beverly Hills, Calif.: Sage.
Tocqueville, A. de. [1835] 1961. *Democracy in America.* 2 vols. New York: Schocken Books.
Turner, F. J. 1920. *The Frontier in American History.* New York: Henry Holt.
Turner, V. 1969. *The Ritual Process.* Ithaca, N.Y.: Cornell University Press.
Wiebe, R. 1967. *The Search for Order, 1877–1920.* New York: Hill and Wang.
Williams, R. 1961. *The Long Revolution.* New York: Columbia University Press.

Contributors

LINDA M. BLUM teaches sociology and women's studies at the University of New Hampshire. She is the author of *Between Feminism and Labor: The Significance of the Comparable Worth Movement* (1991) and *At the Breast* (1999).

JAMES W. CAREY is a professor of journalism at Columbia University and dean emeritus of the College of Communications at the University of Illinois. He has written more than a hundred essays, articles, and book chapters on journalism, communications, culture, democracy, education, and the public sphere. His essays have been collected in *Communication as Culture* (1989) and *James Carey: A Critical Reader* (1997).

CLIFFORD G. CHRISTIANS is a professor at the Institute of Communications Research at the University of Illinois. He recently retired as director of the institute after serving fourteen years. He is the author of numerous books and essays on various aspects of ethics and communications. He is the coauthor of *Good News: Social Ethics and the Press* (1993), *Media Ethics, Cases and Moral Reasoning* (1995), and *Communication Ethics and Universal Values* (1997). He is the former editor of *Critical Studies in Mass Communication* and is on the board of a dozen academic journals.

DANIEL CZITROM is a professor of history at Mount Holyoke College. He is author of *Media and the American Mind: From Morse to McLuhan* (1982) and the coauthor of *Out of Many: A History of the American People,* 3d ed. (2000). He is currently completing *Mysteries of the City: New York's Underworld in Culture and Politics, 1870–1930.*

NORMAN K. DENZIN is a professor of communications, sociology, and humanities at the Institute of Communications Research at the University of Illinois. He has authored numerous books, including *Sociological Methods* (1970), *The Research Act* (1970/89), *The Recovering Alcoholic* (1987), *The Alcoholic Self* (1987), *Symbolic Interactionism and Cultural Studies* (1992), and *The Cinematic Society* (1995). He is the editor of *Studies in Symbolic Interaction* and the *Sociological Quarterly.* He is also coeditor of the *Handbook of Qualitative Research,* 2d ed. (2000).

JOLI JENSEN is an associate professor of communications at the University of Tulsa. She is the author of *Creating the Nashville Sound* (1984) and *Redeeming Modernity: Contradictions in Media Criticism* (1990).

CAROLYN MARVIN is an associate professor at the Annenberg School for Communication at the University of Pennsylvania. She is author of *When Old Technologies Were New: Thinking about Electric Communication in the Late Nineteenth Century* (1988) and coauthor of *Blood Sacrifice and the Nation: Totem Rituals and the American Flag* (1999). She has had refereed articles in numerous mass communication journals.

ROBERT W. McCHESNEY is an associate professor in the Institute of Communications Research at the University of Illinois. McChesney is the author of *Telecommunications, Mass Media, and Democracy: The Battle for the Control of U.S. Broadcasting, 1928–1935* (1994) and *Rich Media, Poor Democracy: Communication Politics in Dubious Times* (1999) and the coeditor of *Ruthless Criticism: New Perspectives in U.S. Communications History* (1993).

ANDREA L. PRESS is a professor in the Institute of Communications Research at the University of Illinois. She is the author of *Women Watching Television: Gender, Class, and Generation in the American Television Experience* (1991), based on interviews with working- and middle-class women about entertainment television, and the coauthor of *Speaking of Abortion: Television, Women's Talk, and the Discourses of Authority* (1999).

LANA RAKOW is an associate professor in the School of Communication at the University of North Dakota. She is author and editor of numerous books, including *The Revolution in Words: Righting Women, 1968–1971* (1990) and *Gender on the Line* (1992), named 1993 Book of the Year by the Organization for the Study of Communication, Language, and Gender. She coedited *Women Making Meaning: New Feminist Directions in Communication* (1992).

LINDA STEINER is an associate professor of communication at Rutgers University. She is the author of numerous journal articles, monographs, and book chapters on histories of women journalists, alternative women's media, and the construction of gender in journalism and mass communication.

RICK TILMAN is the author of *C. Wright Mills: A Native Radical and the American Intellectual Tradition* (1984), *Thorstein Veblen and His Critics, 1891–1963* (1992), and *The Intellectual Legacy of Thorstein Veblen: Unresolved Issues* (1996). He also has a forthcoming book on Dewey.

MARY DOUGLAS VAVRUS is an assistant professor of speech-communication at the University of Minnesota. She writes on feminist media studies and political economy. She is completing a book entitled *Media Representation in a Postfeminist Era: Women, Politics, and Mediated Consumer Culture.*

CATHERINE A. WARREN is an assistant professor in the Department of English at North Carolina State University, where she teaches journalism and gender studies. She is coeditor of *James Carey: A Critical Reader* (1997) and is working on a book entitled *A Trilogy of Silence: Physicians, Sexual Abuse, and Institutional Culpability.*

Index

Composed in 9.5/12.5 Trump Mediaeval
with Trump Italic display
by Jim Proefrock
at the University of Illinois Press
Manufactured by Thomson-Shore, Inc.

University of Illinois Press
1325 South Oak Street
Champaign, IL 61820-6903
www.press.uillinois.edu